The Bible's Authority
in Today's Church

Edited by Frederick Houk Borsch

*Papers on the authority of scripture
presented to the Episcopal House of Bishops*

Trinity Press International
Valley Forge, Pennsylvania

The following were partners in the creation of this book: The House of Bishops, the Conference of Anglican Theologians, the Adult Education and Leadership Development Office and the Communication Unit of the Episcopal Church, and Trinity Press International.

The publication of this book was made possible by the Adult Education and Leadership Development Office through contributions to the Episcopal Church.

Library of Congress Cataloging-in-Publication Data

The Bible's Authority in Today's Church / edited by Frederick Houk Borsch.

    p.   cm.

   ISBN 1-56338-084-6

   1. Bible—Criticism, interpretation, etc. 2. Bible—Evidences, authority, etc.
3. Anglican Communion—Doctrines. I. Borsch, Frederick Houk
BS511.2.B56 1993
220.1'08'823—dc20   93-6017
                                                      .CIP

Published by Trinity Press International, P.O. Box 851, Philadelphia, PA 19482 USA

Printed in the United States of America.

CONTENTS

PREFACE

For several intense days in the fall of 1992 the House of Bishops of the Episcopal Church gathered to reflect on the central role of scripture for our life as a church, and to look at the various ways in which the authority of scripture is expressed. Working in groups of eight, we had an opportunity to share our understandings and be informed by one another. At the conclusion of our time together we were in full accord that it had been time well spent. I believe we were enriched, both individually and as a House of Bishops, by our discussions.

The papers in this book served as a starting point for our reflections. I commend these papers to you for your own reading and study. Perhaps they can focus a discussion group for you, as they did splendidly for the bishops.

I feel certain that you will find in these papers fresh insights and new perspectives. May they make a positive contribution to your own ongoing conversation with God as you meditate on the Holy Word.

The Most Reverend Edmond L. Browning

PART I

Educational Resources

How to Use This Book

This book is designed to be used in a variety of ways by different groups or types of people. Before you begin, you may want to review this section to help you identify how you might best use it.

Included in this resource are the papers on the authority of scripture which were commissioned by the House of Bishops Theology Committee and discussed by the bishops at their meeting in September 1992, and the original writers' responses to each other's papers presented to the Conference of Anglican Theologians. All of this material is quite academic in nature. Additional materials have been prepared which will enable readers to engage the subject matter at different levels. Individuals and groups can select from among these various materials according to their needs, goals, and the time available.

FOR CONGREGATIONAL USE

This resource can be used for adult education groups or as part of programs for laity providing liturgical, pastoral, or catechetical leadership in congregations. While some may choose to read some or all of the papers, others will choose to read the summaries and use the longer texts for reference. It is recommended that you follow the suggestions in the section entitled "A Leader's Guide" or design an educational process that engages people in discussion about their own understanding of the authority of scripture and helps them gain an understanding of various perspectives and respect for other people. The papers can be used as reference material to clarify, support, or challenge one's own understanding.

FOR USE BY THEOLOGICALLY TRAINED PERSONS

The papers can be helpful reading material for individuals or groups where members have had at least some theological training. For example, they might supplement material in a program such as the Education For Ministry program (EFM, Sewanee), or a local training-for-ministry program, or be used as part of a clergy day. The process described under the section entitled "A Leader's Guide" can be utilized or participants may wish to read each paper, prepare responses to the questions found on page 27 and then discuss those questions.

FOR USE BY SCHOLARS AND ACADEMICIANS

All of the papers (including response papers) can be used as course material, supplemental reading material, or reference material. You may wish to skip the "process" section and go directly to the papers themselves.

FOR HISTORICAL USE

These papers represent significant theological thinking on the authority of scripture in the 1990s. Seminaries, libraries, researchers, and historians may want to keep the texts as part of archival materials that will be useful both now and in years to come.

A LEADER'S GUIDE

Linda L. Grenz

It is recommended that you plan on four to six sessions to introduce the subject, discuss the four different perspectives, and help participants clarify their own perspective. This basic outline can be profitably expanded to include time to apply the perspectives to one or more current issues or concerns of the group members.

The following three designs give suggestions for different ways in which a group can engage this material. You may need to adapt the suggestions to fit your group's needs, goals, skills, learning styles, the time available, and the context (such as culture/location/lifestyle differences, seasonal considerations, previous experience of group members). You can also shorten or extend any given session from 1¹/₂ to 2¹/₂ hours or stretch any one session to two or more meeting times.

It is difficult to do any adult educational process in about 45 minutes on a Sunday morning; usually the time is too short to engage any topic on a meaningful level. However, many congregations find that this is the best (or only) time for a group to gather. If this is your situation, you will need to schedule at least eight sessions to cover this material and will have to adapt these session designs to fit the shorter time frame.

FIRST DESIGN

Suggestions for Leading Group Session 1

The purpose of this experience is to enable participants to develop a deeper understanding of the various ways in which Episcopalians see the authority of the scripture and to clarify how they themselves use scripture in their decision making and in their understanding of God, people, the world, and the relationships among them. Participants will also have the opportunity to listen to and reflect on the perspectives of others.

Introductions

If this is a new group, begin by asking people to introduce themselves to the group (name tags are helpful if group members do not know each other). You may wish to use one of the following ideas or design your own way of doing introductions and building community. Select or design a process to fit both your time frame and your context (if everyone is already acquainted, use a shorter method).

- Ask the group members to give their names and say what attracted them to this group (plan on about 30 seconds for each participant and model what you are asking for by introducing yourself first—make sure you keep your introduction short); or,
- Ask each person to find two others and take 5 minutes to exchange names and what they hope to gain from this group; then have the small group members introduce each other and add their hopes to the list you or a group member are writing on newsprint—this enables you to identify people's expectations and clarify what will and will not happen during the group's meetings (plan on 5 minutes plus about 1 minute for each participant); or,
- Ask group members to divide into small groups of five to six persons and take 10 minutes to introduce themselves and write on newsprint what they are most anxious about in participating in this group (their fears) and what they hope to gain from it. Have each small group share their hopes and fears with the larger group. Again, you may want to clarify expectations. (Plan on 10 minutes plus about 3 to 4 minutes for each small group.)

Establishing Group Norms

Ask the group to build a list of behaviors they will expect from themselves and each other. Some of these behaviors may need to be negotiated (e.g., smoking or no smoking). Some of the norms that are helpful for this group include:

- Each person speaks for him- or herself: "I think/feel/believe" versus "They say" or "Everyone knows."
- Each person has a valuable contribution to make to the group and deserves to be heard and respected.
- People will be responsible for meeting their own needs, such as leaving to use the restroom (make sure people know where they are if they are new to the facility), or excusing themselves if they need to leave early.
- Insofar as possible, participants will come on time, and stay for the duration.
- The session will start and end on time.
- Food/drinks will or will not be available, will be provided by _____, will be served before or after the meeting.
- Smoking will/will not be appropriate during a session.

Introducing the Subject

Tell the group that they will develop a personal timeline and discuss it with other members of the group as a way of becoming aware of their personal history with scripture and its place in their life. Give everyone an 8¹/₂" x 11" sheet of paper or a sheet of newsprint and ask them to turn the paper sideways and draw a line from left to right in the middle of the paper. Then ask them to divide the line into ten roughly equal segments by putting a dot on the line and numbering the dots 10, 20, 30 . . . 90. Draw your own timeline on newsprint or a black/whiteboard to demonstrate. Your sheet of paper should look something like this:

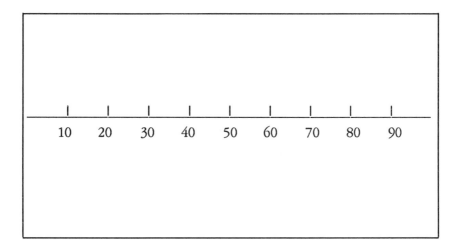

Now ask each person to write a word to two in each decade of their lives that identifies where the Bible(s) in their home were kept in that decade. For example, write in the space before 10 where the Bible was kept in your childhood home; between 10 and 20 write where it was kept when you were a teenager. If there was no Bible in your home, write "none." Give people a minute or two to do this.

Ask each person to think of their first memory of the Bible—ask them when that was and what their perception of the Bible was at that time. Ask them to draw a vertical line on their timeline that marks that date and write a couple of notes about their perceptions in the space above their timeline. Your demonstration should look something like this (use your own information):

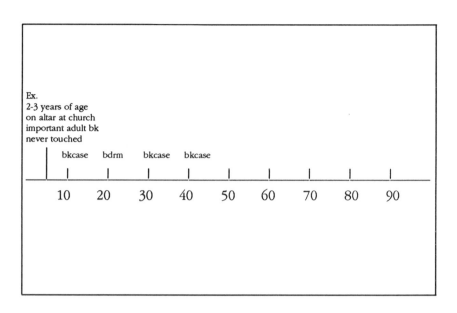

Give people a minute or two to add their notes to their timeline. Then ask them to add any other time when the Bible or a Bible story or passage played a significant role in their lives. Mention a few examples (e.g., carried at wedding, in pocket during combat, story during illness, psalm at time of spouse's death) and add one of your own to your timeline—marking the year and writing notes above the timeline.

Again, give people three or four minutes to make notes. Then ask them to find two people with whom they would feel comfortable sharing their story. Ask each small group to introduce themselves and spend 15 minutes sharing 1) where the Bible was kept in their homes, 2) when they first became aware of the Bible and their perceptions of it at that time, and 3) any other times the Bible played a significant role in their lives.

If you have time, ask each small group to report briefly on their responses and write the response to each of the three points on three sheets of newsprint. This will take about 3 minutes per small group.

After 15 minutes (or after the report back time, if used), ask people to turn their sheet of paper so their timeline runs from top to bottom and then write on the left-hand side their perceptions of the Bible during that decade. Again, demonstrate by doing the first two decades on your sheet. So, for example, you might say:

As a child I saw the Bible as a story book. I mostly remember

Noah, Joseph, and Moses—mostly Old Testament—I'm not sure I knew that Jesus was in the Bible because I was told about him but read "Bible Stories" about OT people. I thought it was like the stories about the presidents of the USA, etc.—historical accounts of what happened. Then the next decade, as a teenager, I began to question the historical nature of these stories—were they literally true or meant to convey a message? Since lots of them didn't make sense literally, I decided they were meant to convey a message. I memorized passages, even whole books for youth Bible contests and knew the content quite well. I was very interested in Jesus and his message and the rest of the Bible became much less important except as a reinforcement of Jesus's message.

Give people 5 to 6 minutes to make notes and then ask them to find two people (other than the two they were with the first time), introduce themselves, and talk about their decade histories. Give the groups about 15 minutes to do this (ask them to give each group member about 5 minutes to tell his/her story).

At the end of this time, ask the larger group to reconvene and spend 5 minutes telling what they learned from their experience.

Preparation for Next Session

Explain the context in which these materials were developed and used (see the introduction, p. 35). Explain that in the next session participants will explore the four different perspectives and identify the similarities and differences they see in them. Before this meeting, number (e.g., Norris = 1, Wondra = 2, etc.) and photocopy the four summaries for each participant. (See pp. 28-34.) Give each participant a set of all four summaries, which will be the content for the next session. They can read the materials before if they wish, but they will be given a few minutes to read one of the perspectives at the start of the next session. You may want to direct them to the author's responses to each other (p.197 ff) which can serve as a helpful introduction to the papers. Explain the Professor Wright's paper (p. 43 ff) provides an historical background for those who would find that helpful.

Before the group disbands, ask for two or three members to be responsible for incorporating any new members into the group next time (welcoming them, explaining what happened in the first session, getting materials for them). Close the session with the following prayer. You may wish to read it aloud, have a group member lead it, or print it on newsprint and have the group read it in unison as a way of closing each session.

Blessed Lord, who caused all holy scriptures to be written for our learning: Grant us so to hear them, read, mark, learn and inwardly digest them, that we may embrace and ever hold fast the blessed hope of everlasting life, which you have given us in our Savior Jesus Christ; who lives and reigns with you and the Holy Spirit, one God, for ever and ever. *Amen.* (Book of Common Prayer, 236)

Suggestions for Session 2:
Studying the Different Perspectives

Opening the Session

This session will usually require two meetings to complete. If you want to fit it into one meeting time, move directly into the discussion of key points. Gather the group members using one of the following ideas or a design of your own.

- Begin with a scripture reflection using one of the methods outlined on p. 23. The longer methods need at least 30-45 minutes; the theological method can be done in 15 to 20 minutes; or
- Begin with devotions: ask a group member to read one of the suggested passages aloud (see p. 23) or the lesson appointed for the day; ask people to reflect silently for a moment; and close with the prayer at the end of Session 1 or one that you or a group member offers; or
- Begin with an opening prayer.

Make sure that everyone has a copy of all four summaries. Explain that the purpose of today's time is to develop a deeper understanding of these four perspectives and to identify the similarities and differences among them.

Ask the group to "number off" from 1 to 4 and to circle their number on their summaries (e.g., if you are a "2" then you will focus on summary number 2). Give the group about 5 minutes to read the one perspective given to them and to underline its key points.

Check at the end of 5 minutes to see if anyone needs a few more minutes. When the group is ready, ask each person to find three others to represent the other three perspectives. Each group of four, therefore, should have someone who has read summary 1, another who has read 2, a third read 3, and the fourth person 4. If you end up with a group size that is not evenly divisible by four, you may need to have from one to three groups of five, each of which will have two persons who have read the same summary.

Ask the small groups to spend 15 minutes taking turns telling each other how they understand the perspective they read and what they see as the key points in the summary. Group members can ask questions for clarification but should not debate, defend, challenge, or argue the perspectives. Encourage people to practice good listening skills. Explain that the purpose of this time is to understand the perspectives.

After 15 minutes, ask the small groups to identify any questions of clarification that their group did not feel they had addressed (5 minutes). List those questions on newsprint without comment, noting only the number of the perspective each question addresses (you can do this by listing all the questions for each perspective on a separate sheet of newsprint, by labeling each question with the number of the summary, or by using four different color markers). Explain that you will return to the questions at the end of the session.

If you will be doing this material in two meetings, this would be a good point to end. Explain that next time you will be looking at similarities and differences. Participants can prepare by reading the paper their group is discussing, and/or the author's responses to each other's papers (see p. 197 ff). These responses identify their sense of the similarities and differences. Close the session with prayer.

If you have time to complete the session in one meeting, you may want to take a break here.

When all the questions have been listed, ask the group to identify the similarities and differences they see between the different perspectives (20-30 minutes). Suggest that participants use the author's responses to each other (p. 197 ff) to help them identify similarities and differences. If you have a large group, you may wish to ask the small groups to do this and list their responses on two different sheets of newsprint which can then be posted with those of the other groups and read aloud so everyone can hear each group's analysis (plan on an additional 15 minutes). Or you may wish to compile a single list, soliciting responses from the entire group and listing them on different sheets of newsprint (perhaps using different markers). If newsprint is not available, ask each participant to record the group's responses on a sheet of paper.

Invite the group to discuss what they experienced in this session. What did they learn? Are there any questions left unanswered (refer to the list generated earlier)? If so, can the larger group resolve them or does someone (or a small group) want to research the question using the full texts of the papers? If you plan on giving each participant a copy of the book, this would be an appropriate time to do so. Explain that they can deepen their understanding by reading some of the papers that were summarized in the handouts you gave them.

Remind participants that all four papers were written by Anglican theologians (seminary professors) and that each represents a perspective held by some Episcopalians. The purpose of this study is not to decide which is "right" and which is "wrong" but rather to develop a deeper understanding of and appreciation for each and to give each participant a way to better understand his or her own perspective.

If you have additional discussion time, ask the group what they think each perspective says about who God is, who human beings are, and what the relationship between the two is. Again, the goal is to engage in a dialogue and not to give any specific answer. Encourage people to resist arguing for or against what someone else says and instead to state clearly what he or she thinks and believes. Encourage people to listen to each other, to respect each other's positions and learn from them.

Preparation for the Next Session
At this point you can continue with the optional session (below) or go directly to Session 3. If you are going to the optional session, explain that it will be a time to explore how the different perspectives might influence how one thinks about a variety of social issues. Emphasize that the purpose will be to understand the relationship between one's perspective on the authority of scripture and perspectives on social issues, not on what should be done about various issues. (To help you prepare for this, see how the author's addressed current issues in their papers.) Ask the group to identify a list of issues they would like to use as "case studies" by jotting down three issues. List the issues on newsprint and guide the group in selecting three or four to use in the next session. Encourage them to select issues that are different from each other, such as personal/global, near/far, "safe"/threatening. Close the session with prayer.

If you are going to Session 3, explain that the next session will be a time for the members to develop their own perspective on the authority of scripture. They do not need to do any preparation but may want to think about it. Some members may also wish to read the paper in the book that they think most nearly fits what they believe. Close the session with prayer.

Suggestions for Optional Session:
Applying Perspectives to Current Issues

Gather the group as in Session 2. Ask the participants to return to the small groups they had at the previous session; adjust any groups that may have missing perspectives by combining groups or asking the one of the "duplicates" in the groups of five to join another group. If you have more than a few people missing you may want to re-form groups. Also, you may want to form three or four larger groups of eight (absolute maximum), one for each of the issues you selected. Each group of eight should have two people representing each of the four perspectives.

Randomly give one of the issues identified at the last meeting to each group, and ask them to spend 20 minutes identifying what position they think a person holding each of the perspectives on scripture would take on the issue and why—how would this person use scripture in developing an approach to the issue? Ask each group to write their response on newsprint using one sheet for each of the four perspectives.

After about 20 minutes, see if the groups are finished; if necessary, give them a few more minutes to complete their work. Then ask the larger group to assemble and have each group in turn give their response. Begin with perspective 1 and ask the group with issue A to say what they think a person holding that perspective would say about issue A and why. Then go to the group that discussed issue B and ask them what they think perspective 1 would say about issue B and why. Continue until you have heard each issue group's response on perspective 1. Then do the same for perspectives 2, 3, and 4. Post the newsprint for each perspective as each group makes its presentation.

If you have time for further discussion, ask the group to review each of the issue responses for each perspective and identify what was similar and what was different in each issue (i.e., for perspective 1, what was similar in issue A, B, C, D? What was different?)

Invite the group to discuss their experience in this session. What did they learn? What was new? What did they find disturbing? What did they find exciting?

Preparation for the Next Session

Explain that the next session will be a time for the members to develop their own perspective on the authority of scripture. They do not need to do any preparation but may want to think about it.

Some members may also wish to read the paper in the book that they think most nearly fits what they believe. Close with prayer.

Suggestions for Session 3:
Forming My Own Perspectives

Begin this session with a time of scripture reflection using one of the methods on p. 23.

Remind participants that until this point they have been discussing perspectives that may or may not be their own. Tell them that this session will be a time to develop or clarify their own perspective. Ask each participant to take 10 minutes in silence to review his or her personal perspective on the authority of the scriptures. Write the following questions on newsprint or a black/whiteboard to guide their reflection.

- I believe the Bible is _____.
- When I have a problem to solve or decision to make, I think the Bible _____.
- The perspective of _____ (writer) is the one I am most comfortable with at this time.

You may also wish to provide art supplies for those who are more comfortable expressing themselves nonverbally. Invite people to develop their response to the first question in whatever way is most comfortable to them (written, artwork, music).

After 10 minutes, ask people to find two others who agree with their answer to the last question (i.e., who have a similar approach to the scriptures). Ask them to spend 15 minutes discussing how they view the authority of the scriptures and how they have used and/or hope to use the scriptures in the future.

After 15 minutes (you may need to adjust the suggested times to fit your time frame), ask each participant to find at least one person who answered the last question differently than he or she did. The ideal is to form groups of about four people with at least two different viewpoints (two of each), but this will have to be adapted depending on the diversity of your group. Form larger groups if necessary. Avoid having three or more people with the same perspective in the same group as the one person with a different perspective may feel outnumbered and uncomfortable. The important thing is to have different perspectives represented in each group and that people are with different people than they had in their agreement triad. (If the entire group agrees or all agree but one or two people, skip this discussion.)

Ask group members to tell each other how they see the authority of the scriptures and how they have used and/or hope to use the scriptures in the future.(10-15 minutes)

Ask the larger group to reconvene and to take a minute to write three things they learned or ways in which their perspective changed. Then invite participants to say how this experience has changed or helped clarify their perspective and/or what they have learned from this experience. Encourage people to speak for themselves—to identify "what I learned," "what I plan to do," "what I think" as opposed to statements that start "I learned we should . . " If people do the latter, ask them to restate what they learned for themselves.

Close the session by asking the group to read in unison the first prayer on page 8.

SECOND DESIGN

Suggestions for Leading Group Session 1
The purpose of this experience is to enable participants to develop a deeper understanding of the various ways in which Episcopalians see the authority of the scripture and to clarify how they themselves use scripture in their decision-making and in their understanding of God, people, the world, and the relationships among them. Participants will also have the opportunity to listen to and reflect on the perspectives of others.

Follow the suggestions for introductions, setting norms, and leading the group in scripture reflection as outlined in the first design above (p. 3).

Preparation for the Next Session
Explain the context in which these materials were developed and used (see the introduction, p. 35). Tell the group that they will divide into four small groups, each of which will study and present one of the perspectives represented by one of the papers. The next session will be a time for them to read the short summary (p. 28-34) and as much of the related paper and responses as they wish and discuss their perspective among themselves. The summaries and the author's responses to each other's papers (p. 197 ff) are the quickest and easiest entry into the content. Since they will need to articulate their perspective, they may want to read the other summary papers

and anticipate what the other groups might present. Each group's task will be to present their perspective on the authority of scripture as clearly and concisely as possible.

Since the purpose of this is to gain an understanding of the various perspectives, participants should not choose which perspective they will present. Rather, groups should be selected randomly—by "counting off" by fours, using four colors on name tags, or some other method. It is important to emphasize that people will be presenting a perspective for the sake of learning and that this may not necessarily be their personal perspective. However, each group member is to make a serious attempt to understand and persuasively present the perspective of their group.

Pass out copies of the book to each group member and help them find the summary pages (p. 28-34) or provide photocopies of those pages. Ask the small groups to meet briefly and identify each other (do introductions if group members are not known to each other). Ask them to take 5 minutes to glance briefly at the summary of the perspective they are to present and to discuss who in their group is interested in doing additional reading (some or all of the corresponding paper and responses).

In some contexts it may be helpful to have the groups select a name or a color or some other identifying moniker. Ask them for their name before they leave so you can assign group meeting spaces by their group names.

Before the group disbands, ask them to identify a convener who will take down the names of the group members and will be responsible for incorporating any new members into the group. Ask the conveners to give you the list of group members so you will have a record of who is in which group.

After 5 minutes, ask the group to reconvene, remind them that they will meet in small groups for the second session, and close with the following prayer. You may wish to print this on newsprint and have the group read it in unison as a way of closing each session.

> Blessed Lord, who caused all holy scriptures to be written for our learning: Grant us so to hear them, read, mark, learn and inwardly digest them, that we may embrace and ever hold fast the blessed hope of everlasting life, which you have given us in our Savior Jesus Christ; who lives and reigns with you and the Holy Spirit, one God, for ever and ever. *Amen.* (Book of Common Prayer, 236)

Suggestions for Leading Session 2:
Studying the Different Perspectives

Opening the Session

Gather the group members using one of the following ideas or a design of your own.

- Begin with a scripture reflection using one of the methods on pages 23–26 (if you have at least 2 hours for this session).
- Begin with devotions: ask a group member to read one of the passages aloud, ask people to reflect silently for a moment, and close with the prayer at the end of Session 1 or one that you or a group member offers.
- Begin with an opening prayer.

Remind the group that they will be working in their small groups for this session. Each group should prepare a 10- to 15-minute presentation of the perspective they are to represent. They can make this presentation in any fashion they choose—by one person, as a presentation, play, poem, or song by the group, or as a panel. If you wish, you can provide art supplies for those who might wish to be artistic.

Remind people that the individual members of each small group may not necessarily hold the perspective being presented but that everyone will make an effort to present the perspective as clearly and positively as possible.

Tell the groups where they will meet and the time they should reconvene to close. Identify any new group members and divide them among the small groups.

Closing

Check with the groups to see if they are ready to present at the next session. If all of the groups want more time, renegotiate the schedule and give them additional small-group time at the next meeting time. If some of the small groups are ready and others are not, ask the groups to negotiate whether they will do preparation at the next regular meeting time or if the group(s) needing more time wishes to schedule an additional meeting, stay later at this meeting, or come early for the next meeting. Help the larger group reach a consensus.

Explain that the next session will be a time for people to present their perspective to the other groups (unless you have renegotiated to include an additional preparation session). Remind them of the meeting time.

Close with the prayer at the end of Session 1 or another prayer led by yourself or a group member, or read in unison.

Suggestions for Session 3:
Discussing the Perspectives

Gather the group as in Session 2. Before starting or at the end of your gathering time, make sure the larger group is seated with the small groups sitting together.

Explain that this session will be a time for the small groups to present the perspective their group studied. Invite any newcomers to sit with you in an observer or cheerleader role (depending on your personality and/or inclinations).

You may wish to encourage a "lively atmosphere" by taking the role of announcer, introducing the groups, and leading applause. Select one of the groups to begin with their presentation and ask them to take center stage, inviting the rest of the groups to become the audience. Tell them you will be the timekeeper and will tell them when their 15 minutes (or whatever length of presentation you have agreed upon) is over. Encourage the group to applaud the group's effort after each presentation.

After the last presentation you can do several different things depending on the length of time in your session and the number of times your group wishes to meet.

Option 1: (short session time and only one session for presentations): After the last presentation, ask people to reflect in silence for 3 to 4 minutes, perhaps making a few notes to themselves. Ask them to reflect on what especially attracted them in the different presentations and what they learned from them.

Option 2: (longer session time, only one session for presentations): After the last presentation, ask each small group to convene briefly and come up with one question they would like to ask each of the other groups. Then ask for one question for the first group and let them respond for 2 minutes; then one for the second group, and so on, for as much time as you have available. End this time as described in option 1.

Option 3: (longer session time and/or additional session for presentations): After the last presentation invite the group to discuss what they heard and ask any questions they may have. Then ask the group to divide into groups of four (or five, if necessary) with each small group having a representative of each perspective. Ask them to identify the similarities and differences they saw in the perspectives (see Design 1, p. 8). Again, end this session as described in option 1.

Debriefing

Ask people to reconvene as a larger group. It is important that the small groups dissolve, so don't just ask people to turn their chairs around or something that basically keeps people in or near their small groups. Moving around is part of "getting out of role" and it is important, especially for people who may have found themselves presenting a position they did not hold. Before you close, ask people to get up and move their chairs or themselves to another part of the room for the closing. Remind people that the presentations just made do not necessarily represent the positions of the people who made the presentation. Ask everyone to take a few minutes to jot down what they learned about the different perspectives and/or themselves. Invite those who want to say what they learned to do so. Ask participants, "How was today's experience for you?" Listen to responses. If people express discomfort with presenting perspectives that they do not hold, agree that it is discomforting to do that. Ask what they learned from the experience. Encourage them to listen to each other and to reflect on what they gained from the experience of "walking in someone else's shoes" for a short time.

Closing

After a time of quiet reflection, close the session with prayer as in Session 1.

Suggestions for Optional Session A: Applying Perspectives to Current Issues

Once the group has a grasp of the different perspectives on the authority of scripture, it can be useful to use those perspectives in thinking about various current issues.

Gather the group with a time of singing, scripture reflection, or whatever opening you have developed.

Ask the entire group to brainstorm a list of current issues they would be interested in exploring. Work with them to select three or four that are interesting to the greatest number of people. Try to get a variety of issues, ones different from each other. For example, a very personal issue (abortion, divorce) and a communal issue (a community environment problem, U.S. armed intervention in the XYZ situation); a "safe" issue (how should I relate to other people?) and a less "safe" issue (how should I deal with my own and others' racism? someone with HIV/AIDS?). These are only examples—let the group generate the list and then encourage them to select two or three that are quite different (close/far, personal/global, clear/conflicted).

When you have agreed on the issues you will use, ask the group to return to their small groups for the remainder of this session to prepare a 5-minute presentation on each of the issues in which they explain how their group, still representing their original perspective, would use the Bible in addressing this issue. What do they think a person holding this perspective would say about this issue and why?

The groups may want to search the scriptures for passages that they can use to demonstrate their perspective, so you will need to have copies of commentaries, concordances, and Bible dictionaries available as well as copies of the Bible in various translations. Encourage them to use the general direction of scripture as well as specific passages (e.g., Jesus' approach to those who came to him for healing as well as a particular incident).

Before they go to work in their small groups, remind them when they are to reconvene to close the group session (if you plan to do that). If the small groups will be "on their own" (e.g., going off to meet in different rooms and or leaving as each group is ready) ask the small group conveners to invite the group to close their time with prayer.

If the small groups reconvene for a general closing time, spend about 5 minutes asking people to say how their meeting went and what they learned. Then close with prayer, singing, or whatever closing ritual you have developed.

Suggestions for Optional Session B: Applying Perspectives to Current Issues

Gather the group with whatever opening ritual you have been using or would like to use. You can use the following suggestion or see the first design above (p. 8).

Select one of the topics and ask each group to present their perspective on how they would use scripture to address that topic. Give each small group 5 minutes to present and then give the entire group 5 minutes to ask any questions of clarification before moving on to the next topic.

Before you open the floor to questions, remind people of two things: 1) people are presenting a perspective that has been assigned to them and they may not personally agree with that perspective; and 2) the goal is not to solve the issues but rather to think about how the different ways of seeing the authority of scripture affects how the different groups approach the issue.

Ask first if anyone has a question about something a group presented that they did not understand and want clarified. Then ask the group to identify how the different perspectives on the authority of scripture affected the way the groups approached the issue. Do not let this get into a debate on the answers to the issue, but get them to focus on how people use scriptures to understand the issue.

Watch your time during this discussion to make sure you have enough time to have the presentations the groups prepared on the other issues. If the group starts debating the answers to the issues, some members are in disagreement on something, or a few people are dominating the discussion and/or "lecturing," move the group along by naming the issue ("It looks like we have strong feelings about our differing positions on this issue") and then suggesting the group do the next presentations and see if more clarity emerges out of that.

If you have argumentative people or people who become highly invested in the issue you may have to take a stronger leadership role in keeping the group moving. One way to get people to disengage and reflect is to ask everyone to take a few minutes to jot down what they learned about how different people use the scriptures in trying to understand issues and make decisions. Then ask people to say what they wrote and just listen to each other. Thank people as they make their contribution and then move on to the next person without comment. The trick is not to allow either yourself or any group member to "tell" the group the "right" answer. Your job as leader is to encourage the group to explore the different perspectives by "trying them on" and by listening to each other.

Debriefing
After you have done the presentations on your selected issues you will again need to help people detach themselves from the position they represented. See the end of the previous session for suggestions on how to do that.

Closing
Close the group time with prayer, singing, or whatever closing ritual you desire.

Suggestions for Session 3:
Forming My Own Perspectives
Begin this session with a time of scripture reflection using one of the methods on p. 23-26.

Remind participants that up to this point they have been representing a perspective that may or may not be their own. Tell them that this session will be a time for them to develop or clarify their own perspective. Ask each participant to take 5 minutes in silence to review their personal perspective on the authority of the scriptures. Write the following questions on newsprint or a black/whiteboard to guide their reflection.

- I believe the Bible is _____.
- When I have a problem or decision to make, I think the Bible _____.
- The perspective of _____ (writer) is the one I am most comfortable with at this time.

After 10 minutes, ask people to find two others who agree with their answer to the last question (i.e., who have a similar approach to the scriptures). Ask them to spend 15 minutes discussing how they see the authority of the scriptures and how they have used and/or hope to use the scriptures in the future.

After 15 minutes (you may need to adjust the suggested times to fit your time frame) ask the group members to find at least one person who answered the last question differently than he or she did. The ideal is to form groups of about four people with at least two different viewpoints, but this will have to be adapted depending on the diversity of your group. Form larger groups if necessary. The important thing is to have different perspectives represented in each group and that people are with different people than they had in their agreement triad. (If you all agree or all agree but one or two people, skip this discussion). Ask group members to tell each other how they see the authority of the scriptures and how they have used and/or hope to use the scriptures in the future.

Ask the larger group to reconvene and to say how this experience has changed or helped clarify their perspective and/or what they have learned from this experience. Encourage people to speak for themselves—to identify "what I learned," "what I plan to do," "what I think" as opposed to statements that start "I learned we should . . ." If people do the latter, ask them to restate what they learned for themselves.

Remind people that these papers have all been written by seminary professors and that each represents a viewpoint within the Episcopal Church. One of the distinctive features of the Anglican communion is that we understand the truth to lie somewhere in the tension between differing perspectives and so value many perspectives as contributing an important part of the truth.

Ask the group to identify what new "truths" or what new perspective they have seen as valuable—something they did not see or understand before and may not necessarily agree with. Encourage group members to continue to listen to each other and to seek to see the value in differing perspectives.

Close the session by asking the group to read in unison the first prayer on page 8.

THIRD DESIGN

Groups that want to read all of the papers (and response papers) can use the same questions used by the House of Bishops (see pp. 27). Each group member would need to read one of the papers before the group session and answer the questions. Small groups of six to eight people could then discuss their answers to the questions. This would be repeated for each of the four papers. The response papers could be incorporated with that discussion or done as additional sessions.

If you choose this design, read the suggestions for doing introductions, establishing norms, and starting and ending the group sessions that are outlined above. You may want to use the introduction for the first design and then distribute four copies of the questions to each participant at the end of that session. Explain the expectations and format for subsequent sessions.

NOTES

1. Twelve additional methods are outlined in the resource *In Dialogue with Scripture: An Episcopal Guide to Studying the Bible*, available from Parish Services, 815 Second Ave., New York, NY 10017, $5.95 book, $5.00 computer disk.
2. This is from *Global Education for Mission*, a guide for leaders of groups wishing to explore any global or local issue. GEM is available through Episcopal Parish Services ($3.00, Part #66-9014).

SCRIPTURE REFLECTION

The following are some passages specifically related to scripture which you might want to use to start or close your group sessions. You can also use the lessons appointed for the day—they often provide more helpful insights than selecting a topical passage.

- Deut. 10:1-5 (Moses receives the Ten Commandments)
- Psalm 119:105-12 ("Your word is a lamp unto my feet")
- Isaiah 55:10-11 ("My word shall go forth . . . and not return to me empty")
- Mark 1:21-28 (Jesus teaches with authority)
- Mark 4:14-21 (Jesus reading from Isaiah in the temple)
- Luke 24:27-32 (Road to Emmaus)
- Luke 24:44-45 ("scripture must be fulfilled . . . opened their minds to understand")
- John 5:31-47 (Testimony to Jesus)
- Acts 8:27-35 (Phillip and the Ethiopian eunuch)
- 2 Timothy 3:16-4:4 ("All scripture is inspired by God")

If you want to include a time for scripture reflection, you may wish to use one of the following approaches to studying the Bible.

A Theological Approach to Studying the Bible

1. Read the passage aloud.
2. Discuss what the passage tells us about God.
3. Read passage aloud a second time.
4. Discuss what the passage tells us about human beings (men, women, and children, young and old, different races, and different places) and the relationship between people.
5. Read passage aloud a third time.
6. Discuss what the passage tells us about the relationship between God and human beings. How might people living in different circumstances or in different cultures perceive the passage's message about the relationship between God and human beings? How does the passage call us (individually and corporately) to change?

7. Read the passage aloud, quietly, meditatively, as a closing prayer; leave a moment of silence and then close with prayer.

An Oral Tradition Approach to Studying the Bible

1. Ask each person to share his or her experience in the area of prayer from the session before. (If this is a first session, begin with step 2.)
2. Ask someone to read the passage slowly. Before the reading, ask people to listen for the word or phrase that catches their attention.
3. Ask participants to take a minute to recall the word or phrase that caught their attention.
4. Invite each person to say the word or phrase with the group (no more than just a word or phrase).
5. Ask someone else to read the passage again (opposite sex of first reader).
6. Invite participants to think/write about: "Where does this passage touch my life, my community, our nation, our world today?" Invite them to think about all the people they encounter, not just those in their own "circle of friends." (3-5 minutes).
7. Invite each person to share the above: "I . . . "
8. Ask someone else to read the passage aloud again.
9. Ask participants to think/write about: "From what I have heard and shared, what does God want me to do or be this week? How does God invite me to change?" (3-5 minutes).
10. Invite each person to share the above: "I . . . " Explain that you will ask each person to pray for the person on their right, naming what was shared in step 10 so they will want to listen carefully and remember any specifics the person names.
11. Ask each person to pray for the person on their right, naming what was shared in step 10 and prays that prayer daily until the group meets again.

- ■ *Note:* In steps 3, 7, and 10, be brief. Do not elaborate, explain, or teach. That which is said is offered to the center of the group. Others do not respond to or build on what is said as if they were in a discussion group.

A Scriptural Conversation Approach to Studying the Bible

1. Explain to the groups what they will be doing: hearing the text read aloud three times with some questions for reflection after each reading. Make sure everyone has pencils and paper. Before

the first reading ask the people to listen for what catches their attention: *words, phrases, images.*

2. Ask someone to read the text aloud.

3. Ask the group members to spend a couple of minutes in silence identifying and, if they wish, writing down the *words, phrases or images* that catch their attention.

4. Ask each person who chooses to, to say no more than one or two *words, phrases,* or *images* he or she has written. Ask the other members of the group to listen and not comment upon, question, or discuss what is said. Tell them to give everyone a chance to speak once and then to wait in silence. (If the group is unable to discipline itself to one word and does not finish after 1 or 2 minutes, quietly interrupt them asking them to limit their response to one word.)

5. Once the group has fallen silent, invite people to listen again and this time to identify which *themes and concerns* they hear raised by the passage. Then ask another person to read the same text aloud for the second time.

6. Ask group members to reflect silently and write down the *themes and concerns* they hear in the passage. Give them a couple of minutes to do this.

7. Ask each person to say what *themes and concerns* he or she heard with the second reading of the text, without discussion or comments from other members of the group. Again, ask each person to speak *once* and then wait until the silence indicates that everyone in the room has finished.

   ■ *Optional:* If you have additional time, you may introduce a voice from the tradition by reading some material from a commentary before the third reading. Keep the reading relatively short, selecting paragraphs that describe the context of the passage, where it fits into the chapter, and any unique or uncommon words or concepts. Do not elaborate on or discuss the commentary. Just offer it as if the writer were just another voice in the group. At the end of the reading ask people to reflect in silence for a moment.

8. Invite people to listen to the passage again; listen for what *insights or challenges* may arise for them in the passage, and for how the passage *relates to issues* they are dealing with in their lives, both personally and communally. Ask another person to read the passage aloud for the third time.

9. After a period of silence, invite people to say what *insights* they

have had, or what they have heard that relates to the issues they identified. Again, ask the other members to listen and not comment upon, question, or discuss what is said.

10. Close the group meeting with prayer.

READING OR DISCUSSION QUESTIONS

1. What is the basic understanding of scripture represented in this paper?

2. How does this paper view the relationship between scripture and God?

3. What is the relationship between scripture and the church in this paper?

4. Within this paper, how is scripture to be interpreted, appropriated, and used?

5. According to this paper, who interprets and determines the authority of scripture?

6. How does your personal use and interpretation of scripture relate to the perspective offered by this paper?

SUMMARIES OF THE FOUR PAPERS

Charles C. Hefling, Jr.

SUMMARY OF THE PRICE PAPER

Words, this paper argues, are the way in which tradition, culture, and common life are shared, so that human beings come to understand not only their world but each other and indeed their very selves by being immersed in words. Like the communities that embody other great religions of the world, the Christian church has a collection of "sacred" words—scriptures—through which Christian selves are formed in being addressed by a transcendent Word. These words rather than others, the canon of scripture, are authoritative for Christianity because the church established its own list of sacred writings. Yet at the same time, and equally, the books of the Bible did and do determine the identity of the Christian community.

Within that community, authority in the full and final sense belongs solely to God in Christ. The power of God's saving work in the words and deeds and risen life of Christ continues to be mediated, by scripture and by those other words which are congruent with the canonical words. But since only God can properly speaking mediate God, the church affirms, on the one hand, that the human authors and editors of the biblical books were *inspired* by God's own Spirit, and, on the other, that this divine inspiration is to be discerned by the community filled with the same Spirit. To perceive the Spirit's work, the work of the Spirit is needed; and while every biblical word *may* become a sacrament of the Word, no biblical word always or automatically *does* convey the Word to every reader or every worshiping community. Prayer and study, the exercise of discernment and reason, play their part as interpreters, in weighing the scripture, are themselves weighed. The process is reciprocal, unavoidable, and unending.

To that process the church brings a variety of gifts, among which *love* is primary. In the continuing process of discerning the divine in human words, the effect of *agapé* has often been gradual. So it was when, after a bitterly long time, the institution of slavery could no longer bear to be judged by love, and the testimony of the Holy

Spirit within the community prevailed over what had been regarded as authoritative biblical texts.

The second part of the paper discusses the use of Scripture under three headings, which are presented as in some sense cumulative. First, and most fundamental, is the use of Scripture in *worship,* public and private. Only by extensive and continuous reading of the Bible is it really possible to hear the Word, to grasp it and praise it and allow it to shape the mind and the will.

One aspect of Scripture's shaping of the Christian *mind* is its use in *determining doctrine.* Here the paper outlines the often complex way in which questions the Bible does not explicitly address have been answered in ways that, while they may go beyond Scripture, do not contradict it. The doctrines of the Trinity and Christ's virgin birth are examined in some detail.

Thirdly, as the words of Scripture shape the *will* of those who worshipfully immerse themselves in them, so Scripture is used in *guiding ethical conduct.* The Bible is no more an ethics textbook than a textbook of doctrine, but in the same way that the believer and the believing community encounter the Word as *logos* in determining doctrine, so they encounter the same Word as *agapé* in relation to ethical questions. After noting the way in which, within the New Testament itself, older, cultural norms of conduct are reshaped—the Law of Moses in the gospels, Hellenistic rules in the epistles—the paper goes on to suggest a way in which the criterion of *agapé* might be analogously applied today in a Christian ethic of homosexuality.

SUMMARY OF THE WONDRA PAPER

Theological terms have their meaning within some interpretive framework, and this paper draws on contemporary theologies of liberation for description and diagnosis of our concrete, human, historical situation. It thus considers the question of biblical authority from the standpoint of human struggles for participation in full humanity—for justice, mutuality, and wholeness.

Redemption, in this perspective, is a solidly historical reality. It takes place, here and now, in release from sin (patriarchal domination, for example) and from the effects of sin (unjust systems, oppression, subjugation). Correspondingly, it is a redeeming God whom oppressed communities encounter in their struggle. In giving this account its theological grounding, the paper argues that the God who is Trinity is inherently both diverse and unified, and that this divine mutuality is the exemplar of that interconnectedness in which efforts directed against domination and towards liberation strive to participate.

Within communities that aim at actualizing in this world such a participation in divine purpose, the Bible may become authoritative. It will not be accorded sole authority, however, because the human embodiments of divine, liberating power are many. Present experience is a primary authority for liberation theologies, and the paper also puts strong emphasis on the authority of the *sensus fidelium* or common mind of a community of faith. Scripture thus takes its place among the authorities that empower liberation, by making it possible to participate in full, mutual humanity.

The authority of the Bible is not, in other words, independent of its effective meaning. Nor is that meaning automatically evident. It has to be discovered. All too often, biblical texts have contributed to the *ideologies* from which social, economic, and cultural structures of domination draw support. Such ideologies commonly identify what humanity as such is and ought to be, with the humanity of those who wield power, and to support the identification they have enlisted scripture. Consequently, the strategy adopted by liberation theologies for appropriating scripture is in the first place fully *critical*. It begins by approaching texts through a "hermeneutic of suspicion" that focuses on those aspects of the biblical tradition which underwrite domination. Not only particular texts and traditions of interpretation, but also the very cultures from which the Bible emerged, are exposed as being pervasively patriarchal.

At the same time, the intrinsically oppressive character of the background, the words, and interpretation of Scripture is not absolute. Again and again, the dominated have found in the Bible a source of hope and empowerment; and the biblical narrative itself, in its ambiguity and variousness, has the potential of undermining its own effects and subverting the idologies it has engendered. Uncovering and displaying this transformative potential, by imaginatively construing the biblical witness, is a second phase of appropriating Scripture. A third phase is constructive. It emphasizes not so much what a given text has *meant* as what it now *means,* and not so much what it *says* as what it *does.* It is here that scripture comes to exercise its authority, inasmuch as it nurtures and enables the liberating drive towards full humanity.

The paper emphasizes that the disclosure, the revelation of sacredness, of which scripture is capable occurs within a community of faith living in a concrete situation. Appropriating scripture authentically depends on dialogue and on emerging consensus, arrived at by relatively free participants, rather than on uniformity of reading or on correspondence to some supposedly objective truth. That is the sense in which it is appropriate to speak of a *sensus fidelium,* a consensus of the faithful whose faithfulness is fidelity to participation in the ongoing, transformative action of God in concrete human history.

SUMMARY OF THE NOLL PAPER

Understanding scripture in its "literal sense," this paper argues, is of fundamental importance for Christian life and teaching. But "literal sense" is a phrase that can mean different things, and the paper is therefore careful to clarify the sense in which "literal sense" may best be used. The definition it begins with is this: "The literal sense is that meaning appropriate to the nature of the Bible as the Word of God in the words of men." Once the key terms that give this definition content are understood, it becomes clear that the literal sense of scripture, so defined, is by no means rigid or simplistic. On the contrary, it is presented as a rich and flexible notion, such that the literal sense of one biblical passage will fit the definition differently from the way another passage does. In order to suggest what is involved in the kind of interpretation this implies, the paper offers a brief but highly concentrated sample, taking Jesus' parable of the wicked tenants as the text.

While such an understanding of the literal sense is flexible, it is not shapeless. The paper takes a position that allows for metaphorical meaning, but does not allow the link between verbal signs and what they signify to be dissolved. Indeed, one implication of the way "literal sense" is defined is that the biblical text does direct its reader beyond itself, to the realities its language signifies. Again, though both experience and reasoning enter into the activity of understanding and interpreting scripture, neither may usurp the authority that the literal sense of the text has exercised, in the view presented here, throughout the Anglican tradition. Again, while there is certainly diversity within the literal sense of scripture, the paper opposes the tendency towards dissecting and fragmentizing the Bible and advocates instead a way of reading that honors scripture's canonical wholeness.

At the heart of the paper is a discussion of three "dimensions" of the literal sense. There is, first, a poetic or *literary* dimension. Literal exegesis will be attentive to the variety of artistic ways in which the Bible uses human words. Secondly, there is a dimension of *truth*. This includes propositional expressions of truth together with the imperatives of exhortation and command—a theme that returns in the discussion of sexuality at the end of the paper. But the truth dimension also includes mimetic, representational, imaginative, "history-like" writing—a fact that is especially important in relation to questions about scripture's historical truthfulness, which the paper discusses with respect to Jesus' resurrection and virgin birth. Thirdly, however, the dimension of truth is bound up with an *eschatological* dimension of the literal sense. "What happened?" ought never to be separated from "Where is all this going?" Considered as a canonical whole, scripture has a directionality, which takes up and carries forward both the propositional and the representational aspects of its truth dimension.

The position argued for in the paper is grounded in a Trinitarian theology, which is presented at the outset and is itself based on a biblical text, the prologue of John's gospel. When "literal sense" has been defined and the definition elaborated and illustrated, the paper turns to the question of how the literal sense of Scripture is *authoritative*. Here the emphasis falls on submitting to the Word of God in human words, and on being transformed by that Word. Thus the paper ends with a recommendation of the same meditative reading that it practices at the beginning.

SUMMARY OF THE NORRIS PAPER

In the account of the Christian scriptures presented in this paper, what these books do defines what they are, and vice versa. A first and fundamental point, therefore, is that "the Bible and the church produce each other." A certain library is recognized as holy scripture, and functions as such, only in a particular community—which, in turn, is constituted as just this community by the fact that it is and has been engaged with just these writings.

The kind of "engagement" involved is *conversation*, an ongoing process that is intrinsically interpersonal. Conversation establishes and manifests relationships between persons, and it does so over time—in this case, over centuries—in a way that makes the past an ingredient in the present. A conversation, in other words, is what it is because of what it has been. Accordingly the paper addresses the question of *what* the scriptures are by noting that it cannot be answered without taking into account the *aim* or concern of the conversation taking place in the Bible and about the Bible—where it is and has been going.

Although there is notable variety of theme and emphasis in scripture, the paper argues that there is nevertheless a unity of aim: concern with attesting and interpreting experiences, events, and persons through which God has called, led, and judged a community of faith. More particularly, the New Testament books aim at guaranteeing the authority of the church's teaching by anchoring it in the witness to Christ that is embodied in a conversation engaged in by apostolic persons.

The next question is how the Scriptures achieve this aim. In what way do they function? Here the paper develops an understanding of *language* that stresses *communication* as an exchange of meaning between persons that is more and other than simply transmitting correct information. Language in this sense includes "body language" and behavior; it is inseparable from *interpretation*; and its medium is *symbol*, the self-expressive sign that makes present to an interpreter the self with whom he or she is communicating. Applying all this to the Christian conversation, the paper proposes that the primary symbol is Christ, and that other symbols play a part only insofar as they too give access, indirectly, to the Word of God.

Finally, a third question: How is the point of scripture conveyed and received? Only by interpretation, the paper suggests. Scripture itself is the record of an interpretive conversation. Successive authors have developed, commented on, interpreted, and carried forward what their predecessors had communicated in writing. But their conversation has not ceased; it is not merely a past but also a present reality. And as with any other conversation the link between *then* and *now* is the history of how successive generations have carried on their engagement with Scripture in the church. Indeed, the paper argues that this history of interpretation is itself a symbol of God's Word. By joining this centuries-long conversation, the church today enters into the mystery of the Incarnation, into "the mind of Christ." And it is out of such interpersonal communication that moral and doctrinal questions are raised and answered. They are raised either by seeming dissonance within the tradition of interpreting scripture, or by dissonance resulting from change in the culture that the church inhabits. But because these books are neither a theological nor a moral data-bank, it is not by turning to them in hope of finding a ready-made answer that the church will best respond to the issues it faces today. Rather, it is by involving the diverse talents, experiences, and perspectives of a variety of people who regularly engage in open-ended study of "the Books" that the church's response will embody the Wisdom those books attest.

Charles C. Hefling, Jr. is professor of systematic theology at Boston College, Chestnut Hill, MA, and the current president of the Conference of Anglican Theologians.

PART II

The Papers

INTRODUCTION

Frederick H. Borsch

From earliest days in the life of the Christian churches there has been no one fixed position regarding the role and authority of the scriptures. Their use and interpretation have frequently been a matter of discussion and have been given different emphases. Certainly the Letter to the Hebrews and the Letter of James, for example, take different approaches to the Jewish scriptures, which were also the scriptures for the first Christians. The first and fourth Gospels have parallels but also many variances in their use of the scriptures. An author may use scriptural quotations or allusions typologically in one place and in a more direct or plain-sense manner in another. Indeed, the third chapter of Paul's Letter to the Galatians employs scriptural materials in a complex of ways.

The early churches also witness to the awareness that the scriptures require interpretation if they are to find their significance and meaning. On the road to Emmaeus, Cleopas and another disciple do not understand the resurrection until Jesus "interpreted to them in all the scriptures the things concerning himself" (Luke 24:27). In Matthew 22:23-33, Mark 12:18-27, and Luke 20:27-40, Jesus uses a reference from the scriptures (Exod. 3:6) to confute the Sadducees who did not believe in the resurrection from the dead because they held, among other things, that such a teaching was not to be found in the authoritative writings. Paul (Rom. 4:3) and James (2:23) offer, in their respective contexts, their own somewhat different interpretations of Genesis 15:6.

As, however, Richard Norris has pointed out in his contribution to this discussion:

> The passion and zealous precision with which believers have argued over the meaning(s) of the scriptures represent not a denial but an affirmation of the Bible's authority, just as the authority of the Constitution of the United States is not questioned but established in the unending debates about how it should be read and what its deliverances imply for present practice.

The several papers and responses included in this volume represent a continuation of study, debate, and conversation about the Bible within the life of the Episcopal Church. For three days in early September 1992, the Episcopal House of Bishops gathered in Baltimore to reflect on their readings of these papers and to share their own thoughts and beliefs about the place of the Bible in their ministries and in the common work and witness of the church.

The process had actually started several years earlier when the Theology Committee of the House of Bishops was charged with the task of deliberating upon these matters on behalf of the other bishops.[1] There may have been an expectation that a single paper or pastoral letter would be produced for discussion by the whole House of Bishops. Indeed, a single essay was commissioned by the committee and proved to be a useful study that encouraged a lively discussion among the committee members.[2]

As that discussion continued, however, it was felt that such conversation and debate was exactly what the whole House—and, for that matter, the whole of the church—could best benefit from. Bishops as well as others in the church expressed difficulty in understanding the different approaches and emphases being used in biblical interpretation. This was especially true with regard to controversial moral and ethical issues in society and the life of the church—most particularly homosexuality. Some bishops felt that certain colleagues were being "unscriptural." The opposing charge was that others were becoming "fundamentalists."

The theology committee next met with the Conference of Anglican Theologians for a weekend of discussion on several papers on issues of scriptural authority and interpretation. With counsel from several members of the conference, the theology committee drew up a plan it believed could effectively engage all of the bishops in a discussion.

It was decided that the study and conversation should be held within the Episcopal Church. There are, of course, many fine theologians and biblical scholars in other denominations and throughout the Anglican Communion. Episcopalians had and would continue to learn much from them, but it was felt that what was most needed at this time was dialogue and new understanding within the denomination.

Professor J. Robert Wright had already drafted his valuable background paper, "The 'Official Position' of the Episcopal Church on the Authority of Scripture," for the joint meeting of the theologians and the bishops. Wright sets out and provides commentary on authoritative statements of the Episcopal Church regarding the Bible, along with statements of other Anglican Communion churches and several ecumenical partners. It was felt that this would also be important background reading for the bishops.[3]

After considerable further discussion, which included other theologians and biblical scholars, it was decided that the committee would commission four other papers that would offer a good representation of perspectives and emphases within the church. The limit of four was not easy to set because there are, of course, any number of permutations and even whole schools of interpretation that could not be fully represented in this way. But there were also important practical considerations if we were to have a manageable conversation. In order to expand the perspectives of the papers, it was determined that each author would be asked to consult with a variety of persons so that all the papers would have received commentary and critique from various ethnic groups, both genders, and different theological disciplines. Further to assist in the selection and guidance of the authors and to help with the logistics of producing and distributing the papers, the Trinity Institute and its Director, Dr. Frederick Burnham, were asked to participate in the process. His advice and the generous assistance of the Institute have been a vital contribution.

It would be easy to try to categorize the papers as "liberal," "conservative," "radical," and so on. The committee, however, sought to avoid labels and to think in terms of questions, issues, and authors who could help us think more deeply—authors who would be generally representative of perspectives and approaches in the Episcopal Church today, but who would also give us their own points of view, be provocative in their diversity, and perhaps surprising in some of their agreements. We asked the authors to select for discussion in their papers some particular concerns—such as the virgin birth, the resurrection, or ethical issues—so that we could better see how their approaches might be applied. The counsel to the authors also included the hope that "the style of the papers will be as nontechnical as possible, winsome and nonpolemical; i.e., far more concerned with stating the benefits of what is believed rather than criticizing the stances of others.[33]

The finished papers were sent to all the bishops some six weeks in advance of the meeting. A planning committee, with the help of Dr. Inagrace Dietterich of the Center for Parish Development, drew up the following six questions for the bishops to respond to while reading the papers and to have in mind as the discussions began.

1. What is the basic understanding of scripture represented in this paper?
2. How does this paper view the relationship between scripture and God?

3. What is the relationship between scripture and the church in this paper?
4. Within this paper, how is scripture to be interpreted, appropriated, and used?
5. According to this paper, who interprets and determines the authority of scripture?
6. How does your personal use and interpretation of scripture relate to the perspective offered by this paper?

The four authors were also invited to the Baltimore meeting. There they were asked briefly to highlight their papers or to present some additional commentary, and then to listen as the bishops—in groups of eight to ten—discussed the papers and their own views and reported their reflections. They also listened as the bishops talked of the distinctions and the convergences they found in the papers and what they believed the discussion meant for them both as individual bishops with teaching and authority roles and as a House of Bishops for the church and in relation to other church bodies.

Major conversation centered, of course, on issues regarding the literal and plain sense of the scriptures, on the manner in which the Bible is to be regarded as incarnate in history and human limitations, and the degree to which it is subject to historical conditions. It would probably be fair to say that the bishops as a group discovered more consensus around the Price and Norris papers, but even those who took exceptions with views set forth in the Wondra and Noll papers said that they learned from them and often found aspects in them with which they agreed.

There was, for instance, a particularly lively conversation regarding Noll's argument for the "literal" meaning of scripture. Perhaps a little surprising was the amount of agreement around the understanding that, while a number of scriptural passages were meant to be read in a variety of figurative ways, much of the Bible did have an intended literal (some bishops preferred the words "plain" or "direct") sense. Others of the papers made this point, too, but it only brought to the fore discussion with respect to the significance of this awareness for the interpretation of the scriptures for today. It was noted, for example, that more than one of the biblical writers intended that the world be viewed with a heaven above and that Jesus be seen as physically ascending into that heaven. But this understanding neither exhausted the significance of these presentations nor solved the matter of the interpretation of the passages for modern disciples.

Perhaps the most positive result of such discussions was the repeated sense that the bishops now had a better appreciation of the views of some of their colleagues and better respect for the seriousness of their concerns and the seriousness with which they approached and studied the Bible. The bishops were, of course, aware of the many ethical and social issues also pressing upon the church and the world at this time, but many of them stated their belief that they would now be better able to confront these issues based upon a stronger common sense of the inspiring power and significance of the Bible for the whole mission of the church. It was also suggested that the process that had brought about the expression and clarification of differing views and had led to new understandings could be a model for the discussion of other issues with the church's life. While the process had deliberately been far more descriptive than prescriptive, it had evidently brought about a larger awareness of being part of a community of interpreters with a host of shared beliefs as well as concerns.

Indeed, there were repeated affirmations regarding the values of diversity in the church and within particular Christian communities. It has long been a fundamental tenet of Anglicanism that the comprehensiveness of a diverse church—the valuing of different experiences—can best bring about a more profound sense of God's presence. Richard Norris had this in mind when he wrote of the ongoing "conversation" spanning many generations which helped bring the Bible into being and "in which new circumstances compel thoughtful folk ever and again to rehearse its earlier stages." It was, however, Ellen Wondra's paper that most stressed not only the value but also the necessity of bringing different views and experiences into the dialogue with and study of the Bible. Not all of the bishops were prepared to follow her emphasis on the liberation theology theme of the "hermeneutics of suspicion" and on the awareness that a number of women interpreters and others challenge or at least want to reinterpret the Bible's authority with respect to basic societal attitudes, particularly having to do with assumptions about male and female roles. At the same time there did seem to be basic agreement among the bishops with regard to the significance of such issues to many Christians, and a collective awareness of the importance of hearing other voices and the necessity of at least some measure, if not of "hermeneutics of suspicion," at least of critical reading and hearing. The history of interpretation teaches, the bishops were aware, how easy it is for one group or culture to read the Bible only through its own eyes.

In one way or another all of the authors pointed out how important it is that this diversity of dialogue be relational, that it is most effective and best able to bring forth the riches of the scriptures when it is not conducted by separated individuals or groups but within the larger community. The papers and the bishops repeatedly emphasized the understanding that the scriptures are the product of communal experience and reflection on God's presence and activity and that their interpretation today requires community study and conversation.[4] It is not, of course, that individuals cannot greatly profit from studying the Bible on their own, but such study only comes to full value when it is brought into community and conversation with others.

Over and again, then, the importance and significance of communal Bible study was raised up. Such daily study was an influential part of the meeting itself and many bishops recalled its important place in the international Lambeth Conference of Bishops of 1988. Testimony was given to the value that a great variety of church groups were finding in giving time for Bible study. Such study seems, for example, to help remind a vestry of its central purposes, to give it new insights, and draw it together more deeply into the common mission of the church.

The bishops had before them the newly issued *In Dialogue with Scripture: An Episcopal Guide to Studying the Bible* with its many suggestions and aids about doing Bible study, and they found much in it for their own benefit and to commend to their dioceses and their congregations.[5]

When the Archbishop of Canterbury, George Carey, joined the bishops for a final day of conversation, he, too, lifted up the significance of various forms of Bible study. Having read the papers earlier and having been briefed regarding the bishops discussions, the Archbishop wanted also to emphasize the importance of bringing the best historical critical and other critical perspectives to Bible study wherever possible. This was only one aspect of Bible study, but it should not be left out. He commended the bishops for their process and for putting biblical issues and concerns at the heart of their deliberation.

Carey, in addition, spoke of the place of the Bible in worship—a repeated interest of the papers and of the bishops' conversations. Anglican and Episcopal liturgy is both thoroughly imbued with scriptural phraseology and makes central the reading and hearing of the scriptures through the liturgical year. There is, then, always much more going on than just "head knowledge" about the Bible. The characters of individual disciples and of communities are being shaped by the Bible, and especially by its great stories, forming, as Bishop Stephen Bayne once put it, "the architecture of faith."

Through the shaping of this worship and these stories modern disciples then seek to understand and interpret their own lives lived before God.

At this point, however, Carey expressed his deep concern about a growing illiteracy with respect to the Bible in almost every society. The Bible could not have its shaping role unless there were more and better forms of Christian education and Bible study. The bishops remembered words from Charles Price's paper: "Biblical illiteracy is the precursor to spiritual death and communal dissolution."

Carey also highlighted a central theme of Price's paper which had earlier affected a lively discussion among the bishops. "Hence within the Christian community," Price wrote, "God in Christ is acknowledged as having ultimate authority. The books of our sacred scripture are deemed to have relative authority because their words bring us into communion with the life-enhancing, saving power of God." While agreeing with the general thrust of Price's statement, some of the bishops nevertheless wanted to be cautious about the word "relative" because of some of its connotations and lest it be understood as lessening the authority of the scriptures to point to Christ. The archbishop, however, was strong in his affirmation of the statement, rightly understood. The church, he maintained, does not worship a book, but God and this God in Jesus Christ of whom we learn through the scriptures. He is "the way, the truth and the life."

Clearly the conversation and dialogue will go on.[6] The bishops have not, for instance, more closely defined the manner in which the scriptures do this pointing to Christ. Much more could be said about the relationship among God, the scriptures, and the church. Many other questions and issues presented in these papers remain open for continued reflection. There is the often debated relationship among scriptures, tradition, and reason, and questions about the interpretation of the teaching that "holy scriptures contain all things necessary to salvation." No doubt some Episcopalians would prefer more clarity and definition for these and related matters, but at least the majority of the bishops seemed to take comfort in the awareness that discussion of these issues has regularly recurred in the life of the church and that it is important that the discussion continue today. They see virtue in a church that is able to continue this discussion openly and to find new insight and new centeredness around the scriptures and renewed community and strength in diversity. The papers of this volume and the process are now commended to the churches and to all communities of faith for their study and ongoing conversation.[7]

NOTES

1. The original members of the committee were Bishops Frederick Borsch, Fitzsimmons Allison, Craig Anderson, Andrew Wissemann, John Spong, Rogers Harris, James Ottley, and Edward McBurney. In the course of the process Bishop Allison retired and Bishops Christopher Epting and Charles Duval were added to the committee.

2. Published now as Philip Culbertson, "Known, Knower and Knowing: The Authority of Scripture in the Episcopal Church," *Anglican Theological Review* 74, no. 2 (1992).

3. Wright's paper has subsequently also been published in two installments, "The Episcopal Church and the Authority of Scripture," *Anglican Theological Review* 74, nos. 3 and 4 (1992).

4. These understandings are underlined in Stephen E. Fowl and L. Gregory Jones, *Reading in Communion: Scripture and Ethics in Christian Life* (Grand Rapids, Mich.: Eerdmans, 1991), a book that was read by a number of bishops before or in connection with the meeting. See also Sandra Schneiders, *The Revelatory Text: Interpreting the New Testament as Sacred Scripture* (San Francisco: Harper Collins, 1992).

5. *In Dialogue with Scripture: An Episcopal Guide to Studying the Bible* (New York: Episcopal Church Center, 1992).

6. The writers of the papers have further continued to the dialogue by adding their own brief responses to the other authors. See page 198ff.

7. See my discussion in "All Things Necessary to Salvation," in *Anglicanism and the Bible*, ed. F. H. Borsch (Wilton, Conn.: Morehouse-Barlow, 1984).

THE CONFERENCE OF ANGLICAN THEOLOGIANS brings together on a yearly basis scholars of the Episcopal Church and the Anglican Church of Canada for discussion of academic papers and other matters of common interest. Its members hold advanced degrees and teach in the various theological disciplines at North American seminaries and universities.

The Secretary of the Conference is the Revd. Prof. Robert D. Hughes III, The University of the South, Sewanee, TN 37375.

The "Official Position" of the Episcopal Church on the Authority of Scripture: Historical Development and Ecumenical Comparison

J. Robert Wright

Although the words "official position" in the title of this essay are chosen deliberately in order to give some boundary to the subject at hand, I do not intend here to take up four preliminary questions that many Episcopalians today, of whatever persuasion, would probably like to have addressed and even answered: First, whether Christianity is primarily a matter of feelings, attitudes, and actions, in such a way that "official positions" expressed in words and written in documents mean very little and are only seen as drawn up to quell immediate arguments and not to have any lasting or binding authority. Second, whether the mass of seemingly authoritative documents that survive (whether various editions of the Prayer Book, resolutions of General Conventions, the Constitution and Canons, pastoral letters of the House of Bishops, resolutions of and reports to the Lambeth Conferences, the Articles of Religion, the decisions of the ecumenical councils, the credal formularies of the early church, and so on) is so vast that virtually no official position is ascertainable on any given topic. Third, who has the authority to determine what the official position is, even if it could be agreed that there is one. And fourth, whether there is or should be any person or persons who have authority to enforce such an official position, even if it could be agreed that there is an authoritative way of determining what it is, or whether in fact any official position is automatically nullified because no authority exists in the Episcopal Church, or could or should exist, to implement it in a binding way.

The present essay has a more limited goal, one that is closely linked with my own interests as a historian and an ecumenist.[1] The goal is to ascertain and to state in words, using the written documents that do exist, what the official position of the Episcopal Church actually is, in this case on the question of the authority of scripture, to trace its historical development backward in time, and then finally to draw it out in comparison with the official positions of some other parts of the Anglican Communion as well as of some other major Christian churches with whom we have been in official ecumenical conversation (but not of them all, for lack of space). Such an exercise, limited though it is, can help us to see more clearly what the official position is that we as a church have taken and inherited, and I claim that this is of first importance as we proceed to discuss whether that position should be retained or modified, whether it should be enforced or abandoned.[2]

This official position, I state at the outset, can be summarized as follows: The holy scriptures of the Old and New Testaments are the Word of God, they contain all things necessary to salvation, and they are the rule and ultimate standard of faith. This official position, thus summarized, is derived from and documented in seven official sources: the Ordination Oath and its questions, the Tradition of Scriptures at Ordination, the Catechism, the Chicago-Lambeth Quadrilateral, the Thirty-nine Articles of Religion, the Apostles' and Nicene creeds, and the Eucharistic Lectionary. This official position, it should be added, was reaffirmed in substance as recently as the 1991 General Convention in the several "whereas" clauses of resolution C-047a, which concluded: "That we hold to the historic appeal of Anglicanism to Scripture as interpreted by the Church's tradition, and applied with reason."

THE POSITION OF THE EPISCOPAL CHURCH, PRESENT AND PAST

The Oath or Declaration at Ordination
The first element comprising the official position of the Episcopal Church on the authority of scripture is the Oath or Declaration, which has been contained in and required by the church's Constitution since 1789, which was also posed as a question to be answered in every service of ordination from the Prayer Book of 1789 to that of 1979, and which since the Prayer Book of 1979 is actually administered in the context of the ordination itself. We look first at the Constitution of the Episcopal Church, from Article VIII:

> No persons shall be ordained and consecrated Bishop, or ordered Priest or Deacon to minister in this Church, unless at the time, in the presence of the ordaining Bishop or Bishops, (he) shall subscribe and make the following declaration: "I do believe the Holy Scriptures of the Old and New Testaments to be the Word of God, and to contain all things necessary to salvation;

and I do solemnly engage to conform to the Doctrine, Discipline, and Worship of the Episcopal Church."

The above portion of Article VIII is traceable back to the same article in the revised Constitution of 1901, which in turn derived from Article VII of the Constitution of 1789. The oath's wording as regards the authority of scripture is virtually identical in all three versions, the only significant development being that in 1901 the governing word "make" was joined to "subscribe," thus clarifying that the person is to recite the declaration and not merely to sign it.[3] For the American church, this oath took the place of subscription to the Thirty-nine Articles, the Prayer Book, and the Ordinal (which at that time was still not officially a part of the Book of Common Prayer) as containing doctrine "agreeable to the Word of God" that had been required by canon 36 of 1604 in the Church of England.[4]

This last point is of special interest, for it has been the consistent position of the Episcopal Church since 1789 that the holy scriptures *are* the Word of God and *contain* all things necessary to salvation. Even granted the limited meaning of the word *contain*, our position that the Bible *is* the Word of God raises the interesting question of whether there is any "more" Word of God, so to speak, outside of the scriptural texts. It was one view held by some at the time of the Reformation that "the Word of God" was itself superior to, and thus the judge of, holy scripture.[5] Our oath, it should be noted, does not require belief that "holy scripture" and "the Word of God" must be taken as coterminous, nor does it expressly deny the existence of some further Word or word(s) of God beyond or above the Sacred Page.

On the other hand, we may wonder if our official position commits us to the belief that *every specific thing* within the Bible *is* "the Word of God" or only that the scriptures are *collectively* "the Word of God"? That some things within the Bible *may not* be "the Word of God" seems at least implied by the distinction made in the second part of the oath, which clearly suggests that only *some* things within the Bible are "necessary to salvation." Such a distinction does seem to be reinforced by the responsive tag "the Word of the Lord" that may now be said (1979 BCP) in the Daily Office or in the Eucharist after the portions of scripture designated for each lesson (OT or NT except following the gospel at the Eucharist). Why designate certain portions of scripture, and only certain portions, to be called "the Word of the Lord"? The fact that this tag is optional has given rise now in some places to endless arguments over which parts of scripture deserve to be so called. In addition, it must be asked, why did our liturgical reformers eventually give us (beginning with the "Blue

Book" of 1976) "the Word of the Lord" rather than "the Word of God" at the end of these lessons? Were they, perhaps, merely opting for the official Roman Catholic revision rather than being faithful to the received text of our own oath at this point? Surely these liturgiologists must have known that the official Anglican position holds the scriptures to be "the Word of God"? We shall return to "the Word of God" later in this essay.

Now we consider the constitutional Oath or Declaration as it is contained within the present (1979 BCP) services of Ordination of a Bishop, Priest, and Deacon (pp. 513, 526, 538), where it comes (for priests and deacons) as an answer to the question "Will you be loyal to the doctrine, discipline, and worship of Christ as this Church has received them?" The answer, which for priests and deacons is prefixed by the statement "I am willing and ready to do so," contains the same text taken from Article VIII of the Constitution: "I solemnly declare that I do believe the Holy Scriptures of the Old and New Testaments to be the Word of God, and to contain all things necessary to salvation." For bishops this declaration stands on its own and is not the answer to a question. The oath is now read and signed publicly within all three rites, whereas prior to the 1979 BCP it was signed by the candidate in the presence of the ordaining bishop just before the service. It thus enjoys a greater prominence and emphasis since the 1979 revision than it did previously.

Prior to the 1979 American book, in the 1928 BCP, although the text of the oath was not contained within the ordination rites themselves, nonetheless its operative clause on the question of scriptural authority was always posed as a question for every future deacon, priest, or bishop to answer (in addition to the subscription required beforehand). We shall examine the texts of these questions, from the 1928 BCP. At the Making of Deacons, they were asked by the bishop: "Are you persuaded that the Holy Scriptures contain all Doctrine required as necessary for eternal salvation through faith in Jesus Christ?" and "Will you diligently read the same unto the people assembled in the Church where you shall be appointed to serve?" And in the 1928 Ordering of Priests, they were asked by the bishop: "Are you persuaded that the Holy Scriptures contain all Doctrine required as necessary for eternal salvation through faith in Jesus Christ? And are you determined, out of the said Scriptures to instruct the people committed to your charge; and to teach nothing, as necessary to eternal salvation, but that which you shall be persuaded may be concluded and proved by the Scripture?"

Such questions for deacons are absent from the ordinal tradition before 1928, where instead we find (for deacons only, and going back to the first English Ordinal of 1550) the question, "Do you unfeignedly believe all the Canonical Scriptures of the Old and New Testament?" The 1928 question for priests, however, goes back in continuity to the English ordinals of 1550 and 1552. At the Consecrating of Bishops in 1928, and extending back to the first English Ordinal of 1550, the Presiding Bishop asked virtually the same question as for the 1928 Ordering of Priests, except for the phrase "to teach *or maintain* nothing, as necessary to eternal salvation." The bishop, like the priest, was expected "to teach," but unlike the priest the bishop was also expected "to maintain" as necessary to eternal salvation that which could be concluded and proven by scripture.[6]

We note immediately how very individualistic these questions were: Each future priest or bishop is to teach (or maintain) only that which he can be persuaded can be concluded and proven from scripture. There is very little ecclesiology in these questions and answers, very little sense of the corporate and received teaching of the church (which may have been assumed, or may have been dismissed), but there is an extremely optimistic view that whatever scripture contains as necessary to salvation will be evident to any sensible and learned individual who reads it.

Looking backwards, the medieval pontificals, no doubt assuming the inherited teaching of the church catholic as well as an external structure of authority that would "settle" all disputed questions, had contained no public examination for prospective deacons or priests, but to the future bishop many questions were asked including these two: "Are you willing by word and example to teach the people for whom you are ordained those things which you understand from the Holy Scriptures?" and "Do you believe that the one author of the New and Old Testament, of the law and of the prophets and of the apostles, is God and the Lord Almighty?"[7] The first of these questions to a bishop is also strikingly individualistic; in Latin it reads "*Vis ea quae ex divinis Scripturis intelligis, plebem cui ordinandus es, et verbis docere et exemplis?*"

The Tradition of Scriptures

The second element that comprises the Episcopal Church's official position on the authority of the scriptures, also found within the services of ordination, is the ceremony that can be called "The Tradition of Scriptures." We look first at the present position as it is contained in the 1979 BCP.

At the presentation of the Bible to the newly ordained bishop these words are said: "Receive the Holy Scriptures. Feed the flock of Christ committed to your charge, guard and defend them in his truth, and be a faithful steward of his holy Word and Sacraments" (p. 521). Similarly, at the presentation of the Bible to each newly ordained priest by the bishop: "Receive this Bible as a sign of the authority given you to preach the Word of God and to administer his holy Sacraments. Do not forget the trust committed to you as a priest of the Church of God" (p. 534). And likewise, at the presentation of the Bible to each newly ordained deacon by the bishop: "Receive this Bible as the sign of your authority to proclaim God's Word and to assist in the ministration of his holy Sacraments" (p. 545).

For deacons and priests, therefore, the Bible is a sign of authority to preach, but for bishops it is also related to something more: to feed and guard and defend the flock in Christ's truth.

Now we move back in time and compare the Tradition of Scriptures in the 1979 BCP with the same ceremony in previous Prayer Books, those of 1928 and of 1792-1892, deriving from the ordinal of the English Prayer Book of 1662. In the 1928 BCP and in those previous, at the Ordering of Deacons, the bishop delivered to each, presumably still kneeling, the New Testament, saying, "Take thou Authority to read the Gospel in the Church of God, and to preach the same, if thou be thereto licensed by the Bishop himself." Thus, whereas since 1979 the new deacon gets the Bible, in 1928 and earlier it was only the New Testament, and whereas in all of these ordinals the deacon gets "Authority," in 1928 and earlier it was only authority "to read the Gospel in the Church" and to preach if licensed, but beginning in 1979 it is a broader but less specific authority "to proclaim God's Word." Looking still earlier, it should be noted that a New Testament has been given (with words similar to 1928) to each new deacon in Anglican ordinations since the first Anglican Ordinal of 1550, where it replaced the book of the Gospels that was given (with no accompanying words) in some medieval pontificals.[8]

Regarding priests in all of these same ordinals, the bishop delivered to each new priest the Bible, just as in 1979, but in the 1928 ordinal and earlier each new priest was to receive it kneeling, a requirement dropped (whether for deacons or priests) in 1979. The bishop said to each new priest, before 1979, at this point: "Take thou Authority to preach the Word of God, and to minister the holy Sacraments in the Congregation, where thou shalt be lawfully appointed thereunto," wording that was altered in 1979 by removing the limitation of such authority to one specific congregation where lawfully appointed. Once again, in 1979 the authority conferred is broader and less restricted than previously. And still earlier, Cranmer's wording in the Ordinal of 1550, "to this Congregation," had made the same limited point. And by the Ordinal of 1552, this Tradition of Scripture had totally eclipsed the medieval (and 1550) Tradition of Instruments. In the medieval pontificals, there was no delivery of Scripture at the ordinations of priests.

For bishops, in the 1928 BCP, the Presiding Bishop delivered the Bible and said to the new bishop, presumably still kneeling, these words: "Give heed unto reading, exhortation, and doctrine. Be diligent in them, that the increase coming thereby may be manifest unto all men, for by so doing thou shalt both save thyself and them that hear thee," followed by additional remarks not directly linked to the delivery of the Bible. In ordinals prior to 1928, and going back to the first English one of 1550, the sentence "Think upon the things contained in this book" was inserted after the words "and doctrine."

Interestingly, neither 1979 nor its predecessors use the word "authority" when the Bible is given to a new bishop, in all cases preferring instead some rather pious words of exhortation, whereas all these ordinals, including 1979, do use the word "authority" when the scriptures are given to new priests and deacons. Is this because they all decline to link the bishop's "authority" with the handing over of scripture, or is it, conversely, because they all assume the bishop already has authority related to scripture and does not need to "receive" the same at Ordination/ Consecration but only to pass it on, to new priests and deacons?

The first Anglican Ordinal of 1550, following medieval tradition, specified that the Bible was to be placed upon the newly consecrated bishop's neck, a tradition not continued in the Ordinal of 1552. The medieval pontificals had specified that a book of the Gospels, not the entire Bible, be held over the new bishop's neck and shoulders following the litany and as the *Veni Creator* was said and the prayer of consecration begun.[9] Again, near the end of the medieval service, the new bishop was given a book of the Gospels with the words "Receive the Gospel and go, preach to the people committed unto you, for God is able to augment within you his Grace."[10]

By stark contrast, finally, we may add that at the earliest point in the history of ordination rites, where such texts first become available, in the early third-century *Apostolic Tradition* of Hippolytus, there are no questions asked of the ordinands, no traditions of the scriptures (or of anything else), and no oaths taken.

The Catechism

There are two questions related to the authority of scripture in the 1979 American BCP Catechism, although they do not seem to have been part of the earlier Anglican catechetical tradition, either in previous Catechisms or in the Offices of Instruction:

"*Q*. Why do we call the Holy Scriptures the Word of God? *A*. We call them the Word of God because God inspired their human authors and because God still speaks to us through the Bible" (p. 853). Interestingly, this answer seems to be the very first textual introduction of the *inspiration* of scripture into documents of the official Anglican position, and although it gives a reason why today we think scripture is the Word of God it is only indirectly related to the question of scriptural authority.[11]

But *should* holy scripture be called the Word of God anymore? This question needs to be asked, because the House of Bishops of the Episcopal Church, at its Spokane meeting in 1983, passed a long "Statement of Guiding Moral and Theological Principles,"[12] which stated that "God's Word is a Person, not a book; the Person transcends all books, even the Bible." Surely the latter clause is true, but the former clause did not state that God's Word is *both* a Person *and* the book of holy scripture but rather that God's Word is a Person, *not* a book. This might have been a momentary and unintentional slip, rather than a corporate violation of the Ordination Oath, were it not for the fact that the very opening line of the bishops' statement of 1983 omits the phrase in question that the Catechism here affirms. The bishops here teach that "the Holy Scriptures of the Old and New Testaments contain all things necessary to salvation, and in that sense are the ultimate standard of faith for this Church." Thus, the bishops' statement omits the first half of the very oath that it is quoting, the declaration that the holy scriptures *are the Word of God* and contain all things necessary to salvation. The only rationale that the bishops' statement offers is that God's Word is a Person, not a book, and whether one agrees with them or not it is difficult to avoid the conclusion that they were contradicting by their 1983 statement the very phraseology of their Ordination Oath that had been raised to greater prominence in the ordination services and Catechism of the 1979 Prayer Book. The bishops' teaching can be explained as a paraphrase of the fourth paragraph of the 1886-88 Chicago-Lambeth Quadrilateral at this point (see below), but the fact that at the same time they took pains to deny that God's Word is a book, "even the Bible," does place a question by the oath to which they had all sworn. Their statement, whether it was a pastoral letter or a position paper or something else, was issued at a level of authority subordinate to the Prayer Book and the Constitution which contain the oath and therefore cannot be taken to supersede them, even though it certainly calls such time-honored phraseology into question, whatever their intention may have been.[13]

"*Q*. How do we understand the meaning of the Bible? *A*. We understand the meaning of the Bible by the help of the Holy Spirit, who guides the Church in the true interpretation of the Scriptures" (p. 853). Here we may note that a logical question to follow, "How does the Holy Spirit guide the Church in the true interpretation of the Scriptures?" is not asked, a question that has been raised acutely in recent international Anglican-Roman Catholic ecumenical dialogue, one that we shall consider later in this essay. It was a question already raised, at least implicitly, in some remarks of Archbishop Edmund Grindal back in the sixteenth century: "You shall understand that Scripture is not so to be taken as the letter sounds, but as the intent of the Holy Ghost was, by whom the Scripture was uttered."[14]

That the ultimate interpreter of scripture remains individual opinion, however, was early recognized by the foundational theologian of post-Reformation Anglicanism, Richard Hooker, who stated in 1594 in his *Laws of Ecclesiastical Polity* (2.7.9):

> Although Scripture be of God, and therefore the proof which is taken from thence must needs be of all other most invincible; yet this strength it hath not, unless it avouch the selfsame thing for which it is brought. If there be either undeniable appearance that so it doth, or reason such as cannot deceive, then Scripture-proof (no doubt) in strength and value exceedeth all. But for the most part, even such as are readiest to cite for one thing five hundred sentences of holy Scripture; what warrant have they, that any one of them doth mean the thing for which it is alleged? Is not their surest ground most commonly, either some probable conjecture of their own, or the judgment of others taking those Scriptures as they do?

The Chicago-Lambeth Quadrilateral

"Lex orandi lex credendi," or in its earlier form as derived from Saint Prosper of Aquitaine in the fifth century, "Legem credendi lex statuat supplicandi," is for Anglicans a basic principle in the determination of doctrine, but we move now from the area of historical liturgics to the fourth and fifth components of the Episcopal Church's official position on the authority of scripture. These components are also contained within the 1979 Book of Common Prayer, but within its "Historical Documents" section.

The fourth is the Chicago-Lambeth Quadrilateral of 1886-88, printed in the 1979 BCP (pp. 876-78, and esp. p. 877). As is well known, the Quadrilateral's four points constitute an Anglican basis for an approach toward church unity, a *terminus a quo* from which other matters may be discussed, and these four points have been authoritative for both houses of the Episcopal Church's General Convention since 1895. The first of these four points constitutes another element in our official position on scriptural authority: "The Holy Scriptures of the Old and New Testaments as 'containing all things necessary to salvation,' and as being the rule and ultimate standard of faith."

Looking backward, we may note that the previous version (Chicago 1886) of the Quadrilateral had read: "The Holy Scriptures of the Old and New Testament as the revealed Word of God" (BCP, p. 877). And the original wording of William Reed Huntington in his book *The Church-Idea* (1870) was "The Holy Scriptures as the Word of God." It is important to note that the key addition to point 1 by the 1888 Lambeth Conference, which significantly altered the earlier wording of the American bishops from Chicago in 1886, as well as the original 1870 formulation of Huntington, is the phrase "containing all things necessary to salvation," taken over from Article VI of the Thirty-nine Articles of 1563-71, a typical Reformation code phrase that has been standard in virtually all Anglican assertions about the authority of scripture since the sixteenth century. By the addition of phrases from the Thirty-nine Articles, in fact, Lambeth 1888 enriched not only the first but also the second and third of the four points coming from the American bishops of 1886, which was just the contrary of what Huntington hoped![15]

The Thirty-nine Articles of Religion

The central place and significance of the phrase "containing all things necessary to salvation" from Article VI has already been remarked above. This is not the place to discuss or determine the exact authority that the Thirty-nine Articles of Religion of 1563-71 may have for the Episcopal Church today, but I think it can be said with confidence that their inclusion (in the version adopted by the American General Convention of 1801) within the section entitled "Historical Documents of the Church" at the back of the 1979 American Prayer Book more certainly signifies some degree of approval than of disapproval. We have not placed in this section documents that we condemn, even though we may disagree about the precise nature of authority they hold today.

Those articles that deal directly with our present subject are Articles

VI ("Of the Sufficiency of the Holy Scriptures for Salvation"), VII ("Of the Old Testament"), XVII ("Of Predestination and Election"), and XX ("Of the Authority of the Church"), and I shall note here certain of their contents. From Article VI:

> Holy Scripture containeth all things necessary to salvation: so that whatsoever is not read therein, nor may be proved thereby, is not to be required of any man, that it should be believed as an article of the Faith, or be thought requisite or necessary to salvation.

Here we find, as has already been noted, the ultimate source for the Episcopal Church's official position on scriptural authority as contained in the Ordination Oath as well as in the examination questions. It states only that whatever is necessary to salvation (and perhaps much else!) is contained within holy scripture, not that everything in holy scripture is necessary to salvation (although presumably the Episcopal Church does hold, with what is now the collect for Proper 27, that "all Holy Scriptures are written for our learning"). Whether everything in scripture is the Word of God, and whether there is any more or different Word of God beyond or above what is written in scripture, has already been discussed.

Article VI is a typical Reformation statement, deriving from Article V of the Forty-two Articles of 1553, which read:

> Holy Scripture containeth all things necessary to salvation: so that whatsoever is neither read therein, nor may be proved thereby, [although it be some time received of the faithful as godly, and profitable for an order and comeliness:] yet no man ought to be constrained to believe it as an article of faith or repute it requisite to the necessity of salvation.

The words in brackets were omitted in 1563 when other minor changes were made. And this article is in turn related to Cranmer's book of 1551-53, the *Reformatio Legum Ecclesiasticarum* (which never became fully official), where the reference is made to "sancta Scriptura, qua omnia creditu ad salutem necessaria, plene et perfecte contineri credimus."[16]

Yet it is also necessary to observe that such assertions about scriptural authority, even in such sweeping terms, do not originate with the Reformation but have considerable grounding in the early church. Here are some illuminating examples of the patristic foundation of this Anglican position: Origen, Homily 5 on Leviticus: "If any thing remains which Holy Scripture does not determine, no other third scripture ought to be received to authorize any knowledge." Athanasius, *Contra Gentes* 1: "The holy and divinely inspired

Scriptures are of themselves sufficient to the enunciation of truth."
Athanasius, *Festal Epistle* 39: "These are the fountains of salvation,
that whoever thirsts may be satisfied with the words they contain. In
these alone is proclaimed the doctrine of godliness. Let no one add
to them, neither take ought from them." Basil the Great, Homily no.
29: "Believe those things that are written: the things which are not
written, seek not." Cyril of Jerusalem, *Catechesis* 4.17: "Do not
believe even me merely because I tell you these things, unless you
receive from the inspired Scriptures the proof of the assertions. For
this saving faith of ours depends not on ingenious reasonings but on
proof from the inspired Scriptures." Augustine, *De Doctrina
Christiana* 2.9: "In those things which are plainly laid down in
Scripture, all things are found which embrace faith and conduct."
And even the later Eastern writer John of Damascus, *On the
Orthodox Faith* 1.1: "All things that are delivered to us by the law,
the prophets, the apostles, and the evangelists we receive, acknowledge, and reverence, seeking for nothing beyond these."[17]

Article VI furthermore discusses which are the canonical books of
the Old and New Testaments, asserting also that the books of the
Apocrypha are useful for example and instruction but not for estab-
lishment of doctrine. The statement about the authority of scripture
made earlier in Article VI is thus governed by the principles of
canonicity established in the second part of this article, just as that
authority is further governed for the Episcopal Church by the various English translations of scripture that General Convention decides
to authorize and by which scriptural passages the lectionary selects
to be read on particular days. In a sense, therefore, questions of lectionary and of translation, as regards the authority of scripture itself,
are best understood as related to the process whereby the canon is
established. And by implication, likewise, any other extra- or non-
canonical writings, whether contemporary or not, do not for the
Episcopal Church possess the same authority as the canon, even
though they may be spiritually edifying or academically useful.

From Article XVII:

> We must receive God's promises in such wise, as they be gener-
> ally set forth to us in Holy Scripture: and, in our doings, that Will
> of God is to be followed, which we have expressly declared
> unto us in the Word of God.

Here we seem to have an even more limited statement of the scriptures' authority: it extends only so far as there is an *express* declaration of God's will, and the Word of God clearly does not extend
beyond the text of scripture itself.

Article XX:

> The Church hath power to decree Rites or Ceremonies, and authority in Controversies of Faith: and yet it is not lawful for the Church to ordain any thing that is contrary to God's Word written, neither may it so expound one place of Scripture, that it be repugnant to another. Wherefore, although the Church be a witness and a keeper of Holy Writ, yet, as it ought not to decree any thing against the same, so besides the same ought it not to enforce any thing to be believed for necessity of Salvation.

The confidence that scripture is itself somehow self-authenticating, reflected in these articles (especially the last) and quite characteristic of the Reformation's reaction against the authoritative church of the Middle Ages, can be seen as firmly established for the Church of England in the Act of Supremacy of 1559 which provided that no one in the Church of England would "in any wise have authority or power to order, determine, or adjudge any matter or cause to be heresy" but rather that appointees of the Crown would declare as heretical

> only such as heretofore have been determined, ordered, or adjudged to be heresy by the authority of the canonical Scriptures, or by the first four general Councils, or any of them, or by any other general Council wherein the same was declared to be heresy by the express and plain words of the said canonical Scriptures, or such as hereafter shall be ordered, judged, or determined to be heresy by the High Court of Parliament of this realm, with the assent of the clergy in their Convocation.[18]

In this act we have the legal foundation for Articles VI and XX, as well as a hint of the confidence or assurance that is expressed in Article XVII. We also have a willingness for anything previously found to be heresy to be still considered as such, scripture being the ultimate criterion, but on the other hand we find a reluctance to allow any such authoritative function to the church of the present era. How can the church have "authority in controversies of faith," especially if one or more persons declare that it has made a pronouncement not consonant with scripture as they understand it?

Still others of the Articles of Religion, in a sense dependent on Article VI because they make judgments about whether particular points can be proved by scripture (notably Articles VIII, XVIII, XXI, XXII, XXIV, XXV, XXVI, XXVIII, XXXII, XXXIV, and XXXVII), are part of the general Anglican doctrinal inheritance but less directly tied to the current official position of the Episcopal Church than is Article VI by reason of its being the verbal and conceptual source of the constitutional oath for ordinations. In yet another, Article XXXV, the Episcopal Church "declares the Books of Homilies to be an explication of Christian doctrine, and instructive in piety and morals," so that any points in them that may touch upon scriptural authority can be said, but only in a rather indirect way, to be commended by this article to the extent that it is received in the Episcopal Church.

The Creeds

In a sense, of course, the classical catholic creeds, Apostles' and Nicene, are themselves also official statements that establish for the Episcopal Church the particular way in which scripture is authoritatively interpreted on major points of doctrine. Their authority is grounded not only within Article VIII ("for they may be proved by most certain warrants of Holy Scripture"), but also in the church's liturgical use whereby we require the Niceno-Constantinopolitan Creed to be said at every Eucharist on all Sundays and major feasts, and the Apostles' Creed to be said in the Baptismal Covenant and the Daily Office. By such liturgical requirements, then, we are here asserting that scripture is authoritatively interpreted by us in the way in which we receive the doctrinal formulations of the creeds that we use.

The Lectionary

A seventh and final component of the official teaching on scriptural authority is to be found in the official Eucharistic Lectionary of the Book of Common Prayer. Here, for the Sundays throughout the year, the Old Testament readings are chosen to match the Gospel readings Christologically, either by anticipation or by type, so that the unity of the Old and New Testaments is set forth on a basis of salvation history with Christ at the center, not on some principle of historical criticism or of linear chronology as it is often taught in seminaries. And scripture is also read throughout the liturgical year in relation to the developing life of Christ, with the implication that public preaching is likewise to be based thereupon. Just as with the requirement for saying the creeds, therefore, scripture is authoritatively interpreted in the Episcopal Church by the Christological principle upon which it is to be publicly read in the principal act of Christian worship on every Lord's Day and other major feasts (BCP, p. 13). Scripture for Episcopalians/Anglicans is thus used not so much for dogmatic theologizing as it is to shape the hearts and minds of those who worship so that they may grow as one body in Christ.

COMPARISONS WITH OTHER CHURCHES

Having now outlined the official position of the Episcopal Church on the authority of scripture as well as its historical development, we next turn to some lateral (but not historical) comparisons with other churches in the present era, beginning with the Anglican Church of Canada and the Church of England, and then extending ecumenically to look at the official positions of the Lutherans, the Orthodox, and the Roman Catholics.

Anglican Church of Canada

The official position of the Anglican Church of Canada was set forth at its foundation in its Solemn Declaration of 1893, traditionally printed in the front of all Canadian Prayer Books: "Hold the One Faith revealed in Holy Writ, . . . receive the same Canonical Scriptures of the Old and New Testaments, as containing all things necessary to salvation; teach the same Word of God." And for the latest statement of this position, we turn to the ordinal in the Canadian *Book of Alternative Services* (1985), where we find for all three orders of ministry virtually the same oath (within the service) and the same words at the Tradition of the Bible as in the 1979 American BCP. The most notable difference is that at in Canada the ordination of a priest the chalice and paten are given in addition to the Bible (p. 649).

The Church of England

For the Church of England, we turn to *The Alternative Service Book* of 1980, which may reasonably be taken as the latest restatement of its official position. At the conferral of each of the three orders, the bishop (archbishop) asks the same question about scriptural authority: "Do you accept the holy Scriptures as revealing all things necessary for salvation through faith in Jesus Christ?" Somehow, it seems to me that the choice of "revealing" is a less specific, but also more dynamic, word than the American church's consistent retention of the word "containing," derived as the latter is from Article VI of the Thirty-nine. The enduring authority of the articles for the Church of England today, however, is a question that can only be raised here and not discussed further than has already been done for their authority within the Episcopal Church.

Following each English ordination, a New Testament is given to the new deacon, a Bible to the new priest or bishop. The words said at each of these Traditions of Scripture, however, are different from one another as well as from their North American counterparts.

To a new deacon the bishop says, "Receive this Book, as a sign of the authority given you this day to speak God's word to his people. Build them up in his truth and serve them in his name." The deacon in the Church of England, we thus note, is to "speak" God's word, whereas the deacon in the Episcopal Church is to "proclaim" it. And whereas the Church of England links the deacon's New Testament with God's word, the Episcopal Church links the deacon's Bible with both word and sacraments. Whichever book is being presented, though, both churches connect it with "authority" that is being given to the deacon.

To a new priest the bishop says, "Receive this Book, as a sign of the authority which God has given you this day to preach the gospel of Christ and to minister his Holy Sacraments." Here there is more agreement of the Church of England with North American usage, both presenting the Bible to the new priest, both connecting it with "authority to preach," both refusing to restrict this authority to a particular congregation, both distinguishing the priestly ministry of preaching from the diaconal one of speaking or proclaiming, and both linking the new priest's Bible with the sacraments as well as with the Gospel (Church of England) or Word (North America).

To a new bishop the archbishop says, "Receive this Book; here are the words of eternal life. Take them for your guide, and declare them to the world," followed by additional remarks not directly linked to the delivery of the Bible. Here there is little similarity to the words now used in the two North American churches, except that the Church of England, like them, makes no mention of scriptural "authority" when the Bible is given to a new bishop, preferring some rather pious words of exhortation, whereas it does (like them) use the word "authority" when the scriptures are given to new priests and deacons.

This last point, however, may be related for the Church of England to the fact that only for a new bishop, and not for all three orders as in North America, is there in the *Alternative Service Book* the requirement to take an oath as part of the ordination service itself: "I . . . declare my belief in the faith which is revealed in the holy Scriptures and set forth in the catholic creeds and to which the historic formularies of the Church of England bear witness" (p. 388). Here again, as in the question asked of all three orders in England, we note the preference for "revealed" over the traditional Anglican (1662) verb "contained," and thus it cannot be said that for the Church of England any longer the operative phrase descriptive of scriptural authority is "containing all things necessary to salvation," as it still is for the Episcopal Church in the USA and the Anglican Church of Canada.

Inasmuch as the Church of England has a firmer legal foundation than any other church of the Anglican Communion, it will also be necessary to note its official position in canon law, which is governed by Canon A-5 of 1964/1969:

> The doctrine of the Church of England is grounded in the holy Scriptures, and in such teachings of the ancient Fathers and Councils of the Church as are agreeable to the said Scriptures. In particular such doctrine is to be found in the Thirty-nine Articles of Religion, the Book of Common Prayer, and the Ordinal.[19]

This canon, passed by the convocations of Canterbury and York and repealing any related canons of the Code of 1603, now has the force of ecclesiastical law within the Church of England. It should be noted that the ordinal to which it refers is that of 1662, which, rather than that of the ASB 1980, is still technically the "official position" of the Church of England, even though the Ordinal of ASB 1980 probably comes closer to representing its present mind. We may note, however, the lack of clarity when the canon says that such doctrine "is found in" such documents but only "grounded in" the Bible.

The position of the Church of England on scriptural authority is somewhat strengthened by one other canon, number C-15, which prescribes and requires a "Declaration of Assent" to be taken by every bishop before confirmation of election or consecration and by every priest and deacon before ordination and again before institution to any cure, whereby the person swears the doctrine of the Church of England as set forth in the Thirty-nine Articles of Religion and in the Book of Common Prayer and Ordinal "to be agreeable to the Word of God."

At least by implication, Anglican doctrine is by this canon authoritatively subordinated to "the Word of God," with echoes of the sixth Article of Religion, although the classical Anglican statements that the scriptures are the Word of God and *contain* all things necessary to salvation are no longer employed.

The Lutheran Churches

For the official position of the Lutherans, we turn first to the Evangelical Lutheran Church in America (ELCA), the Lutheran body that is now the Episcopal Church's closest ecumenical partner, and here we find their official position on scriptural authority expressed in their new (1988) Constitution, chapter 2, which makes the following statements:

2.02.c "The canonical Scriptures of the Old and New Testaments are the written Word of God. Inspired by God's Spirit speaking through their authors, they record and announce God's revelation centering in Jesus Christ. Through them God's Spirit speaks to us to create and sustain Christian faith and fellowship for service in the world."

2.03. "This church accepts the canonical Scriptures of the Old and New Testaments as the inspired Word of God and the authoritative source and norm of its proclamation, faith, and life."

2.04. "This church accepts the Apostles', Nicene, and Athanasian Creeds as true declarations of the faith of this church."

2.05. "This church accepts the Unaltered Augsburg Confession as a true witness to the Gospel, acknowledging as one with it in faith and doctrine all churches that likewise accept the teachings of the Unaltered Augsburg Confession."

2.06. "This church accepts the other confessional writings in the Book of Concord, namely, the Apology of the Augsburg Confession, the Smalcald Articles and the Treatise, the Small Catechism, the Large Catechism, and the Formula of Concord, as further valid interpretations of the faith of the Church."

2.07. "This church confesses the Gospel, recorded in the Holy Scriptures and confessed in the ecumenical creeds and Lutheran confessional writings, as the power of God to create and sustain the Church for God's mission in the world."

Related but subordinate to this Constitution, and at a lower level of authority than the *Lutheran Book of Worship*, is the new book of *Occasional Services* (1982), which in the service that may (but not must) be used for Ordination to the Pastoral Office in the ELCA provides the following question:

The Church in which you are to be ordained confesses that the Holy Scriptures are the Word of God and are the norm of its faith and life. We accept, teach, and confess the Apostles', the Nicene, and the Athanasian Creeds. We also acknowledge the Lutheran Confessions as true witnesses and faithful expositions of the Holy Scriptures. Will you therefore preach and teach in accordance with the Scriptures and these creeds and confessions? (p. 194)

Here then we do not find the characteristically Anglican description of scriptural authority as "the Word of God and containing all things necessary to salvation," but we find two phrases that are possibly its substantial equivalents: "the inspired Word of God and *the authoritative source and norm of its proclamation, faith, and life*" (Constitution 2.03) and "the Word of God and *the norm of its faith and life*" (ordination promise). By such phrases as I have italicized, however, do Lutherans accord scripture a more extensive authority than do Anglicans? Is the territory of *adiaphora* for Anglicans, perhaps, wider than it is for Lutherans?

The Augsburg Confession of 1530, which is considered "binding" for all Lutherans and not just those of the ELCA, has very little to say directly about the authority of scripture, but we do find authoritative statements on this topic elsewhere within the Book of Concord, most especially in the Epitome of the Formula of Concord (1576):

> We believe, teach, and confess that the prophetic and apostolic writings of the Old and New Testaments are the only rule and norm according to which all doctrines and teachers alike must be appraised and judged. . . . Other writings of ancient and modern teachers, whatever their names, should not be put on a par with Holy Scripture. Every single one of them should be subordinated to the Scriptures and should be received in no other way and no further than as witnesses to the fashion in which the doctrine of the prophets and apostles was preserved in post-apostolic times. . . . Holy Scripture remains the only judge, rule, and norm according to which as the only touchstone all doctrines should and must be understood and judged as good or evil, right or wrong.[20]

It should be noted finally, for the ELCA, that the above statement is nonetheless of a lower level of authority than the Augsburg Confession itself, the Confession being accepted in the ELCA Constitution "as a true witness to the Gospel" and the Epitome of the Formula being accepted merely as "a further valid interpretation of the faith of the Church.

The Orthodox Churches

Looking now at the churches of Eastern Orthodoxy, with whom the Anglican Communion and the Episcopal Church have had their oldest ecumenical dialogue, we find almost no trace of any explicit authoritative statement at the highest level on the authority of scripture. Overall, the Orthodox position on scriptural authority is summarized by the ex-Anglican Timothy Ware, now well known as "Bishop Kallistos" and currently the Spalding Lecturer in Eastern Orthodox Culture at Oxford University:

> The Christian Church is a Scriptural Church: Orthodoxy believes this just as firmly, if not more firmly than Protestantism. The Bible is the supreme expression of God's revelation to man, and Christians must always be "People of the Book." But if Christians are People of the Book, the Bible is the Book of the People; it must not be regarded as something set up *over* the Church (that is why one should not separate Scripture and Tradition). It is

from the Church that the Bible ultimately derives its authority, for it was the Church which originally decided which books form a part of Holy Scripture; and it is the Church alone which can interpret Holy Scripture with authority. There are many sayings in the Bible which by themselves are far from clear, and the individual reader, however sincere, is in danger of error if he trusts his own personal interpretation. "Do you understand what you are reading?" Philip asked the Ethiopian eunuch; and the eunuch replied: "How can I, unless someone guides me?" (Acts viii, 30-31). Orthodox, when they read the Scripture, accept the guidance of the Church. When received into the Orthodox Church, a convert promises: "I will accept and understand Holy Scripture in accordance with the interpretation which was and is held by the Holy Orthodox Catholic Church of the East, our Mother."[21]

The same position was put in words that sound more familiar to Anglican ears by Bishop Kallistos's predecessor in the Spalding chair at Oxford, Nicholas Zernov:

> The Orthodox believe that the Holy Scriptures contain the word of God, not because they were written by the Apostles, but because these books were unanimously chosen by the Church under the guidance of the Holy Spirit as the true record of Christ's life and teaching.[22]

We may note his choice of phrase, "contain the word of God," to describe the Orthodox position.

There is one classical Orthodox statement of scriptural authority, and this is the Longer Russian Catechism of 1839, which was approved by the Holy Synod at Moscow and published in that year. On our topic it gives the following questions and answers:

19. What is that which you call Holy Scripture?
Certain books written by the Spirit of God through men sanctified by God, called Prophets and Apostles. These books are commonly termed the Bible. . . .

21. Which is the more ancient, holy tradition or holy Scripture?
The most ancient and original instrument for spreading divine revelation is holy tradition. From Adam to Moses there were no sacred books. Our Lord Jesus Christ himself delivered his divine doctrine and ordinances to his Disciples by word and example, but not by writing. The same method was followed by the Apostles also at first, when they spread abroad the faith and established the Church of Christ. The necessity of tradition is further evident from this, that books can be available only to a small part of mankind, but tradition to all.

22. Why, then, was holy Scripture given:
To this end, that divine revelation might be preserved more

exactly and unchangeably. In holy Scripture we read the words of the Prophets and Apostles precisely as if we were living with them and listening to them, although the latest of the sacred books were written a thousand and some hundred years before our time.

23. Must we follow holy tradition, even when we possess holy Scripture?
We must follow that tradition which agrees with the divine revelation and with holy Scripture, as is taught us by holy Scripture itself. The Apostle Paul writes: "Therefore, brethren, stand fast, and hold the traditions which ye have been taught, whether by word or our epistle." 2 Thess. ii.15.

24. Why is tradition necessary even now?
As a guide to the right understanding of holy Scripture, for the right ministration of the sacraments, and the preservation of sacred rites and ceremonies in the purity of their original institution. . . .

56. What rules must we observe in reading holy Scripture?
First, we must read it devoutly, as the Word of God, and with prayer to understand it aright; secondly, we must read it with a pure desire of instruction in faith, and incitement to good works; thirdly, we must take and understand it in such sense as agrees with the interpretation of the orthodox Church and the holy Fathers.

This Catechism, however, is not among those documents listed by Timothy Ware or Nicholas Zernov, nor by any other Orthodox writer that I can locate, as being of "chief" or "authoritative" standing.[23] Its position does follow the general lines of Ware and Zernov on scriptural authority, although its official status remains uncertain.

To be fair to the Orthodox, I think they would in no way consider the absence of any official position at the highest level on the authority of scripture to be a deficiency, holding to the contrary that in the one true church (which they believe themselves to be) such an official position statement is entirely unnecessary and that the emergence of such statements in the churches of the West is merely evidence of the confusion and disagreements that have been brought about by the Reformation of the sixteenth century.

It is only when pressured in ecumenical dialogue by the churches of the West, however, that the Orthodox have been moved to put such views in writing at anything like an official level, and we find them, almost incidentally, within the Orthodox statements made at the second and third World Conferences on Faith and Order. At Edinburgh in 1937 the Orthodox said, on the topic at hand:

We consider the Church and not the "Word" (i.e. the written and preached Word) as primary in the work of our salvation. It is by the Church that the Scriptures are given to us. They are God's gift to her; they are the means of grace which she uses in the work of our salvation.

And at Lund in 1952 they stated:

The Orthodox Church cannot accept that the Holy Spirit speaks to us only through the Bible. The Holy Spirit abides and witnesses through the totality of the Church's life and experience. The Bible is given to us within the context of the Apostolic Tradition in which in turn we possess the authentic interpretation and explication of the Word of God.[24]

Probably the most explicit written statements of an official Orthodox position on the authority of holy scripture are those that emanate from the official international Anglican-Orthodox Joint Doctrinal Discussions, and to these we now turn. First, in the Moscow Statement of 1976,[25] we find the following agreements (which do not, interestingly, include or even mention the "containing all things necessary to salvation" phrase that was still the official Anglican position at that time):

4. The Scriptures constitute a coherent whole. They are at once divinely inspired and humanly expressed. They bear authoritative witness to God's revelation of himself in creation, in the Incarnation of the Word and in the whole history of salvation, and as such express the Word of God in human language.

5. We know, receive, and interpret Scripture through the Church and in the Church. Our approach to the Bible is one of obedience so that we may hear the revelation of himself that God gives through it.

6. The books of Scripture contained in the Canon are authoritative because they truly convey the authentic revelation of God, which the Church recognizes in them. Their authority is not determined by any particular theories concerning the authorship of these books or the historical circumstances in which they were written. The Church gives attention to the results of scholarly research concerning the Bible from whatever quarter they come, but it tests them in the light of its experience and understanding of the faith as a whole. . . .

9. Any disjunction between Scripture and Tradition such as would treat them as two separate "sources of revelation" must be rejected. The two are correlative. We affirm (i) that Scripture is the main criterion whereby the Church tests traditions to determine whether they are truly part of Holy Tradition or not; (ii) that Holy Tradition completes Holy Scripture in the sense that it safeguards the integrity of the biblical message. . . .

11. The Church cannot define dogmas which are not grounded both in Holy Scripture and in Holy Tradition, but has the power, particularly in Ecumenical Councils, to formulate the truths of the faith more exactly and precisely when the needs of the Church require it.

And the Dublin Agreed Statement of 1984 stated:

We agree in our basic understanding of the inspiration and authority of Scripture, and we agree more particularly that the Church gives attention to the results of scholarly research concerning the Bible. . . . We agree likewise in our view of the fundamental relationship between Scripture and tradition: they are not two sources, but correlative. We agree that the Church cannot define dogmas which are not grounded both in Scripture and in tradition.[26]

Even an intelligent and forward-looking interpreter of Eastern Orthodoxy such as Father Demetrios Constantelos, eminent scholar and professor at Stockton State College in New Jersey, does not in his introductory *Understanding the Greek Orthodox Church*[27] cite any explicit and authoritative written Orthodox statement or statements that govern the official position of the Eastern Orthodox on scriptural authority, not even the ones I have quoted above. He does have much to say that is positive about the central position and authoritative role that the Bible plays in Orthodox liturgy, making helpful counts of the (very large) numbers of scriptural quotations appearing in various liturgical texts. Nor does he mention the Moscow or Dublin statements in his book on ecumenism, *Issues and Dialogues in the Orthodox Church since World War Two*.[28] Of course there is some uncertainty as to what degree of authority such statements possess for the Orthodox, and it may be for this reason that they are seldom cited. The Dublin Statement was commended in an ecumenical resolution of the Episcopal Church's 1991 General Convention.

The Roman Catholic Church

Finally, but by no means least, we come to the present and official position on the authority of scripture as held by the largest church in the world, the Roman Catholic Church. Surprisingly, however, the present position will not take long to describe, although a historical treatment could easily occupy an entire book. We begin with the new Pontifical of 1968, which contains the services of ordination, and here we find no oaths or questions relating to the authority of scripture.[29] There is a Tradition of the Book of the Gospels for new deacons, which they receive kneeling as the bishop says, "Receive the Gospel of Christ, whose herald you are. Believe what you read, teach what you believe, and practice what you teach." And at the ordination of a bishop, an open book of the Gospels is placed upon his head (*super caput*), held there throughout the prayer that consecrates him, and later given to the new bishop by the principal consecrator, who says, "Receive the Gospel and preach the word of God, always teaching with the greatest patience." Neither of these statements, we may note, links the Tradition of Scripture with any kind of authority. The scriptures are not given to new priests.

The historical development of the Roman Catholic church's official position on the authority of scripture is well told in chapter 72 of *The New Jerome Biblical Commentary* (1990), but for the present position we need pick up the story only with the Dogmatic Constitution on Divine Revelation, *Dei Verbum*, of the Second Vatican Council (1965), whose background is precisely the classical debate over scriptural authority since the Reformation. Are scripture and tradition two independent sources of revelation (the traditional Roman Catholic view), or is there only one source and that scripture alone (the traditional Protestant view)? Overall, it seems that at the Second Vatican Council the Roman Catholic Church moved somewhat from a position of "two independent sources" toward a more highly nuanced position that affirms *one* source of revelation that is transmitted through *both* scripture *and* tradition. Thus, whereas the original title of the first draft of chapter 1 of *Dei Verbum* was "On the Two Sources of Revelation," the final title was simply "On Revelation Itself." Also, the word "tradition" occurs in none of the final chapter titles, although the titles have very much to say about "scripture."

Holy scripture, of course, does not consist of theological propositions or decrees, and one example of the way in which the Roman Catholic position shifted to a more dynamic and less propositional view of scriptural authority at Vatican II can be seen by comparing the opening sentence of chapter 1 of *Dei Verbum* with the corresponding opening of Vatican I's document on the same subject (*Dei Filius*, 1870). Vatican II begins, "In his goodness and wisdom, God chose to reveal himself and to make known to us the hidden purpose (*sacramentum*, or, from Eph. 1:9, *mysterion*) of his will," whereas the corresponding sentence at Vatican I had read "eternal decrees (*aeterna decreta*) of his will." The authority of scripture, therefore, is for Vatican II more of a sacrament or a mystery, whereas for Vatican I it was more a matter of decrees or propositions.

The other key statement of Vatican II, *Dei Verbum*, for our purposes is found in paragraph 10, where we read:

> Sacred tradition and sacred Scripture form one sacred deposit of the word of God, which is committed to the Church. . . . The task of authentically interpreting the word of God, whether written or handed on, has been entrusted exclusively to the living teaching office (*vivo magisterio*) of the Church, whose authority is exercised in the name of Jesus Christ. This teaching office is not above the word of God, but serves it, teaching only what has been handed on, listening to it devoutly, guarding it scrupulously, and explaining it faithfully by divine commission and with the help of the Holy Spirit; it draws from this one deposit of faith everything which it presents for belief as divinely revealed. It is clear, therefore, that sacred tradition, sacred Scripture, and the teaching authority of the Church, in accord with God's most wise design, are so linked and joined together that one cannot stand without the others.

Here we find four assertions interwoven: 1) Scripture and tradition form one deposit of the word of God, 2) which may be interpreted only by the church's teaching authority,[30] 3) which is not above the word of God but serves it, and 4) all three form a triad of scripture, tradition, and authority—which may be contrasted with the traditional Anglican triad of scripture, tradition, and reason.

And this brings us, finally, to the question of authority as it has played itself out in the Anglican-Roman Catholic International Commission, known as ARCIC-I. It is a broad and complex subject that occupies the last 50 percent of that commission's *Final Report*, but for our purposes the question of the authority of scripture is addressed most directly in the report's assertion (1981) that "if [an infallible papal] definition proposed for assent were not manifestly a legitimate interpretation of biblical faith and in line with orthodox tradition, Anglicans would think it a duty to reserve the reception of the definition for study and discussion."[31] Cardinal Ratzinger of the Congregation for the Doctrine of the Faith later commented upon this point, asking "who decides whether what you say is in accord with Scripture or not?"[32] And that, in an extended way, is the question upon which I conclude this survey: Who decides, for Episcopalians, which of the things contained in holy scripture are necessary for eternal salvation, and by whose authority are they to be interpreted and to be implemented? Who decides, on behalf of Article XX, whether something is "contrary to God's Word written"?

NOTES

1. This essay in an earlier form was first presented as the opening address to the Conference of Anglican Theologians meeting in Berkeley, California, on September 20, 1991, and it was subsequently published (in two parts) in the *Anglican Theological Review* 74, no. 3 (Summer 1992) and 74, no. 4 (Fall 1992). Bibliographical references are not given for conciliar, liturgical, canonical, and scriptural texts in common use.

2. For a viewpoint, and a survey of the thought of some individual Anglican theologians on scriptural authority, see Philip Culbertson, "The Authority of Scripture in the Episcopal Church," *St. Luke's Journal of Theology* 34, Special Issue (May 1991): S20-S37. A useful collection of essays may be found in *Anglicanism and the Bible,* ed. Frederick H. Borsch (Wilton, Conn.: Morehouse Barlow, 1984). For a helpful historical essay, but largely related to the English scene, see Reginald H. Fuller, "The Authority of the Scriptures in Anglicanism," in *Lutheran-Episcopal Dialogue: Report and Recommendations: The Report of the Lutheran-Episcopal Dialogue Second Series 1976-1980* (Cincinnati: Forward Movement Publications, 1981), 87-113.

3. Edwin A. White and Jackson A. Dykman, *Annotated Constitution and Canons for the Government of the Protestant Episcopal Church in the United States of America otherwise known as The Episcopal Church,* 1981 rev. ed. (New York: Seabury Press, 1982), 1:110-12.

4. J. V. Bullard, *Constitutions and Canons Ecclesiastical 1604: Latin and English* (London: Faith Press, 1934), 40.

5. John Guy, "Scripture as Authority: Problems of Interpretation in the 1530s," in *Reassessing the Henrician Age: Humanism, Politics, and Reform 1500-1550,* ed. Alistair Fox and John Guy (New York: Basil Blackwell, 1986), 200.

6. Paul V. Marshall, *Prayer Book Parallels (Anglican Liturgy in America,* vol. 1) (New York: The Church Hymnal Corporation, 1989), 590-91, 608-9, and 632-33. There are omissions on p. 608.

7. William Maskell, *Monumenta Ritualia Ecclesiae Anglicanae* (London: William Pickering, 1847), 3:246, 251.

8. This was especially common in medieval England: Ibid., 199.

9. Ibid., 255-56.

10. Ibid., 275.

11. Cf. Reginald Fuller in *The Study of Anglicanism,* ed. Stephen Sykes and John Booty (Philadelphia: Fortress, 1988), 80-82.

12. H.B. Resolution B-16, *The Journal of General Convention 1985* (New York: Episcopal Church Center, n.d.), part 2, pp. 311-13.

13. Title III, canon 21, section 2 (f) and (g); *Journal of the General Convention 1964,* 312-13, Resolution on "Levels of Authority within the Church." The

report to the 1958 Lambeth Conference on "The Holy Bible: Its Authority and Message" was more carefully nuanced than the 1983 resolution of the American bishops: "It is clear that if we are to understand the way in which the Bible is the Word of God we need to take as our central thought the fact that Jesus Christ is the Word of God" (1958 Lambeth Conference, committee reports, page 2.7; cf. resolution 2: "The Conference affirms that our Lord Jesus Christ is God's final Word to man, and that in his light all Holy Scripture must be seen and interpreted").

14. *Remains*, Parker Society, p. 40, as cited in George H. Tavard, *Holy Writ or Holy Church* (New York: Harper and Brothers, 1959), 228.

15. J. Robert Wright, ed., *Quadrilateral at One Hundred* (Cincinnati: Forward Movement Publications, 1988), 12-15, 30.

16. *De Summa Trinitate et Fide Catholica*, chap. ix.

17. E. J. Bicknell, *A Theological Introduction to the Thirty-nine Articles of the Church of England*, 3d ed., rev. by H. J. Carpenter (London: Longmans, Green and Co., 1955), 131; Edward H. Browne, *An Exposition of the Thirty-nine Articles* (London: Longmans, Green and Co., 1865), 140-42 (original texts); William Palmer, *Treatise on the Church*, part 3, chap. 1.

18. I Elizabeth I, cap. i, sect. 36, later cited with approval by Hooker in his *Ecclesiastical Polity* 7.2.17.

19. *The Canons of the Church of England: Canons Ecclesiastical Promulged by the Convocations of Canterbury and York in 1964 and 1969* (London: SPCK, 1969), 3-4.

20. *The Book of Concord*, ed. Theodore G. Tappert (Philadelphia: Fortress Press, 1959), 464-65, and cf. 503-4.

21. Timothy Ware, *The Orthodox Church* (Baltimore: Penguin Books, 1964), 207-8, citing Decree no. ii of the *Confession* of Dositheus, Patriarch of Jerusalem, which received synodal ratification in 1672. A helpful bibliography of pertinent works by Orthodox writers is given by Theodore Stylianopoulos in *The Anchor Bible Dictionary*, ed. David N. Friedman (New York: Doubleday, 1992), 5:1023.

22. Nicholas Zernov, *Orthodox Encounter* (London: James Clarke and Co., 1961), 95.

23. English translations in William Palmer, *A Harmony of Anglican Doctrine with the Doctrine of the Catholic and Apostolic Church of the East, being the Longer Russian Catechism, with an Appendix* (Aberdeen: A. Brown and Co., 1846), 7-8, 13, and in Philip Schaff, *The Creeds of Christendom, with a History and Critical Notes*, vol. 2. rev. (New York: Harper and Brothers, 1905), 449, 454. Lists of authoritative doctrinal statements, but not containing the Longer Russian Catechism, are found in Ware, *The Orthodox Church*, 211, and in Zernov, *Orthodox Encounter*, 90.

24. *The Orthodox Church in the Ecumenical Movement: Documents and Statements 1902-1975*, ed. Constantin G. Patelos (Geneva: World Council of

Churches, 1978), 84, 94.

25. *Anglican-Orthodox Dialogue: The Moscow Agreed Statement* (London: SPCK, 1977), paras. 4-12, pp. 83-85.

26. *Anglican-Orthodox Dialogue: The Dublin Agreed Statement 1984* (Crestwood N.Y.: St. Vladimir's Seminary Press, 1985), paras. 90-92, pp. 42-43.

27. Demetrios J. Constantelos, *Understanding the Greek Orthodox Church: Its Faith, History, and Practice* (Brookline, Mass.: Hellenic College Press, 1990), esp. 119-28.

28. Demetrios J. Constantelos, *Issues and Dialogues in the Orthodox Church since World War II* (Brookline, Mass.: Holy Cross Orthodox Press, 1986).

29. *Pontificale Romanum ex Decreto Sacrosancti Oecumenici Concilii Vaticani II Instauratum auctoritate Pauli PP. VI Promulgatum: De Ordinatione Diaconi, Presbyteri et Episcopi*, editio typica (Vatican City: Typis Polyglottis Vaticanis, 1968).

30. This assertion has recently been emphasized just before the conclusion to the 1991 Vatican Response to The *Final Report* of ARCIC-I (*Origins* 21, no. 28 [19 December 1991]: 446).

31. Anglican-Roman Catholic International Commission, *The Final Report* (Cincinnati: Forward Movement Publications, 1982), para. 29, p. 95.

32. Joseph Ratzinger, "Anglican-Catholic Dialogue: Its Problems and Hopes," *Insight* 1, no. 3 (March 1983): 2, 4.

HOLY BOOK, HOLY PEOPLE
A STUDY OF THE AUTHORITY AND USE OF THE BIBLE

Charles P. Price

The first two sections of this paper are introductory. The first, *"The Words"*, using Sartre's autobiography by that name, seeks to establish the importance of an ambience of words for mediating a culture and affirming the selves shaped by that culture. The second, *"The Scriptures of the World"*, aims to show that human beings regularly surround themselves with *sacred* words, the "sacrament" of the divine. The transcendent Word addresses human beings in all times and in all places, giving them the capacity to respond in words. They become selves in a world.

The main body of the paper has two main sections, the first on the *Authority of Scripture*, and the second on the use of scriptures as in first sectoring in the context provided by the introduction, the Christian canon of Scripture is seen to give a norm of judgment for discerning the divine in all these words. The growth of the canon is traced to show that as the church shaped the canon, the canon shaped—and shapes—the church. The relationship between church and canon is found to be dialectical, neither having priority over the other. The canonical books are given the authority they possess because they are inspired. On the one hand, the writers of the sacred books are declared to be inspired *objectively* by the action of the Holy Spirit upon them; on the other hand, this judgment is made *subjectively* by hearers and readers of the biblical words by virtue of what Calvin called the internal testimony of the spirit.

The Incarnate Word of God is identified as God's normative communication with the world. In Jesus alone do the divine and human appear in complete hypostatic union. Jesus is therefore the Word of God absolutely. The Bible is the Word of God relatively. Yet the only vehicle possessed by the church for knowing the Incarnate Word is the written Word of the Bible. Church and Bible are found to be in a continuous and never-ending dialogue whose purpose is to discover the character of the Word of God with ever more faithfulness.

In the second half of the paper, on the *use of scripture* three uses are discussed. The primary use is claimed to be in worship. Here the need for *lectio continua* is insisted upon. The second use of scripture is in determining doctrine. Although scripture is not a textbook of doctrine, scripture as read in certain epochs of the church asks of its readers questions which doctrine is formulated to answer. Such doctrine may not contradict scripture, but may go beyond it. The doctrines of the Trinity and the virgin birth are cited as examples. The third use of scripture is as a guide to ethical behavior. Scripture is found not to be a textbook of ethics, but it records the encounter between God's love in Christ (*agape*) and-first-Jewish society, and-second-Hellenistic society. Its effect on Jewish divorce law and Hellenistic provisions for slavery and marriage are explored. A survey of the possible implications of this approach to scripture for establishing a contemporary ethic of homosexuality brings the paper to a close. It is suggested that homosexuality, though not itself sinful, may be a mark of sin in a fallen creation, that homosexuals are not necessarily greater sinners than the rest of human kind, and that a more open attitude toward permanent and faithful homosexual unions and toward the ordination of homosexual persons would not contradict the thrust of scripture any more than our changed attitudes toward slavery and the equality of women. The Theology Committee of the House of Bishops has requested four papers on the authority and use of the Bible. This study is the second in that series, representing, in the words of the invitation, a point of view "more open [than the first] to the historical conditions of passages," written from a perspective that might be described as "more evangelical" than the third. I am glad to occupy such a position; I call myself evangelical, in the sense that I believe that God's work, accomplished through the life and death of Jesus of Nazareth, is good news for the whole creation, and that the document which communicates that good news, the gospels in the setting of the whole Bible, is the primary empirical evidence on which my faith rests. I call myself liberal, in the sense that I hold that the gospel, like the Sabbath which "was made for humankind and not humankind for the Sabbath" (Mark 2:27), was made for us and not we for it. To be liberal with respect to the scriptures is not only to be open to an examination of the historical conditions behind any passage, but to be free to ask of the text any questions which life makes insistent, and free to weigh all argument with our reason, that "best member that we have." Through the engagement of our reason with the biblical text, our reason (always a historically conditioned reason) is converted to Christ; and so the Bible, which we study like any other book, discloses itself as unlike any other. These premises underlie this study.

THE WORDS

Jean-Paul Sartre, the French existentialist philosopher of the last generation, entitled his autobiography *The Words.*[1] Sartre grew up in his grandfather's house in Alsace. His grandfather, Charles Schweitzer—Albert's older brother—was a teacher. His house contained a large library. The early chapters of *The Words* tell how Jean-Paul felt himself to be surrounded by the words in those books, how he loved them before he could understand them, and how, in the end, they communicated to him the meaning of the culture in which he was raised.

> "I began my life as I shall no doubt end it: amidst books . . . Though I did not yet know how to read, I already revered those standing stones: upright or leaning over, close together like bricks on the book-shelves . . . Books were my birds and my nests, my household pets, my barns and my countryside . . . It was in books that I encountered the universe: assimilated, classified, labeled, pondered, still formidable". (pp. 40, 49)

At the end, he observes.

> "I write and will keep writing books; they're needed; . . . Culture doesn't save anything or anyone; it doesn't justify. But it's a product of man: he projects himself into it, he recognizes himself in it: that critical mirror alone offers him his image (p. 254)

One doesn't need to be an existentialist or to agree with Sartre in every respect to sense the power of what he has to say about words, especially about being immersed in words and finding in them an affirmation of one's own image. Human beings come to understand themselves and their world from the words with which they are surrounded. Not only written words, of course, and more than words, to be sure. A culture is a treasury of relationships and artifacts. But it is the filter of words which enables us to see and articulate who we are, and to understand the events which shape us, and to establish our basic communities. Words mediate to us the explicit form of the tradition which underlies and shapes our common life and therefore plays such a large factor in shaping us. If we are losing out supply of common words, as seems not unlikely, we lose our community, our culture, our world, and in the end our very selves.

SCRIPTURES OF THE WORLD

Readers of this paper, of course, are not concerned primarily with the survival of Western culture but with the health of the Christian church and the formation of Christian selves. What words are decisive for us? What words enable us to understand and articulate what the church is and who we are as Christians? What words interpret the events which influence the church and establish the quality of our lives in it? For Christians there are in fact very particular words which in our tradition are charged with this function—the words of the library of books gathered as the Bible, the sacred scriptures of the Old and New Testaments.

In April 1992, Wilfred Cantwell Smith delivered an address to the American Theological Society entitled "Scripture—What is it? and Why?" In the address (still unpublished, Smith, who describes himself as a "comparativist" in religion, confesses that he is struck by the fact that most of the world's great religions have collections of books, their scriptures, on which they base their faith and their way of life. What is there about being human, he asks, which causes human beings with some regularity to surround themselves with words which are on the one hand written by human beings and on the other hand elevated by them into a special role, because they are felt to mediate the divine? "May we suggest calling scripture, and the various scriptures of the world, sacrament?" he asks. "The notion bespeaks divine initiative, and human involvement, plus the empirical object that mediates" (p. 16).

Smith's provocative point is that the one God of all the world seems to make the presence and power of God available to human beings at all times and in all places through words. One might press beyond what Professor Smith indicated in his address, though not beyond the tenor of his thought, to speculate that human beings are called into their humanity by a transcendent Word which addresses them and gives them the capacity to respond to that address in their own words. Christians are clearly of the opinion that God the Word spoke to chosen prophets in Israel and in the church through words which the prophets were able to "hear" and express to the communities whose servants they were. We also hold that God has never been without witnesses (Acts 14:17). Christians, therefore, might agree that in all times and places God the Word has summoned prophets and that those prophets have heard some form of the Word of God. It is obvious, to be sure, that not all have heard with the same clarity or amplitude. There are many words and many scriptures. Not all say the same things. Some principles of discrimination are needed to discern truth beneath all the words. What words supply our canon of judgment as Christians What words most truly and amply represent the Word of God? How do we know?

THE CANON OF SCRIPTURE AND THE CHURCH

The Christian community acknowledges canonical books. When the church recognizes the Bible as a canon, it indicates that its contents are normative for us. They hold up a yardstick or norm to Christian life and thought. What are these Christian scriptures? "The Holy Scriptures," replies the Catechism in the Book of Common Prayer, "commonly called the Bible, are the books of the Old and New Testaments; other books, called the Apocrypha, are often included in the Bible."[2]

Why have just these books come to be included in the sacred volume? The question turns out to be not an easy one to answer. From one point of view these collections, both the Hebrew Scripture and the New Testament, grew "silently". There is no indication that during the period when the books were being composed that were designed to be part of a larger whole They were written piecemeal and collected gradually. As far as the Hebrew Bible is concerned, it was not until A.D. 90 at the Council of Jamnia that rabbis made a definitive judgment about which books should count as scripture. They finally gave their approval to Esther and the Song of Solomon, about which there had been questions earlier, and excluded the fourteen books which we now call the Apocrypha. Those apocryphal books had appeared in the collection of writings used by Greek-speaking Jews in Alexandria, the Septuagint. In the Septuagint, these fourteen books were not separated out in any way, but were simply distributed throughout the regular collection. The Septuagint as a whole was, in turn, accepted by Greek-speaking Christians as their Old Testament. Thus the apocryphal books appear in Roman Catholic and Eastern Orthodox Bibles to this day. Some Orthodox churches include even more books. For sixteenth-century doctrinal reasons, most Protestant churches replaced the longer septuagintal canon with the canon authorized by the rabbis at Jamnia. The issue was that some of the apocryphal books had been used in the Middle Ages to justify doctrine contested by the Protestants In the end, Anglicans and Lutherans decided to print the fourteen apocryphal books between the testaments. "The church doth read (them) for example of life and instruction of manners; but yet doth it not apply them to establish any doctrine".[3]

As far as the New Testament is concerned, lists of books used in Christian worship are extant from the late second century on. The first list, which includes just the twenty-seven we recognize as canonical today, appears in an annual Easter letter of Athanasius in 367, although it includes a supplementary list of books which are given as much authority and dignity as the others. The Council of Hippo in 393 cites exactly our present list as scripture, but that decree was not authoritative for the universal church.[4]

Not until the Reformation in the West were the precise books to be included in the canon of scripture specified by acts of councils legislating for the whole church, or, alas, a whole church. Article VI of the *Articles of Religion* lists the Old Testament and Apocryphal books by name, but, significantly, not the New Testament books. The silent growth of the New Testament canon seems to be recognized by the silence of the article. "All the books of the New Testament, *as they are commonly received,* we do receive, and account them Canonical"[5] (emphasis added). They are not named.

Thus, in some sense the church has established the list of canonical books. The church existed before the books. Members of the church wrote the books. Churches in various centers collected, preserved, and exchanged the books. There was obvious human activity involved.

But more needs to be said. There is also a sense in which the books determine the church. The church allowed itself to be instructed and formed by the books as the canonical list was taking shape. The list was shaped as the church was shaped, and it grew organically out of the life of the church. Appearances of the list in theological writings, in the letters of bishops. and in the decrees of popes and later of councils simply confirmed what already existed. This spontaneous process is what lies behind Karl Barth's famous dictum that "the Canon canonized itself."

We conclude that the relationship between the list of canonical books and the church is dialectical. The canon grew as the church grew. The canon told the church what the church was; the church preserved the canon. And when, as happened in the sixteenth century, the churches of the Reformation altered the canon by dropping the Apocrypha, the change reflected a change in the church.

If this point is taken seriously, it becomes impossible to maintain the superiority either of church over canon or of canon over church. It also becomes impossible to contemplate adding to the canon, as was suggested a few years ago in connection with the Dead Sea

Scrolls. Such additions would either be congruent to the canon and hence be unnecessary, or would add to the "things necessary for salvation" (Art. VI) and hence change the church. Of course, new discoveries such as apocryphal gospels and the Dead Sea Scrolls may not be disregarded. They have to be studied and their bearing on existing documents determined with the greatest care. But we do not add them to the canon lest we find ourselves out of communion with the church of the ages.

AUTHORITY AND INSPIRATION

What makes these particular books canonical or normative? This question is really the question of authority. What makes these particular books authoritative? Why just these?

A brief excursus is in order to consider the nature of authority itself. The derivation of the word is instructive. *Authority* is the English translation of the Latin word *auctoritas. Auctoritas* in turn is formed from the perfect participle of *augeo*, which means to increase or to originate. Persons or institutions are recognized as having authority when they cause one's life to be increased or enhanced in some way. An institution has authority if it improves the quality of life, and a person connected with an institution has authority if he or she represents that life-enhancing source. Scientists speak with authority when they represent life-increasing, life-improving knowledge.

Legitimate representatives of a government have authority *if the government itself has authority*, because they speak for an organization which has established communal life of a recognizably positive quality. One might nuance this description almost endlessly, but for the purposes of the present discussion, this much will suffice. Authority depends on personal relationships which make life "more abundant." It is to be distinguished from mere power.

We are led to virtually the same conclusion by examining the etymology of the Greek word for authority, *exousia*—literally, "out of being." What has ultimate authority for us is what comes from the heart of Beings-Itself, to indulge in a kind of philosophical word-play.

Within the Christian community, God in Christ alone has authority, for in the framework of Christian belief, God is shown to be the ultimately life-enhancing source through the resurrection of Jesus Christ from the dead. Jesus in his living, his teaching, his acting (his life-affirming miracles), his passion, his dying, but supremely in his risen life, showed himself to come from God, out of Being-Itself. Hence, within the Christian community God in Christ is acknowledged as having ultimate authority. The books of our sacred scripture are deemed to have *relative* authority because their words bring us into communion with the life-enhancing, saving power of God.

To be sure, other words can mediate this saving power to us. Every sermon, for example, holds the possibility for doing so. But the ability of other words to communicate God's work in Christ depends on their congruence to the canonical words. Over the first two centuries or so, the church defined itself, its structure of belief and its way of life, by these words. New words have to be tested by the canonical ones. If there is a genuinely new departure, and not simply a new way of looking at the once-for-all deliverance of which the canonical books speak, not simply a fresh statement necessitated by new historical circumstances, then the new words make a new community, beyond the pale of the church established in the resurrection of Christ. The Book of Mormon presumably represents such a new departure, for example, although Mormons would not think so. The task of determining whether new words pass the crucial test of congruity with the canon is a delicate one. We shall return to it in a later connection.

We repeat the question. What is there about these particular books, Old and New Testaments alike, which marks them as authoritative? We suggest that it is their continuously experienced capacity to mediate to the community of Christian faith a fresh grasp of the saving work of God in Christ. God revealed in Christ alone has true authority in the church.

How do these books acquire that power? The answer to this question moves us beyond historical and sociological considerations toward a theological examination of the way God acts in the world and in the church. We enter the realm of action of the Holy Spirit of God and ask the question of the inspiration of the biblical books.

Human words, no matter how eloquent, cannot of themselves mediate God's self to us. Only God can do that. The traditional language for expressing the way that words of scripture, written by human beings, mediate the reality of God is to say that the writers were inspired by God to write them. Some of the Hebrew prophets were quite explicit about the process. "The Lord God has spoken. Who can but prophesy?" (Amos 3:8). "The word which Isaiah the son of Amoz *saw* [N.B.] concerning Judah and Jerusalem" (Isa. 2.1). "The word of the Lord came to me saying . . . ." (Jer. 2.1). There are more comparable instances than one could list. Among New Testament writers, Paul also *saw* visions (2 Cor. 12:1), and John of the

Apocalypse saw the whole revelation of God, translated into those vivid and unforgettable verbal images. The writers of the four Gospels, on the other hand, provide little description of how their material was composed. Luke says that he edited existing documents. In every case, it would be said from a modern theological point of view (at least from the point of view represented in this essay!) that the Spirit of God has been at work both in the composition and in the editing and compilation of the biblical writing.

What is the basis for such a judgment? It would be futile and self-defeating to argue from the inspiring character of the writings themselves. They are too varied to permit such an appeal. For every Second Isaiah there is a Leviticus. The basis for discerning the inspiration of the Holy Spirit in the production of the canonical books is the operation of the same Spirit within the community which receives the books. As Saint Paul put it, "Now we have received not the spirit of the world, but the Spirit which is from God, that we might understand the gifts bestowed on us by God" (1 Cor. 2:12). John Calvin spoke of the "*internum testimonium Spiritus sancti*"— the inward testimony of the Holy Spirit.[6] The inspired character of the biblical books is recognized within the Spirit-filled community which continues to be shaped by them—recognized by individual Christians and proclaimed by the church. *It takes the work of the Spirit to perceive a work of the Spirit.* (Cf. 1 Cor. 2:11-13).

Lest this conclusion seem to be self-defeating, circular, or eccentric, it should be pointed out that this fundamental Christian *theologoumenon* applies not only to scripture but also to the Christ and to every item of Christian worship through which human beings encounter the divine. For example, "No one can say 'Jesus is Lord' except by the Holy Spirit" (1 Cor. 12:3). Here we meet Saint Paul's language for the inner testimony of the Spirit. There is no doubt in his mind, on the other hand, or in the mind of the Christian community down through the ages, that Jesus is Lord by the operation of the Holy Spirit. The narrative of the Annunciation makes it explicit, and the creeds proclaim it. In the same vein, bread and wine are *recognized* as the Body and Blood of Christ through the *epiklesis* of the Spirit upon the worshiping congregation. This *epiklesis* is explicit in the fullest forms of the Eucharistic prayer, and it is always implicit through the baptism of the participants. The sacraments, too, depend on the inner testimony of the Spirit. At the same time, all the Prayer Book Eucharistic prayers express the objective transformation of the bread and wine into the Body and Blood of Christ by the work of the Spirit. For example, in Eucharistic Prayer D we find,

"Lord, we pray that in your goodness and mercy your Holy Spirit may descend upon us [*inner testimony*], and upon these gifts [*objective reality*], sanctifying them and showing them to be holy gifts for your holy people, the bread of life and the cup of salvation, the Body and Blood of your Son Jesus Christ." Still in the same vein, newly baptized persons are *recognized* as adopted by God as his children by the congregation of already baptized persons in whom the Holy Spirit bears its inner witness; but the newly baptized are objectively "sealed by the Holy Spirit in Baptism and marked as Christ's own forever."[7]

The Bible belongs in this series of items which Christians believe to be touched by the Spirit. It, too, is an outward and visible sign of God's presence among us in Christ. It is recognized to be such by Spirit-filled congregations. The Spirit fills the church with the very power of God, the most real entity. The eyes of the church are opened to that reality by the same Spirit, beholding it in the scripture and in all these other places as well.

THE CHARACTER OF INSPIRED WRITING

What does the inspiration of the Holy Spirit entail for the writing of the books themselves? We suggest several positive and negative responses.

On the positive side, to declare that the biblical books are inspired means that they have all, at least one point in the formation of the canon and in the life of the church, mediated the truth to some worshiping community. Consequently, every biblical word should be read by a present-day community expectantly, as if God would once again speak through it. Having once been a "sacrament" of the Word, every biblical word may become a sacrament of the Word again. "We call the Scripture the Word of God," declares the Catechism, "because God inspired their human authors *and because God still speaks to us through the Bible*" (emphasis added).

Negatively, by taking this position we do not claim that every Biblical word is always and automatically a Word of God to every reader and every worshiping community every time it is read. Only in Jesus of Nazareth is there a complete, unequivocal (hypostatic) union between the divine and something finite. *The Bible is not another Christ. It did not die for us nor was it raised from the dead.*

Furthermore, to claim the scriptures as inspired does not mean that they are inerrant. God's Spirit, being holy love, does not destroy or negate the human spirits of those who are inspired, frail and limited though they are. The inspiring Spirit does not eliminate or circumvent human shortcomings. God reveals God's love and even God's own self, to persons—finite and even sinful persons—who do not have a perfect understanding of the operation of the physical world or a complete knowledge of the past or a detailed knowledge of the future. In the New Testament tradition, even God's incarnate Son was understood not to know the time of the end (Mark 13:32).

In short, scripture is not primarily a textbook of science or history. It is, to be sure, our sole source for much of the history of the period which it covers, and it gives us apparently reliable information about the flora and fauna of Palestine, for example. But the Bible is primarily a book about God. It yields inerrant knowledge about God sufficient for our salvation, but only after careful study and much prayer.

Finally, to claim that the scriptures of the Old and New Testament are inspired does not mean that they are inspiring. Although such passages as Isaiah 53 and First Corinthians 13 rank with the world's greatest literature, the place of scripture in the life of faith does not depend on such considerations.

THE LIMITS OF INSPIRATION

Are only canonical books inspired? Ancient authors, both Jewish and Christian, did not limit the list of books which they regarded as inspired to the list we now declare to be canonical. For example, both Philo and Josephus, on rather different grounds, recognized a distinction between "mere inspired utterance" and canonical scripture.[9] Philo regarded some of his own writing as inspired, and within the church the Shepherd of Hermas and the epistles of First Clement were sometimes so regarded. From a systematic theological point of view, there is no reason why, on one hand, there should be any limit on the number of *inspired* writings, recognized as such, ultimately, by the inward testimony of the Spirit. On the other hand, the *canonical* list is closed. It includes only those documents which from earliest times Christians have found to contain "all things necessary to salvation." The list is closed around what was originally believed to be the first-generation witness to the Christ, together with the Hebrew scriptures which constitute the preparation for that gospel.

> Contemporary scholarship recognizes later dates for a number of New Testament books, but in the words of E.C. Hoskyns, they were written by people "who, though belonging to a later gener-

ation, have been so created by apostolic witness and formed by apostolic obedience, that they are veritably carried across into the company of the original disciples of Jesus, and invested with the authority of their mission."[10]

The canon constitutes the norm by which any other inspired works must be evaluated. Apart from such a norm, the judgment that a particular work was inspired would readily become a "wax nose which any knave can mould to fit his own face." Only those works deserve to be called inspired which are found congruent to the canon. The decision about the canon is an ecclesiastical decision, made by the whole church. A decision about inspiration is a theological decision, which may be made by an individual inspired by the Spirit. The power and effect of such an individual decision, of course, depends on whether it is accepted by a wider community. A quarter of a century ago, for example, a number of people regarded Dag Hammarskjöld's *Markings* as a profound and searching statement of faith even inspired. Today it is scarcely remembered.

INCARNATE WORD OF GOD AND SCRIPTURAL WORD OF GOD

We have already used the phrase *Word of God* in connection both with scripture and with the Incarnate Son. What is the relationship between these two manifestations of the Word of God? In the first place, the provenance of these two manifestations of the Word is different. In the Old Testament and in some New Testament passages, the Word of the Lord is the agent of inspiration of Hebrew and Christian prophets. That Word so impinges upon them, or inspires them, that they utter words. The psychology of the prophet by which the divine Word is translated into human words is not clear. Ecstatic utterance is a fairly common phenomenon among religious people the world over, including the Christian community. However their psychology may be conceived, though, prophets believe themselves to be uttering the Word of God, which they "see" or "hear" directly.

The Word which "was in the beginning with God" and which "was God" has a different origin. It suggests the Logos of Greek philosophy, although no Greek philosopher would have gone so far as to make the identification of the Logos with God or to have uttered the unutterable words, "the Word became flesh." To accept Karl Barth's phrase, the Word in this context is God's "second way of being God." The Word is God-in-relation to finite creation. God's "second way of being God" is God with a capacity for relationship with creatures. If this understanding of God the Word is accepted, it is not very far distant to claim that God the Word has sought entrance into the worded minds of his human creatures from the beginning. "I held out my hand all day long to a rebellious people" (Isa. 65:2). Some of God's human creatures in every place, presumably aided by the grace of God's Spirit, responded to the Word and uttered words. These utterances more or less faithfully expressed the meaning of the Word. In the fullness of time, after a long and stormy period of preparation through the life of the sometimes obedient and usually disobedient nation of Israel, Mary, by the aid of the same Spirit, responded to the Word and became the bearer of the Incarnate Son, "born of a woman, born under the Law." Jesus, the incarnate Son of God, is God's Word most perfectly translated into the terms human beings can best understand—the form of a human life.

All we know about the Incarnate Word—the preparation for him, his life, his death, his resurrection, the recognition of his risen life by his disciples—we know through the scriptures. On the other hand, the Incarnate Word of God is the touchstone by which all the words of the scripture must be judged. To read the scriptures in the Christian community of faith is to engage in a never-ending dialogue by which the meaning of the whole scripture can be discerned. The scriptures make Christ known to us. In the end, there is simply no other source. Faithful preaching and teaching is dependent on the scriptures. They "preach Christ," in Luther's phrase. Then, as we grow in our knowledge of Christ, the revelation of God to us, we turn back to the scriptures and perceive their meaning at deeper and deeper levels, "one text at a time," as Walter Bruggemann has been quoted as saying. It is a continuous dialectical process.

THE ROLE OF THE INTERPRETER

The process which we have been describing involves three centers, not two. There is first the Bible, comprising the words within which the Word of God is to be found. It "containeth all those things necessary to salvation," as the Article holds and as we have said several times. Through the Bible we discovered the Word of God (second in experience but first in importance), who in Jesus of Nazareth became flesh, whose nature and character are communicated by the words of scripture. In third place, by no means the least important in understanding the process, there is the community of faith which reads, proclaims, and hears these words, by means of the words discerns the Word, and so is formed and illuminated by the Word.

The community of faith comprises individuals of different gifts and different degrees of commitment. It lives in the world, and is shaped not only by the Word of God as contained in the scriptures, but also (since the church does not live in a vacuum) by historical and cultural forces, all of which in some way owe their origin and existence to the Creator of all things, but which at any given time will be partly obedient and partly disobedient to the creative Word. At any given time, the community of faith has but a partial grasp of the Word since the community is finite, and but a distorted grasp, since it is sinful. But because the Christian community has been granted the gift of the Spirit—the gift of the Spirit of Christ which is love—it is able to love the Word, to open itself before the Word, therefore, in this continual dialectic, to submit itself to the words of the scripture, to be grasped afresh by the Word which speaks through the words, and so to be transformed.

This process of discerning the Word of God through reading, proclaiming, and hearing the scripture is dynamic and complex. Part of the complexity results from the fact that the readers, preachers, and hearers always come with a history. There is never a zero-base. The community of faith is never a *tabula rasa*.

The community approaches the scripture through its several members. Initially only individuals can make the necessary discerning judgments. Community judgments are made by the interaction of the members until a group judgment emerges. Consensus is desirable, but probably not always possible. To this consensus different members contribute their different gifts: wisdom about divine and human things, scholarly research, poetic insight, practical experience, spiritual thirst—doubtless many others. All gifts are necessary to illuminate the text, but in this respect as in every other, the most necessary of all is love. Members of the community of faith must love both each other and the text itself.

In the end, there will be a new decision on how to interpret the text, and it will be based on a reasonable judgment in the light of all the input. Archbishop Laud's words to "Mr. Fisher, the Jesuit" are helpful in this matter.

> "The books called the scripture are commonly and constantly reputed to be the Word of God, and so infallible verity to the least point of them. Doth any man doubt this? The world cannot keep him from going to weigh it at the balance of reason, whether it be the Word of God or not. To the same weights he brings the Tradition of the church, the inward motives in scripture itself, all testimonies within, which seem to bear witness to

it; and in all this there is no harm. For the Word of God, and the Book containing it refuse not to be weighed by reason. But the scale is not large enough to contain, nor the weights to measure, the true virtue and full force of either."[11]

What Laud did not examine in his conference with Mr. Fisher was the quality of that reason, which we now understand, as he did not, to be culturally conditioned and sin-skewed. By that reason, in weighing the scripture, the one weighing it encounters the Word and is in turn weighed. The Word corrects and enlarges the reason which weighs it and enables it more accurately to grasp the sense of the biblical words. There is simply no way around this dialectical conversation. The Word of God, the Christ, in some such sense as this, is the final judge and interpreter of the scriptures, even as the church and its individual members do the weighing.

In this intense interaction between the Word of God and the hearers and readers of scripture in the believing community, the individual members are grasped by the words and the Word. In the course of time, therefore, accepted interpretations of scripture change as the common grasp of the Word changes. In Wilfred Cantwell Smith's paper cited above, for example, five views of the Song of Songs are examined, from five different periods of time and settings.

Other examples are more germane to our purposes. One is the process by which during the course of the nineteenth century the mean of scripture *for the church* changed from one which supported the institution of slavery to one which opposed it. Saint Paul returned Onesimus, the runaway slave, to his owner, Philemon. In his covering letter to Philemon Paul raised no questions about the institution as such. He appealed to Philemon "for love's sake" (Philemon 9) to treat the returning Onesimus "as a beloved brother" (Philemon 16). With that appeal, Paul introduced into the institution of slavery the Christian idea of *agapé* as the judge of the relationship between master and slave. In the end, after a bitterly long time, the institution could not bear to be judged by love. In the twentieth century, slavery is not an option for Christians, despite the plain meaning of Philemon and several other New Testament texts.[12]

Modern readers of the New Testament bring to it a new initial understanding of the Word, which revises and reforms the older interpretation of the words. The new initial understanding was formed amid considerable anguish in the encounter between a believing community which once accepted slavery on one hand, and on the other the Word of God, finally liberated from these scriptural words. The community finally had to ask itself what *agapé* required of it when it was forced by a new historical situation to confront what slavery did to human beings—both slaves and masters. Not all members of the community came to that understanding at the same time. Some had "prophetic insight." Some resisted to the shedding of blood. But in the end the *internum testimonium Spiritus sancti* has claimed the heart and mind of the whole believing church, to deny slavery as a possible christian relationship. Slavery could not contain *agapé.*

Two conclusions may be drawn from these considerations. The first is that the meaning of scripture cannot be discerned once for all from the literal sense of the text, *although the process of discernment always must begin with the literal sense.* The second is that on reflection, *the process of discernment is found to be throughout the work of the Holy Spirit, in the world, in the text, and in the partially obedient, partially recalcitrant interpreter in the process of being transformed.*

THE USES OF SCRIPTURE
We turn now to the second major part of this essay, the use of scripture. Three uses, in fact, will concern us: in worship, in determining doctrine, and in giving ethical guidance.

The Use of Scripture in Worship
If the contention of this paper is correct, that the holy Scriptures of the Old and New Testaments are sacred words in which the believing community is immersed and in which they discover the Word of God through a process of dynamic interaction, it follows that the primary use of the Bible is in worship. Today, when the church gathers in the presence of God, scripture is read. God's presence is articulated and focused in these words.

As far as we can tell, the *reading* of scripture probably did not form a part of temple worship in Israel. Passages of Torah were recited to keep Israel immersed in the sacred story. Newly composed prophetic oracles were probably declaimed in the liturgy. In postexilic times Hebrew scripture—the Torah, Prophetic Books and Writings—were read in the course of regular synagogue services as acts of worship, establishing in the ears of the hearers the milieu in which God's Word resounded. This practice of reading documents as part of a service of worship was picked up in the nascent Christian communities at an early date. Old Testament writings continued to be read, in Greek for a Greek-speaking church,and gospels and apostolic writings were quickly added. The goal was the same as in the synagogue: to hear the Word of God when these words were read.

This goal implies some kind of continuous reading. The early Latin church spoke of *lectio continua.* The fact is that the significance of any given passage of scripture can adequately and truly be discerned only when it is seen in its place within the whole drama of salvation, just as the significance of any part of a vast painting can be rightly determined only by seeing it as part of the entire canvas. Evidence of early eucharistic lectionaries indicated that *lectio continua* was a common practice in primitive times. As the Middle Ages progressed this pattern tended to be obscured, for lessons became shorter and shorter. Cranmer attempted to restore a form of it in the 1549 Book of Common Prayer. Psalter and scripture lessons in the Daily Office were to be read for the most part in continuous sequence, as is well known, although even the 1549 lectionary provided for the omission of large sections of Ezekiel, for example. Subsequent Anglican prayer books for better or worse followed the medieval push for shorter lessons, and they frequently break sequential reading for the sake of special commemorations. Nevertheless, it remains true that large sections of the main service lectionary in the 1979 Book of Common Prayer and of the Daily Office lectionary utilize the principle of *lectio continua* almost completely except for major feasts.

Thus, for those who are able to follow the prayer book provisions for daily worship, the words of all the sacred books come to reverberate and resound in their ears and minds and hearts. One must recognize, however, that many church members do not and perhaps cannot live up to that Prayer Book prescription. Those members, perhaps the majority in our church, depend in large measure on being filled in and brought up to date by the preaching at Sunday services, programs of instruction, and other forms of devotion. One thinks of the function of stained glass windows in the Middle Ages and the current interest in "story telling." Unless the church at large can somehow be helped to hear the words of the scripture in sufficient measure to hear the Word of God and—perhaps even more importantly—to know it when they hear it, there will overtake us that "famine of hearing the words of the Lord" of which Amos warned (Amos 8:11). Bibical illiteracy is the precursor to spiritual death and communal dissolution.

The primary use of scripture is to hear the Word of God through the words of that old, old story, to grapple the Word to ourselves, to praise God in the Word, and to give the Word free rein to shape our minds and wills.

The Use of Scripture in Determining Doctrine

To allow scripture to shape our minds is to grant it a role in the determination of doctrine. Nevertheless, the Bible is not a textbook of doctrine. Article VI, far from asserting that scripture makes infallible statements of Christian doctrine, in fact is content with stating the case for scripture with a curious double negative. "Whatsoever is not read therein, nor may be proved thereby, is not to be required of any man that it should be believed as an article of faith, or be thought requisite or necessary to salvation." We notice that the authority of scripture maintained by this Article has to do with salvation. "Holy Scripture containeth all things *necessary to salvation*," and not simply "all things."[13] Hooker made this point tellingly in his controversy with the Puritans.

> The schools of Rome teach scripture to be so unsufficient, as if, except traditions were added, it did not conteine all reveled and supernatural truth, which absolutely is necessarie for the children of men in this life to know that they may in the next be saved. Others, justly condemning this opinion grow likewise unto a dangerous extremities, as if scripture did not only contain all things in that kind necessary, but all thing simply, and in such sort that to due any thing [*or to think anything!*] according to any other laws were not only unnecessarie, but even opposite unto salvation, unlawful and sinful.[14]

Pursuing this line of thought, one might say that the proper subject matter of Christian doctrine is contained in scripture, and in that sense doctrine is determined by scripture. Also doctrine must not contradict scripture. Doctrine, however, is not simply texts, especially texts without context. As we observed earlier, the meaning of scripture is determined by the saving Word, the Logos. The proper subject matter of Christian doctrine is given by the Logos. Doctrine comes from the impact the Logos makes upon the minds of Christian believers when they open themselves in love and humility before the words of scripture. The result of that encounter, when formulated, examined, discussed, and authenticated by the church, frequently after long periods of uncertainty and stormy debate, becomes doctrine. The Word makes its impression upon individual believers and also upon the church as a whole by the reading and hearing of the scripture; resulting formulations of doctrine must not contradict scripture as the Article stipulates; but we understand that at this late point in the process scripture has already been interpreted and judged by the Word as the community of believers best understands the Word. Moreover, the possibility is always open that in this process the church may be grasped by a profound new understanding of the Word in the power of the Spirit. Then, as in the sixteenth-century Reformation, a radical reformulation of doctrine may result, in order to keep doctrine true to the Word.

Before we show in several examples how that complex process works itself out, it should be observed that doctrine is always hammered out in response to questions which people of different languages, cultures, and thought-forms ask *of the Scripture*. The need for doctrinal formulation arises when scripture is taken seriously and anomalies arise. Then it is discovered that scripture itself does not always resolve the anomaly. Scripture mediates the Word of God, but it does not as such answer all questions, since it was written in still a different culture by authors of still different mind-sets. To be authentic, doctrine must be stated in language and categories which the people who ask the questions can understand. They should be able to perceive that their questions have been addressed, and to comprehend that the abiding mystery with which all Christian doctrine is surrounded is not simply obfuscation.

Some examples are in order.

The Doctrine of the Trinity

Scripture itself raises the questions to which the doctrine speaks, but as is well known, scripture does not state the doctrine of the Trinity. Scripture speaks of God, the Father of Jesus; it speaks of Jesus Christ, the Lord, the Son of God, "in whom all the fullness of God was pleased to dwell" (Col. 1:19); it speaks of the Holy Spirit, who is from time to time equated with the Lord—"the Lord who is the Spirit" (2 Cor. 3:18). Scripture also has other ways of speaking about these actors in the divine drama of salvation. Jesus was said to "increase in wisdom and in stature, and in divine and human favor" (Luke 2:52). He spoke of himself on the cross as "God-forsaken" (Mark 15:34). Apparent contradiction could be multiplied. Also, scripture from beginning to end insists on the unity of God: "The Lord our God is one Lord" (Deut. 6:4). Almost no other sentence of scripture has more resonance. Can there then be three Gods?

In the Hellenistic world, Christians were asked and asked themselves how to approach this perplexing question of the relationship among Father, Son, and Spirit. To settle for an understanding that there were three divinities would not have been foreign to that polytheistic world; and at the other extreme, a subordinationist version of the relationship could be made to seem very reasonable. It took 381 years to form a definitive doctrine on this subject. It was affirmed at the Council of Constantinople that the Son is "one in

Being with the Father" and that the Spirit "with the Father and the Son is worshiped and glorified."[15]

Athanasius, the chief proponent of this doctrine of the Trinity, stood for a while virtually alone "contra mundum" for this formulation. He perceived that the issue had to do with salvation. If the work of the Son were not fully God's work, it was not fully accomplished. To acknowledge any inequality of "Persons" would threaten the once-for-all character of the work of Christ. If salvation had not proceeded from the highest quarters, it might be undone. The resulting doctrine of the Trinity, which described God as Three-in-One and One-in-Three, using such unbiblical words as essence and substance, (even *Persona* is not a biblical category), provided the key by which thoughtful Hellenistic Christians could read the scripture. The doctrine opened their minds to scripture, as scripture opened their minds to the doctrine. It confirmed and did not contradict the scriptural *thrust* of understanding the Wisdom and Word of God, who *was* God (John 1:1; cf. Prov. 8:22).

We must note that such a salient agreement within the church about so central and sensitive a matter of Christian belief as the very essence of the Godhead constitutes a permanent deposit in the theological tradition. It is, of course, subordinate to scripture; but subsequent generations of Christians have learned to read scripture with minds attuned to the questions and insights which this doctrine represents. This doctrine, or any doctrine so universally held for so long a time, may not lightly or easily be circumvented or discarded. Even if scripture should be introduced (by people who read it in the light of the doctrine of the Trinity) to a culture which does not ask the questions which the doctrine addresses, the doctrine will simply of necessity (since the presenters are informed by it) accompany that introduction as part of our "cumulative tradition." Because the doctrine has been so crucial for the introducers, they cannot simply disregard it. It may not be good missionary strategy to emphasize it within the new believing community, but it will remain part of the patrimony, and eventually theologians in the new situation will make their own peace with it.

In this case, scripture was found to necessitate a doctrine which went beyond scripture, although did not contradict scripture. In fact it safeguarded the scriptural witness to Christ.

The Doctrine of the Virgin Birth

The doctrine is expressed in the Nicaeno-Constantinopolitan Creed (the creed "commonly called the Nicene") in the words, "by the power of the Holy Spirit he became incarnate from the Virgin Mary, and was made man."[16] Scripture seems to underwrite this doctrine unequivocally, in contrast to its silence regarding the Trinity (Matt. 1:18-25; Luke 1:26-38).

The *Report of the Commission on Doctrine Appointed By the Archbishops of Canterbury and York in 1922* indicated that we are agreed in recognizing that belief in our Lord's birth from a Virgin has been in the history of the Church intimately associated with its faith in Incarnation of the Son of God."[17]

Fundamentalists and others to this day hold that the virgin birth as taught in the scriptures, implying the physical virginity of Mary, constitutes the *evidence* for the divinity of our Lord. This doctrine for such believers is a major underpinning for Christian faith. To weaken it is to overthrow the whole structure.

Yet serious questions have been raised about the doctrine in modern times. The *Report* had to admit that even some members of the commission held that "full belief in the historical Incarnation is more consistent with the supposition that our Lord's birth took place under normal conditions of human generation." What can be said about such a disagreement from the point of view represented in this essay?

One begins by assessing the possibility of a biological virgin birth. No one can rule it out *a priori*. If it happened, it happened. Enough research has been done on parthenogenesis to know that it can occur for small animals under certain specifiable conditions. These births are apparently always female. They lack a chromosome which, so far as we know, comes only from males. From a scientific point of view, the birth of a male human being by parthenogenesis is extremely, even wildly, improbable.

One then asks the historical question. Did it happen? Are the texts reliable historical evidence? The narratives in which the account of the birth are embodied are disarmingly mythological, with their account of the activity of angels, stars, unlikely night-visitors, and the general presence of the supernatural. Moveover, the stories are not attributed to Mary, who would be the sole reliable witness to her virginity. The birth narratives on their face are not the best evidence. Although, as is the case with any document, it is impossible to prove that the facts which these stories contain are in error, it does seem that the event, considered as history, is improbable.

How then is the doctrine of the virgin birth to be evaluated? On one hand, it lies far too deep in the tradition simply to be denied. The approach adopted in this essay insists that in such an instance one must persist in asking, "Why would such stories be related?" What is the point of them? What do they mean in the broad context of the scriptural narrative? When one is open to the full range of scripture, one perceives that Jeremiah, for example, was given to understand that before he was formed in the womb, God "knew him." (Jer. 1:4). In the same vein, Second Isaiah says of the Servant, "The Lord . . . made you . . . [and] formed you in the womb" (Isa. 44:2). Somewhat similarly, the author of Psalm 139 recognized that God had created his inmost parts and had knit him together in his mother's womb (Ps. 139:12). One recalls also the extraordinary births of Isaac, Moses, and Samuel, and concludes that in the horizon of Hebrew scripture the language which expresses God at work in a person's life even before conception is a not unfamiliar way to communicate the profoundest truth about election and grace—Jeremiah's election and call as a prophet, the Servant's call to be a "light to the nations," the psalmist's inspiration as a poet and trusting Israelite.

It would be consistent with this understanding of scripture to observe that if God chose Jeremiah for the work of a prophet before he was born and elected the Servant of Second Isaiah "from the womb"—so that their whole lives and ministries were to be conceived as being wholly of grace from the beginning—inspired New Testament writers might readily appropriate the language of virginal conception in order to present God as active in Jesus' life, electing and empowering him for the work of messianic deliverance from his very beginning. If these stories are improbable as history, they are profound as myth. From this point of view, one could wholeheartedly affirm the virginal conception of Jesus and still maintain some skepticism about Mary's physical virginity, and even suggest that the full humanity of the Savior would be better imaged if he had had two human parents.

However, if one elects this route to affirm the doctrine of the virgin birth, one may not use the birth to *prove* Jesus's divinity. Things are quite the other way around. Knowledge of Jesus' messianic election, assured by the results of his death and resurrection, lead to the affirmation of the virgin birth. Jesus' saving work authenticates his special relation to God, and in the tradition of Hebrew scripture this relationship can be effectively communicated as his conception by God, or (in later and more developed terms) by the Holy Spirit.

Those who understand the virgin birth in this way gladly utter the credal words, but would argue that a contemporary understanding of history and science, a new appreciation of the theological power of mythical narrative, and a clear grasp of the saving action of the Word of God in Christ have provided a new, perhaps profounder, reading of the scriptural words, which are nevertheless taken with utmost seriousness, faithfulness and courage.

The Use of Scripture in Guiding Ethical Conduct

From the perspective of this paper, when the believing community immerses itself in the words of scripture, scripture comes to have a role in shaping conduct as well as thought. Nevertheless the Bible is not a textbook of ethics any more than it is a textbook of doctrine—perhaps less so. Hooker's words cited earlier to the effect that scripture contains *all things necessary to salvation* but not *all things*, apply even more to ethics than to doctrine. The quotation comes at the end of an extended argument to show that it is both self-defeating and contradictory to hold that unless scripture says you can do something, you should not—"even so far as to the taking up of a rush or a straw" (on the Sabbath). The use of scripture to determine action, Hooker continues, should be kept "within the compass of moral actions, actions which have in them vice or virtue"; and we should not be required to give chapter and verse for each ethical precept. Rather, "it sufficeth if such actions be framed according to the law of reason, the general axiomes, rules, and principles of which law being so frequent in holy scripture, there is no let but in that regard, even out of scripture such duties may be deduced by some kind of consequence."[18]

The fact is that, considered as a whole, scripture constitutes quite a mixed bag of prescriptions for behavior. Article VII of the *Articles, Of the Old Testament*, begins to make significant discriminations among them. It recognizes that the "law given from God by Moses, as touching Ceremonies and Rites" is not binding on members of the Church of England. Perhaps even more significantly, it concedes that "the civil precepts" of the Mosaic law do not have to be enacted by a Christian commonwealth as his own law. Of course, all the provisions of the Law were regarded as binding by the Jews. It took them all to shape Israel's life, both individual and corporate, both civil and religious. The Article implies that the Hebrew scripture, at least, if not the New Testament, must be brought under some kind of judgment before its ethical provisions could be accepted in the sixteenth-century English church. A Christian community engages in a work of interpretation before it can know which of the Old Testament "commandments which are called Moral"[19] continue to claim the obedience of its members.

We have been arguing that the meaning of the scripture is determined by the impact of the Word on the believing person and the believing community who hear or read the words. In the case of doctrine, we said that the Word imposes itself on the community as Logos. In the case of ethical behavior, the Word imposes itself on the community as *agapé*. *Agapé* gives the believing community the touchstone for discerning the kind of behavior which the laws and various other ethical prescriptions included in both testaments require of believers. "Love is the fulfilling of the law" (Rom. 13:10).

This consideration puts us in the same dialectical relationship to scripture that we have discovered before. On the one hand, *agapé* is the norm for evaluating the ethical demands of scripture. On the other hand, scriptural words are ultimately the only means available to the church for discerning what *agapé* is.

What we turn to the Bible to find out about *agapé*, we discover first of all that it is described by the life and death of Jesus. "We know love by this, that he laid down his life for us, and we ought to lay down our lives for one another" (1 John 3:16). We know what the life of Jesus was like and the story of how he died for us only from the Bible.

However, although we might say that the most concrete and specific instance of *agapé* is Jesus, yet it is notoriously difficult to translate a biography into ethical precepts and a code of action. We need something at one remove from that concrete and specific life toward a more abstract definition, precisely so that we can know how to apply it to our lives, which are so very different from his, in circumstances very different from his. Indeed we find a canonical and widely accepted *definition* of *agapé* in the scripture: the thirteenth chapter of First Corinthians, whose vivid phrases have etched themselves into nearly every Christian's consciousness as providing a basis for ethical behavior. *Agapé* "bears all things, believes all things, hopes all things, endures all things" (1 Cor. 13:7).

Those who allow themselves to be formed by such words come to have a grasp of what Christian ethical behavior is; but even this definition of *agapé* in First Corinthians is not a set of "Commandments which are called Moral." What are the rules?

The rules which prescribe ethical behavior are the products of a culture, and the church is not now, nor has it ever been, a culture of its own. It has lived in many different cultures. It is an *ecclesia*, a people called out "from every nation, from all tribes and peoples and tongues" (Rev. 7:9). The church does not have, nor did it ever have, a ready-made all-purpose set of habits, customs, or morals. The church came into the Hebrew world, which had its own moral laws. They were not specifically Christian laws. The church has continued to live in alien cultures, each of which takes place between a culture where the church takes root and the Christian ethical norm, which is *agapé*.

In the New Testament, we find the "new" Christian people in just this kind of an encounter successively with two "old" cultures, with Israel and its Mosaic covenant, with its ceremonial and civil laws regulating all aspects of personal life; and then with Hellenistic society of the first century, with quite a different set of laws and customs.

Jesus and Torah

One looks through the New Testament in vain for a code of ethical principles of a system of ethical teaching. A large part of Jesus' teaching, or course, had to do with ethics—with money, marriage, divorce, citizenship. But in all that teaching there was nothing particularly new. Matthew records Jesus as saying, "Do not think that I have come to abolish the law or the prophets; I have come not to abolish but to fulfill" (Matt. 5:17).

Yet Jesus did teach about the law in a new way. He used it to lay bare the sickness of the human spirit. He reached behind the region of overt actions in order to reveal the human condition which made the law necessary. In the Sermon on the Mount he used the law against murder to pinpoint the hatred and contempt out of which murder springs. He subjected the old law to his own scrutiny, which the church has taken to be the scrutiny of *agapé*. Some people who were completely obedient to the law against murder turned out by this new criterion to be far from the kingdom of God. Jesus thus opened a whole new range of ethical considerations. Yet neither he nor any responsible Christian has ever questioned the validity of the law against murder *as a law*. At least that law still stands, along with the other nine commandments, as "Commandments which are called Moral."

Some modern New Testament critics do not recognize that the Sermon on the Mount reports Jesus' own words. It is rather the reflection of a primitive Jewish-Christian community on the words and deeds of Jesus. To put the point in the terms of this essay, the Sermon on the Mount would represent the impact of the person of Jesus and his teaching of *agapé* on the life and thought of a group of first-century Jews. If the Sermon on the Mount does indeed represent that kind of material, it would demonstrate the thesis of this section even better than if it were Jesus' own words, since it would show the church reshaping Torah under the power of *agapé*.

The situation with regard to divorce was different. Jesus used his analysis of the Jewish law about divorce to show that it too was given "because of your hardness of heart" (Mark 10:4). Under Torah a husband was allowed to dismiss his wife simply by giving her a bill of divorce (Deut. 24:1-4). In this case, Jesus not only revealed the sickness of the human situation, but also brought this provision of the Torah under the judgment of God's institution of marriage in Creation (Gen. 2:24). As things turned out, the church did not retain the Jewish law of divorce in its own regulation of marriage, although it has upheld the provision of the Torah against murder. The church has developed divorce legislation of its own, however, despite the clear recognition that Jesus did not countenance divorce in the kingdom of God. The church has had to come to terms with the fact that divorce is neither a good nor a right, but under the unruly and disorderly conditions of existence, it is sometimes a lesser evil. Divorce laws have varied from culture to culture, and undoubtedly will continue to do so. The New Testament yields no model legislation. It does show how the church began to deal with divorce by including Matthew's famous exception for adultery (Matt. 5:32), despite Mark's (and Jesus') prohibition (Mark 10:2-9).

It is impossible to be more specific than this without going far beyond the mandate of this essay. But we have given an example of a section of Torah (Deut. 24:1-4) which Jesus criticized and the Church disregarded because it did not meet the test of *agapé*.

St. Paul and Gentile Congregations

The New Testament also records the encounter between *agapé* and the Gentile mission. When Saint Paul or someone writing in his name addressed the congregations in Ephesus and Colossae about ethical duties of husbands and wives, parents and children, masters and slaves, the author did not insist that these Hellenistic Christians adopt the Jewish law in these matters, any more than circumcision was required of them. Instead, they were urged to maintain familiar *Hellenistic* ethical rules, as recent studies have shown.[20]

Whether Saint Paul wrote these epistles or not, they reflect the impact which the teaching of *agapé* had on these congregations. In these epistles we see *agapé* shaping Hellenistic laws and customs as in the synoptic gospels we see how *agapé* shaped Jewish laws and customs. Significantly, in the Gentile case, Saint Paul or the person writing in his name made some "in course corrections" in the relationship between husbands and wives, for example; husbands are to love their wives "as Christ loved the church and gave himself for her," and, as we have already noticed, Philemon, the master, was to love Onesimus, the slave, "as a beloved brother." Nevertheless, wives were still to obey their husbands and Onesimus was returned to slavery.

Why the writers of these documents did not require the end of slavery is a matter for speculation. Whether they were so convinced that the kingdom of God was imminent, as seems likely, that radical changes in society would not be useful; or whether they did not apply the claim of *agapé* to the institution with sufficient rigor it is not now possible to determine. The fact is that this literature countenanced slavery as well as a certain subjection of women to men in marriage and in the life of the church in general. At the same time, faithful to the Spirit of the risen Lord, these inspired writers turned loose a Spirit of love and joy and freedom which in the course of 2000 years, after much pain and travail, has shown slavery and any form of involuntary subjection of one person to another to be a violation of the kingdom of God. For "there is no longer Jew or Greek, there is no longer slave or free, there is no longer male or female; for all of you are one in Christ Jesus" (Gal. 3:28). *The church cannot be at rest until this vision of heavenly reality is translated into rules and laws and precepts for the governing of the life of both church and its society here on earth, as much as may be in a fallen world.* There will always be a distance to go to reach this goal. We have come some way already in these 2000 years, though not far enough.

This discussion leads up to the use of the Bible in determining a Christian ethic of homosexuality. This is not the occasion to review all the biblical evidence on the subject, which is considerable. Some things, however, can be suggested within the perspectives of this essay.

1. The first use of the Bible to determine ethical behavior in this matter, as in the others we have considered, is to study the evidence. What are the texts? What are the contexts? The texts must be taken seriously, and they are largely negative.

2. As in the other cases we have considered, however, what either the Old or the New Testament has to say about homosexuals cannot be applied mechanically to late twentieth-century society. A careful study would have to determine what homosexual behavior entailed then and what it is like now before any inferences can be drawn.

3. Such behavior—then and now—would have to be brought under

the scrutiny of *agapé*. What does it mean to be related in love to people who are gay or lesbian? What does it mean for lesbian or gay persons to be related to each other in *agapé?* Are such relationships possible? Is there any analogue to faithful life-long heterosexual relations? I believe that such relations are possible.

4. What does *agapé* require of the laws under which homosexual persons live in our society and in our church? Are present laws and canons depersonalizing and even unjust? I believe that our laws and canons are in need of review and reform.

5. On the other hand, it has yet to be proved beyond any doubt that homosexual persons are such *by nature*, by virtue of their genes. Can homosexuality really be understood as an aspect of the world as God created it, as an "alternative lifestyle"? I think that in this case, as for the rest of creation, God has concluded all under sin that in the end God may have mercy on all.

6. I regard it as at least a possible and perhaps a desirable outcome of the present debate on this subject that our church might conclude that homosexuality is a *mark* of a sinful world—like poverty, for example,—but that individual homosexual persons, like the poor, are not necessarily any more responsible for their condition, and therefore not necessarily any more sinful, than the rest of us.

7. It might be possible for the church to countenance a life-long faithful (agapaic) relationship between homosexual persons. *Agapé* would preclude predatory and promiscuous behavior for homosexuals as it does for heterosexuals. An agapaic relationship between homosexuals, moreover, is not marriage.

8. It might be possible for the church to put the ordination of homosexuals under the same regulations as pertain to heterosexuals.

9. Such conclusions might be found to be no more contradictory to the thrust of scripture than the stand against slavery or for the equality of men and women.

10. The chance of discerning the best laws and rules governing homosexual behavior will be improved when all of us discern from the scripture that we are all sinners together and are all candidates in our several ways for the grace and forgiveness of God.

ACKNOWLEDGMENTS

An earlier version of this essay has been reviewed by the persons whose names appear below. Either by conversation or correspondence they have made a number of significant and helpful suggestions, many of which have been incorporated into the paper in its final form. The reviewers should not be implicated in the infelicities and shortcomings which remain, however; nor is any of them committed to agree with everything in it.

Ms. Verna Dozier	The Rev.Frederick Quinn
Washington, DC	*Chevy Chase, MD*
The Rev. Prof. Reginald Fuller	The Very Rev Richard Reid
Richmond, VA	*Virginia Seminary*
Prof. Barbara Hall	The Rt. Rev. Philip Smith
Virginia Seminary	*Bishop of New Hampshire (Ret'd)*
The Rev. Prof. Charles Hefling	The Rev. Robert Trache
Boston College	*Alexandria, VA*
Ms. Evelina Moulder	Ms. Betty Wanamaker
Alexandria, VA	*Alexandria, VA*

(Biblical citations in this essay are from The Holy Bible, New Revised Standard Version, copyright 1989, Division of Christian Education of the National Council of Churches of Christ in the United States of America.)

NOTES

1. Jean-Paul Sartre, *The Words* (New York: George Braziller, 1964).
2. Book of Common Prayer, 853.
3. Article VI, Book of Common Prayer, 868.
4. Cf. Edgar J. Goodspeed, "The Canon of the New Testament," in *The Interpreters' Bible*, vol. 1 (New York: Abingdon-Cokesbury, 1952).
5. Article VI, Book of Common Prayer, 868.
6. Cf. Calvin, *Institutes* 1.7.5, vol. xx, Library of Christian Classics (Philadelphia: Westminster Press, 1960).
7. Book of Common Prayer, pp. 375, 858, 308.
8. Ibid., p. 853.
9. Cf. George T. Ladd, *The Doctrine of Sacred Scripture* (New York: Scribner's, 1883), 39ff.
10. Edwyn Clement Hoskyns and Francis Noel Davey, *The Fourth Gospel*, 2d rev. ed. (London: Faber and Faber, 1947), 92.
11. William Laud, *A Relation of the Conference between William Laud, Then Lord Bishop of St. David's, now Archbishop of Canterbury and Mr. Fisher, The Jesuit*, in More and Cross, *Anglicanism* (Milwaukee: Morehouse Publishing, 1935).
12. *Vide* Eph. 6:5-6; Col. 3:22-23; 1 Pet. 2:18.
13. Book of Common Prayer, 868.
14. Richard Hooker, *Laws of Ecclesiastical Polity* 2.8.7, Folger Edition (Cambridge, Mass.: Belknap Press, 1977), 1:191.
15. Nicene Creed, Book of Common Prayer, 358-359.
16. Book of Common Prayer, 358.
17. *Report of the Commission on Doctrine Appointed by the Archbishops of Canterbury and York in 1922* (London: SPCK, 1938), 82.
18. Hooker, *Laws of Ecclesiastical Polity* 2.1.2, vol. 1, 145.
19. Ibid.
20. Cf. E. Lohmeyers, *Die Philipper, Kolossie und an Philemon* (Göttingen: Vandenhoeck und Ruprecht, 1953), 154.

"For Freedom Christ Has Set You Free": The Interpretation and Authority of Scripture in Contemporary Theologies of Liberation

Ellen K. Wondra

INTRODUCTION

In any age, Christians are called to reflect deeply and conscientiously on the relation between their faith and the world in which they live. No less is true today. The call to continuous reflection comes from the Incarnation itself: in Christ, God becomes flesh and lives in the midst of the changes, chances, and particularities of human history. Because in Christ God is Emmanuel, "God with us," historical existence is the place where God acts as creator, sustainer, and savior. Thus our attention is drawn constantly by God to contemporary events and movements of history. Our faith seeks both understanding and the clarity of its cause where we live. The presence of God with us in contemporary events also draws our attention to the sources that shape our faith, and we encounter these sources anew. Thus, the scriptures and the communities of tradition—the church—which names them scriptures (rather than, say, great literature) must also be understood anew.

In the contemporary world, deep and conscientious reflection is prompted by events of massive suffering and by the cries of the suffering that the injustice of their plight be recognized and that their own voices be heard. Much massive suffering is the consequence of social oppression; so the voices of the suffering draw attention to their marginal place in human history, even as they cry out for full participation in human societies. Their voices also draw attention to the contributions Christianity has made both to their oppression and to their liberation. That is, the voices of the marginalized and the oppressed remind us that it is through Christianity that they encounter the saving grace of God offered through Christ to all humanity; but their voices also remind us that Christianity has accompanied and even justified the conquest and oppression that are at the root of their massive unjust suffering.

This essay is a discussion of how the theologies emerging from contexts of massive unjust suffering understand the authority of scripture. The ambiguous character of the scriptures—which are themselves many texts rather than a text—is intensified in these contexts by the fact that the scriptures may be and are used both to justify domination and to empower liberation. This being the case, a basic question emerges: On what basis do communities of liberation recognize the scriptures as having authority? My contention here is that, in contexts of struggle, the authority of the scriptures resides in their capacity to empower liberation by authorizing persons to seek full humanity. Before exploring this contention, it will be helpful to understand both the situation that gives rise to theologies of liberation, and some possible responses to it.

Many persons of European and American heritage experience the protests of the suffering against their plight as an eruption of "the other." Specifically, the eruption of the other refers to the insistence by those who are marginalized and suppressed by social, political, economic, and cultural systems and structures that their unjust suffering cease, that their voices be heard, and that they be heard in their own languages and inflections. The peoples of the "Third World," the lower and underclasses in Europe and North America, racial and ethnic minority groups, women of all races and classes, gays and lesbians, and the earth itself have all been making new claims on our attention, both through massive global suffering and through movements of protest, resistance, and liberation. Their common goal is participation in full humanity—in meaningful human life, and in the promises of God made to all persons.

Also claiming our attention is the presence of "the other" within— within our own culture, in the often unfamiliar and (to some) disruptive presence of racial and ethnic minority groups who maintain their particular identity, of women, of gays and lesbians who insist on defining their own identity, and of the underclasses, the homeless, and the ill. The consequence of this eruption in the postmodern West is that our understanding of human society is shifting from a model of unity to one of pluralism and diversity.

But "the other" is also within ourselves, in the equally unruly presence of the subconscious and unconscious, and in the insistent presence of our bodies and our feelings. The recognition of the other within ourselves means that it is increasingly difficult and almost impossible for any given person to see him- or herself as autonomous, objective, rational, and static. It is increasingly difficult and almost impossible for any of us to see ourselves as formed, completed, fully conscious selves in any significant way separable from each other, from our bodies, from our historical circumstances, from our ways of thought. And it is increasingly difficult and almost impossible to say what the human self is when we are surrounded by radically differing selves and cultures, and by radically differing claims to meaning and truth, each of which can be—on its own terms—plausible, consistent, and cohesive. The consequence in the postmodern West is that our understanding of the human self or person is shifting from a paradigm of autonomy to a paradigm of relationality.

These two shifts in Western consciousness—to pluralism and to relationality—may be experienced as a fragmentation of familiar and necessary structures and systems, and as a breakdown in authority. When the interpretation of this experience is attributed to the eruption of the other, the response is often a forceful defensive reassertion of these familiar systems and structures, and of the customary notions of authority.

But another response is possible, and that is the affirmation of the value and generative possibilities that come with pluralism and with the ambiguity that accompanies it. A positive valuation of pluralism turns our attention to how differing things are connected, how they pile up on top of each other, with overlaps, extensions, and pressures, so that they press down on each other and overflow, like grapes in a wine press. These connections and overlaps and extensions are not neat. They involve continuity but also difference, complementarity but also opposition, mutual affirmation but also contradiction, complex harmony but also difficult conflict. That is, they are ambiguous. But ambiguity has its own resources as well as its own challenges. Because of its challenges, "it is in the areas of ambiguity that transformation takes place; in fact, without such areas, transformation would be impossible."[1]

Living with plurality and ambiguity requires more than tolerance. It requires a basis in confidence that the rubs, gaps, and fissures as well as the agreements and overlaps that we encounter are generative. That confidence is based in a certain faith in the power of the divine as "God with us," such that we can be sure in religion while tentative in theology (as Ian Ramsey put it). That confidence requires that we understand faith as always in the "process of seeking, contending, wrestling, like Jacob with the angel until dawn, wanting to be blessed. . . ."[2]

Related to this positive valuation of plurality and ambiguity are theological presuppositions. The first is that God is a communion of difference (of which I will say more later). Second, what it means to be human is to be historical; history really matters. As historical beings, we are finite and limited. We are constructed by what mediates our existence: social arrangements, language in the broadest sense, and our own ability to make something of the "blooming, buzzing confusion" that surrounds us. All of our existence is mediated. The mediations make us what we are. They also keep us from being something else. Third, as humans we are also made in the image of God. In part, this means we are relational by nature, because God is relational. Finally, we are sinful. Sin is pervasive; everything is affected. The glass through which we see only darkly because of our inherent limitations is darkened further by sin. So we have to deal not only with the mediations but also with the distortions of our existence.

I view our contemporary situation as one of irreducible plurality, which I see as revelatory of God and God's saving presence with us. The ambiguity of this contemporary situation is very sharply presented by social movements for liberation, which are prompted by resistance to social and symbolic systems of oppression and marginalization. Many of these movements have significant roots in Christian churches and in the Christian faith. I here suggest transformation of Christian theological reflection (and particularly as it relates to the scriptures) to an approach based on the mutual participation of all involved and affected, and on an understanding of authority as dispersed among the constituents of complex and interactive communities. This response is akin to that of the suffering and the marginalized as they struggle for liberation; and it is deeply and richly based in the biblically shaped Christian faith that empowers and sustains their struggles.

My discussion here focuses on the work of Christians for whom the transformation of the present world is focused by liberation from unjust systems and structures. Theologies of liberation are always and explicitly concerned with the material forms of domination (economic, political, and social). What is of concern here, however, are the more covert forms of oppression that affect consciousness, experience, and thought.

My discussion of these covert forms is principally informed by liberation theologies produced by Americans of African descent and by white feminists, two approaches that are found within the Episcopal Church as well as within North American Christianity as a whole.

This discussion is also informed by Latin American liberation theology, an approach that has significantly defined the nature and purpose of liberation theologies worldwide, and which has explicitly considered the interpretation of the scriptures in considerable depth. While my primary interest here is with those liberation theologies already mentioned, I will also use sources from other historical and contemporary theologies to relate my discussion to the consciousness of the contemporary Episcopal Church. I will discuss the plurality of human experience and the factors that unify it; the related dispersal of authority; the nature of the scriptures as multivocal narrative; and the interpretation of the scriptures through disclosure and recognition. To make the discussion more concrete, I will discuss how liberation theologies understand the circumstances of the birth of Christ (including the role of Mary the God-bearer), and how a faith in "God with us" manifests itself in movements for economic and social justice.

These points are elaborations of a basic theme of liberation theologies: participation in full humanity. This theme is often expressed in contemporary terms within the context of struggles against oppression and for liberation, but it also reflects a significant continuity with the Christian tradition of communion among human persons as a reflection of the eternal communion of the Persons of the Trinity. A brief discussion of participation will set the stage for a more detailed discussion of the authority and interpretation of the scriptures. This discussion is followed by a brief elaboration of underlying views of human experience, the nature of authority, and the Bible as authoritative text.

PARTICIPATION AND LIBERATION

Following a tradition stemming from the Gospel of John, the Cappadocian Fathers, and Thomas Aquinas, Richard Hooker defines participation as "that mutual inward hold which Christ hath of us and we of him, in such sort that each possesseth other by way of special interest, property, and inherent copulation."[3] Hooker emphasizes both the distinction between the human and divine, *and* their unbreakable connection.[4] While the connection is the more significant, both aspects of participation are based in the very nature of God, who is one substance in which each Person participates in a different way. God, that is, is both diverse and unified:

> The persons of the Trinity are not three particular substances to whom one *general* nature is common, but three that subsist by

one substance *which itself is particular,* yet they all three have it, and their several ways of having it are that which maketh their personal distinction.[5]

What is true for God is true for Christians: "Participation thus means both union and distinction in the Godhead and between Christ and the Christian."[6]

Brazilian liberation theologian Leonardo Boff describes participation in more contemporary terms: the Persons of the Trinity "co-exist simultaneously and the Three are co-eternal from the beginning." The unity of the Three is found in their communion; and that communion is one of "permanent interpenetration, the eternal co-relatedness, the self-surrender of each Person to the others" such that "each Person contains the other two, each one penetrates the others and is penetrated by them, one lives in the other, and vice-versa." In other words, without differentiation between the Persons there can be no union.[7]

The communion of the Trinity flows outward and is expressed in the interconnectedness of all aspects of the created universe. Each created thing reflects the nature of its creator, and so is related with all other created things in the same sort of communion of permanent interpenetration, eternal co-relatedness, and self-surrender as is true for God. The divine communion is thus the basis and the form of human longings for community and for justice. As Boff writes,

> The oppressed struggle for participation at all levels of life, for a just and egalitarian sharing while respecting the differences between persons and groups; they seek communion with other cultures and other values, and with God as the ultimate meaning of history and of their own hearts. As these realities are withheld from them in history, they feel obliged to undertake a process of liberation that seeks to enlarge the space for participation and communion available to them.

Thus, in the quest for justice and communion, struggles for liberation are the human expression of the life of the Trinity in history. These struggles seek always to mirror the life of God more fully. "The community of Father, Son and Holy Spirit becomes the prototype of the human community dreamed of by those who wish to improve society and build it in such a way as to make it into the image and likeness of the Trinity."[8]

Participation or communion, then, is a relation of both intimate connection and individual distinction, to which diversity or difference is inherent. Because this relation is itself the very nature of the divine who creates, sustains, and redeems all that is, creation itself ideally should strive to embody this same relation. To the extent that relations among creatures fail or refuse to embody and nurture participation, they depart from their divine ground, and are therefore sinful. To the extent that relations among creatures increasingly embody and deepen communion, they increasingly participate in divine creativity and sovereignty. Thus, the appropriate goal of human quests for holiness, goodness, and truthfulness is to reach toward this divine mutuality. This goal is made concrete among persons and in systems and institutions through increased and deepened communion and mutual participation among all involved and including all affected.

THE CONTEXTS OF LIBERATION

As Boff suggests, the oppressed have been denied the opportunity for full participation in communion. This denial is abundantly evident in historical systems of patriarchal domination[9] and subjugation. These systems are expressed in social, economic, and political structures of inequality and injustice. Because of these structures, the marginalized and oppressed—predominantly women of every race, men as well as women of color, gays and lesbians, the poor, and their children—suffer real deprivation of the basic material needs of life (food, shelter, health care, meaningful work, and so on), and they live in situations where their primary aim is one of day-to-day survival.

These unjust socioeconomic systems are undergirded by ideologies of domination, which support marginalization and subjugation by equating normative humanity and human historical existence with the humanity, history, and experience of powerful male elites. This construction of gender, race, class, and sexuality shapes human consciousness, experience, and self- and other-regard through language, symbol systems, and structures of authority. By identifying the powerful as the human norm, systems of domination relegate the experience and existence of the dominated to the margins of history. This marginalization deprives the oppressed of their histories and denigrates their modes of expression and relationship (their "voices"). These multiple forms of domination and subjugation are considered to be "natural," and even of divine origin. Because these systems and ideologies operate largely unconsciously, consciousness-raising and criticism are inevitably major components of the struggle for liberation from domination, and for full participation in human history.

Theologies of liberation begin from within but at the margins of existing societies and structures. They are first and foremost theologies that emerge within the church, committed to Christianity but critical of its contributions to systems of domination and marginalization. Although theologies of liberation may begin with critique, they move readily to recovery and reconstruction of the liberating aspects of Christianity.

Once the oppressive character of patriarchal culture is recognized, it is possible to "break the silence" of cultural deposits and traditions to render visible the varied and active presence and participation of various differing "others" throughout history. This reconstruction provides a more adequate understanding of human history as a whole. This process also challenges the cultural presuppositions of contemporary readers because it discloses that received texts and traditions present a reality genuinely different from our own. This critique and recovery of tradition makes available resources for expanding consciousness and transformed thought, allowing the marginalized and suppressed to contribute more freely to the continuance and development of the societies and cultures with which they are connected.

Liberation theologians understand that human existence is made up of certain inherent polarities, such as existence and transcendence, nature and history, actuality and potentiality, spirit (or mind) and body, and so on. The tensions of the interconnections within these polarities have historically been resolved through dualistic distortions that identify one pole as superior to and dominant over the other; for example, spirit as superior to body, history and culture as superior to nature, and male as superior to female. Dualistic distortions of this sort are at the root of all forms of domination. The distortions therefore must be healed through transformation in order for the original interconnections to emerge once again. Dualism and the social structures (including patriarchy) through which it finds expression violate the order of creation. They also sunder creation from existence, and existence from redemption; they are, therefore, sinful.

In stark contrast to sinful distortions and their consequences stands the possibility of a divinely based full humanity. For the marginalized and subjugated, moving toward the eschatological vision of full humanity requires the renewal of the interconnections that are inherent to human existence. Concretely, the process of such renewal is evidenced by struggles to create a just society in which the well-being of each human person is integral to the well-being of all, such that all have access to the material necessities of daily living. Further, just well-being integrally includes mutual participation in the creation and interpretation of history, of symbolic, artistic, and cognitive modes of expression, and in the envisioning of the future.

Liberation theologians insist that God is known relationally. They claim that the divine is itself inherently relational, as previously described. When the divine is understood in classical Trinitarian terms as mutually giving and receiving, divine relationality is the empowering source and model of just and mutual human relationality. Human sin is the sundering of those just and mutual relations that reflect the internal life of the Trinity.

The divine (as distinct from the human) may be imaginatively understood as the matrix—both ground and substance—of both being and new being, the source of the original polarities of human existence, the empowering energy for transformation of historical dualisms and their sinful consequences, and the lure into a future of completed transformation beyond history. It is by participation in the ongoing activity of the divine relationship with creation that human historical liberation takes place.

Liberation theologians rely heavily on hope-filled vision grounded in a biblically based understanding of inaugurated eschatology. Redemption is already available and experienced partially now; but it is to be fully actualized only in the future. In past and present struggles for justice, just mutuality, and liberation, concrete signs of this historical *and transhistorical* future may be found, and hope and courage for further struggle generated. Signs of this future are also found in exemplary figures in human history, including Jesus, who is revealed as the Christ in his incarnation or embodiment both of liberated humanity and of the restored mutual relation between humanity and divinity.

What is notable here is the identification of historical, finite, and ambiguous human existence as the place where the ultimate connection of creation, existence, and redemption begins to occur. Particularly in struggles for economic and political liberation, the pervasive effects of sin and the continuous offer of redemption are disclosed, experienced, recognized, and articulated in part through the problematics of overcoming domination and moving toward transformative healing. Present struggles of this sort, historically and critically understood, disclose a past where such struggles are also continuous. However, these struggles are often obscured by the operations of domination in recording history as the history of the dominant group(s). Reconstructions of the suppressed past along with present struggles are then the ground from which fruitful (but not absolute) visions of a transformed future emerge.

To put it another way: present struggles for liberation have authority precisely because they actively seek to move into a future where the connection between creation and existence and between existence and redemption is restored and renewed; in this longed-for future, the possibility of mutual participation throughout creation and with the divine is increasingly approximated. The authority of struggles for liberation is not one of force; it is, rather, one of disclosure, appeal, and nurture.

In appealing to present experience understood in the light of an emerging transformed future, liberation theologians both tacitly and explicitly appeal to divine authorship and authority, with God seen as the ultimate liberator and nurturer, and as the ultimate source of struggles for liberation. The divine is understood as fully present in human history as fellow-sufferer. God is God with us, rather than a distant, imperial Lord. Human authority is then measured by its coherence with its divine source. And claims of divine authority for anything that hampers or counters divinely empowered impulses toward liberation—for example, proclaiming texts or traditions of domination as "the Word of God"—are unwarranted and even blasphemous: God, who is both creator and redeemer, cannot support domination.

The God who is creator and redeemer is the source of the norm against which human experience is evaluated. This same God also constitutes the norm against which other authorities—including the scriptures—are evaluated. Thus, the scriptures have authority in that they may empower and nurture liberation, that is, in that they may contribute to participation in a full humanity.

This view of the authority of the scriptures is part of an ongoing process of recovering the scriptures from their role in establishing, justifying, and perpetuating various systems of domination. Each form of liberation theology points to biblical texts that have been and continue to be used as texts of domination and terror. In each case, what is at issue is not only how the scriptures are used or interpreted; also significant are the texts of the scriptures themselves.

For example, African-American theologians critique not only the proslavery elaboration of the "Hamitic curse"; they also point to Genesis 9:25, upon which the Hamitic curse is based, and Leviticus 25:44-46, which provides for the acquisition of slaves. Feminist and womanist[10] theologians bring under suspicion not only the Eve/Mary paradigm of the early church; they also point to Genesis 2 and 3 and to sections of the Epistles of Paul (including 1 Corinthians'

Adam-Christ motif). These texts themselves undergird other biblical texts, such as the "household codes" of Ephesians 5:21-6:9, Colossians 3:18-4:1, and 1 Peter 2:18-3:7, and the Epistle to Philemon.

But it is not only the specific texts that are found in Genesis or the Epistles of Paul that are problematic. These texts themselves rest on the patriarchal ethos of the biblical world in which the subordination of women, servants, slaves, and strangers was routine. The sociohistorical context of the biblical world thus undergirds and informs the biblical texts themselves, even as these texts seek to give expression to encounter with the divine, whose life is beyond as well as in history. In turn, scriptural texts have generated a long "history of effects" that continuously shapes how these texts are understood and appropriated by subsequent believers.[11] That is, scriptural texts both reflect the biblical world and shape the postbiblical world.

Consequently, the approach of liberation theologies to the authority and interpretation of the scriptures has three central tasks: critiquing scripture's patriarchal aspects; recovering scripture's transformative potential; and incorporating contemporary experience into interpretive processes.

The most obvious of these tasks is the disclosure and critique of the relation of the patriarchal aspects of the scriptures to their overall character and status. This task arises directly from the role the scriptures play in shaping consciousness and mediating religious experience. That is, the immediacy of religious experience is always mediated by the structures, processes, and contexts in which religious experience occurs: the language, symbols, and everyday experience available to us provide the means by which we understand experience precisely as religious. In contexts of domination and subjugation, the subjugated must submit and consent to patriarchal domination even to encounter the biblical text as readers, because the language and symbols available reflect domination. This requirement is also placed by the patriarchal formation of the scriptures themselves, as well as by its attributed authority in contexts of domination; that is, women (for example) must hear or read as if they were male simply to follow the story.[12]

Biblical texts—like all other texts and traditions—must therefore be engaged with the suspicion that they reinforce subjugation. Liberation theology asks questions like these: To what extent is patriarchy so inherent to the biblical witness and religion that these can do nothing other than support domination? To what extent are the scriptures also a force for liberation? How can the witness of the scriptures be unentwined from patriarchy? And can this be done without ignoring or suppressing the "dangerous memory" and the ongoing reality of its real contributions to systems of domination?

The second task is more subtle. Consciousness is a construct within concrete contexts, and "the cultural matrix founds its own interrogation." Thus, theologians of liberation point to the fact that Christianity—*despite* its patriarchal character—is also a primary source for the hope of present transformation as well as of the redemption that will be fully actualized in the future. Transformative influences come not just through texts that explicitly treat the full humanity of the oppressed. Rather, the possibility of liberating transformation is suggested even by those texts that are implicitly or explicitly patriarchal. This second task takes seriously the fact that the oppressed "have actually experienced these 'negative' texts as liberating."[13]

The third task focuses on the appropriate use of experience as a constructive hermeneutical source. Awareness of the presence and effects of patriarchal domination puts distance between the dominated and familiar religious beliefs and practices. At the same time, it destabilizes the authority of the familiar. This throws theologies of liberation

> back upon the primary intuitions of religious experience itself, namely, the belief in a divine foundation of reality which is ultimately good, which does not wish evil nor create evil, but affirms and upholds our autonomous personhood . . . , in whose image we are made.[14]

The pervasiveness of patriarchy, the ambiguity of received texts and their history of effects, and the importance of contemporary religious experience—these three issues and their related questions constitute three critical, analytic, and constructive "moments" in liberation biblical hermeneutics. Regardless of the various ways that liberation theologies approach these three tasks, each comes to biblical texts with a suspicion of its support of domination. Once this suspicion is fully explored, each approach answers the question of the patriarchal character of the scriptures by arguing that while that character is pervasive it is not absolute. This judgment is based in part on an understanding of the scriptures as a web of narratives that are sometimes continuous, sometimes complementary, sometimes confusing, sometimes contradictory. To see the scriptures as a uniform unit, then, is contrary to the character of the scriptures themselves. The recovery of ignored, suppressed, and forgotten biblical texts and their interpretation through the experience of the subjugated and marginalized confirms this point. Along with other contemporary theologians, liberation theologians recognize that narrative—by nature—provokes interpretive response in those who encounter it. These responses will be plural, in part because the experience of persons differs, but—as significantly—because narrative itself contains surpluses of meaning that necessarily evoke multiple responses.

Nevertheless, the patriarchal character of the scriptures is sufficiently significant that the authority of scripture must be redefined: the scriptures are not automatically normative, and their authority is, in any event, balanced by the authority of the theological presuppositions sketched at the beginning of this essay, and by contemporary experience of a specifiable sort. In other words, the first of the three "moments" is incomplete without the other two, each of which involves scriptural interpretation.

THE HERMENEUTICS OF LIBERATION

The issue of the ambiguity of the scriptures and their interpretation in situations of domination and the issue of the importance of contemporary human experience are addressed by liberation biblical hermeneutics through a variety of interpretive strategies involving critical suspicion, proclamation, remembrance, and creative actualization.[15] These strategies judge the authority of theological texts on the basis of their relation to struggles against domination and for liberation. At the same time, this judgment is enhanced by the use of historical-critical methods that reclaim the "dangerous memory" of human suffering and the subversive memory of ongoing resistance to domination, both of which are understood to be reflected in and occasioned by biblical texts and their historic usage.

Further, liberation hermeneutics relies on an "imaginative characterization of the central reality of Christianity"[16] as bearing on human historical freedom as well as on transhistorical transformation. Liberation theologies profess a God who is inherently relational, and so is the source of just, mutual relations among human persons and societies, and between humans and the earth itself. This God constantly offers redemption and lures creation into a transformative and transformed future. Human persons experience the divine gift of redemption as freedom from sin and as liberation from the historical effects of sin.

For example, the liberation theologies of feminists, womanists, African Americans, and Latin Americans interpret the texts and traditions surrounding the birth of Jesus and the person of Mary his mother in light of their concern for the oppressed and marginalized. The decision of God to become incarnate through the cooperation of a poor woman, in a land subjected to colonial occupation, and as one of the homeless proclaims God's solidarity with the poor, God's own refusal of the idolatry of patriarchal privilege, and a divine humility that is mirrored in the simple lives of the subjugated and outcast. Mary's voluntary consent to God's gracious request—in the face of her increased marginalization because of the apparent illegitimacy of her child—manifests the courage of the poor and of women in resisting the degradations of their subjugated condition. This resistance and its basis in faith are proclaimed in the Magnificat. The announcement of Jesus' birth to the shepherds is further indication of God's favor toward the poor, while the journey of the Magi (and especially their refusal to betray the Holy Family to Herod) indicates the possibility of the conversion of the rich to the cause of the God of life.

Thus, the circumstances of Jesus' birth are of a piece with his life and teachings, in which he supported and encouraged the lowest in word and deed, using their lives to illustrate the gracious action of God and the nature of God's reign in creation. Jesus' unjust suffering and violent death are the direct outcome of his living his life as one of the marginalized: God does not abandon the suffering—even to escape death. Finally, Jesus' resurrection proclaims that death is not the meaning of life. God's "reign is built on a pact with women and men—a pact on behalf of life, and a pact against whatever might threaten that life."[17]

The fundamental theological affirmation here—that God is the God of life, and therefore of those who are denied life by their historical conditions—then shapes *what* sort of authority the scriptures have, *which* parts of the scriptures are granted authority, *how* the scriptures are used, and in *what* contexts. Thus, liberation theologies appropriate *any* biblical story or tradition that is empowering and transformative to those engaged in struggles for survival and liberating transformation. This appropriation involves reading scriptural texts from the perspective of the oppressed, that is, from within the context of domination and collective struggles for transformation.[18] These readings are then subject to the evaluation and response of other readers inside and outside particular communities of resistance and transformation.

Nevertheless, precisely because the scriptures have been used both to enslave and to liberate the oppressed,[19] the Bible is not *automati-*

cally a primary authority for liberation theologies. Scripture has authority in liberation theology not primarily when it provides content (although it may do so), but more basically when it nurtures and empowers persons toward freedom. That is, scripture is an authority in liberation theology when it *authorizes,* when it frees and empowers the subjugated to act.[20]

This understanding of the scriptures as authorizing thought and action leads to a dialogical method of Bible study in which all are authorized participants. Communities of faith involved in struggles for liberation bring to their study of the scriptures the historical-critical tools familiar to the scholarship of Europe and North America. These methods, which often focus on the development of the canonical text, are generally applied by those participants with formal theological education. Of equal significance, however, is the community's own analysis of its context, and the historical effects of scripture and theology within that context. For this aspect of study, the tools of critical social analysis and research are crucial. Thus, the study of scripture involves a shift in methodological paradigms, from a literary approach to critical social analysis. The intent of Bible study, in this model, is to generate understandings of what the text *means* in contemporary situations, rather than what the text *meant* as it developed.

Thus far, I have provided a summary overview of the constructive theological claims of liberation theologies, and have related those to the interpretation of scripture. The discussion will now turn to the understandings of human experience and authority that are related to these claims.

THE NATURE OF HUMAN EXPERIENCE

One of the primary constructive tasks of liberation theologies has been to provide a relatively adequate description of human experience, one which recognizes that human experience is irreducibly plural but nonetheless connected. This description (which entails redefining human subjectivity and consciousness, as well as experience) is made necessary by the inadequacies of the dominant view of human persons as autonomous, constituted by a single universal essence and essentially unaffected by historical existence. It is this dominant view of the self that has marginalized and suppressed the experience of women of all peoples, men as well as women of color, the poor, and gays and lesbians.[21]

Movements of resistance and liberation rely on forms of consciousness-raising to develop analysis of the human situation, plans of action to address that situation, and solidarity among participants. Corporate, critical, and self-critical exploration of and reflection on persons' concrete lives provide significant bases for new, interactive, process-oriented understandings of the human person, of consciousness, and of human experience. This epistemology is, in turn, based on a complex view of the human subject. Subjectivity is grounded neither in some human core or essence unaffected by the changes and chances of existence (as with idealism), nor in subjects' material conditions (as with Marxian materialism). Rather, subjectivity is constituted "by one's personal, subjective engagement in the practices, discourses, and institutions that lend significance (value, meaning, and affect) to the events of the world."[22]

The emphasis here is on the social as well as the personal construction of reality: "practices, discourses, and institutions" are human products that organize material conditions in particular ways, giving them their significance, and providing suggestions for how they are to be perceived, interpreted, and understood. Such constructs include sociopolitical systems, economic arrangements, cultural and religious institutions, and linguistic structures. They also include constructions of gender, race, class, and sexuality, which further serve to place individuals' and groups' lives, desires, and hopes within social reality.

Human persons are thus understood to be socially and historically constituted through their involvement in multiple communities of discourse and practice, and human consciousness develops and changes within the limits of historical identity and humanly construed concrete situations. At the same time, how individuals live and act within their situations reconstructs both the situation itself and their consciousness of it.[23]

Human experience is nevertheless common in its most basic processes and structures. Each and every person is constituted by the interaction of their internal and external worlds; what differs are the concrete elements of those worlds, and how particular elements in all their concreteness are interrelated in value, meaning, and significance. When either meaning or experience changes—as do both, with changes in their constituent parts—consciousness itself changes. The impetus for such change arises within the existing context of experience.

> Experience itself is interpreted. The data of our existence is filtered through some organizing matrix in order for us to categorize it, order it, and make it sensible . . . Only when anomalies

> grow do we ever question the matrix itself. Even at that point,
> however, our questions are guided by the same interpretive grid.
> The cultural matrix founds its own interrogation.[24]

To understand experience and consciousness in this way is to recognize that human experience is itself plural and diverse. That is, the varieties of human experience are irreducibly interstructured on the basis of gender, race, class, and sexuality; and these factors cannot be eliminated or ignored in order to understand "who we really are." Nevertheless, *all* human experience is connected. First of all, every human person has a gender, a race, a class. Beyond this, the elements that constitute experience are tied together in relations of conflict, domination and subjugation, mutual support, and overlapping struggles for survival, liberation, and transformation. Genders, races, classes are irrevocably related to each other. Thus, concrete human experiences are at the same time different and similar; and the interplay between them makes it possible for persons to understand and learn from each other's differing concrete experience without suppressing the differences and conflicts of their historical existences. In other words, human experience is diverse in its concreteness. But it is also unified both in the formative connections among concrete groups and in conscientious human attention to these connections and their consequences. The human person, in sum, is *always* a self-in-relation.

Experience understood as relational and critically reflective is a highly appropriate source for liberation theory and practice because, as an ongoing critical and self-critical process, experience resists the forces of domination. Critically reflective experience breaks the silences and suppressions that are a consequence of domination, thereby interrupting patriarchal subjugation, disclosing the participation of the subjugated in all areas of human existence, and revealing the social and historical construction of all experience.

THE NATURE OF AUTHORITY IN CHRISTIAN COMMUNITY

Christian liberation theologians bring this view of the human as relational to bear directly on the problem of authority. To understand the authority of the scriptures, the nature of authority of all sorts must be examined.

The authority granted to any person or thing is related to power, the ability to "make a difference to the world,"[25] which may be expressed (individually, collectively, or systemically) through request, persuasion, argumentation, or the fostering of consensus. Or authority may be expressed through the use of force, coercion, domination, or manipulation. Power is therefore related to the exercise of human freedom and agency, and to the ability of individuals to discern truth, meaning, and value and to act in the midst of their existence.[26] Authority, in other words, derives not only from the forcefulness of observable structures and functions external to the individual; it is also conferred by factors residing in the inner life of individuals.

Authority thus may be understood as primarily a type of relationship among persons and between persons and the conditions of their existence. As John Skinner writes, authority is "that kind of structured reality, whether social or personal, which through nurture and cultivation [anchored ultimately in the source of all reality] enables individuals to become truly centered selves or persons, and thus, relatively free beings."[27]

Ideally, I suggest, authority encourages voluntary consent.[28] Mutuality in relationships is violated when the exercise of power shifts from the persuasive to the coercive, from evoking relatively free consent to forcing compliance.

The operation of authority, then, is not primarily a matter of an external standard that confers legitimacy on certain acts, or that "grants the right to hold an opinion." Rather, authority operates (ideally) by nurturing and cultivating the ability to think, to act, to discern truth, and to strengthen the connection between persons and between experienced reality and the ultimate, the divine.[29] In other words, authority draws its power from its ability to make an appeal, a claim on the human subject, and its ability to evoke a response— positive or negative—to that appeal. This type of authority is compelling for precisely this reason: "The result of refusing to respond is not some kind of sanction such as physical violence, [or] ignorance . . . ; it is the diminution of the self"[30] in relation to all others to whom the self is related, including the divine.

It is the relation between human existence and the divine as it is encountered in the context of finite and sinful human history that has led theologians to claim that the basis of all religious authority is in God, the author of all that is. When this is the case, the status of more observably proximate authorities—including the scriptures—is secondary and derivative: they have authority in that they are related to the divine. Thus, for example, the 1948 Lambeth Conference argued that authority is single in that it is based in the divine life of the Trinity. The Lambeth Conference went on to state that secondary authority is dispersed or distributed interactively among a variety of human elements, including scripture, tradition, creeds, ministry, "the witness of saints," and the *consensus fidelium*.[31] This dispersal presumably protects against any secondary authority claiming primary status for itself. Thus, for example, protection is rendered against any claims that the Word of God is coterminous with the scriptures rather than conveyed by them.

On this view, the church, made up of "relatively free human beings," is to be a "transparent medium" for "creativity and redemption."[32] Further, as the 1968 Lambeth Conference pointed out, authority must "refuse to insulate itself against the testing of history and the free action of reason,"[33] even—and perhaps especially—when such testing strikes at long-cherished and deeply held presuppositions and convictions. The church must also form, protect, and nurture the informed consciences of its members, seeking to generate a *consensus fidelium* rather than either assuming or dictating it.

Now, if this is something like the way the Episcopal Church understands authority—and in practice I think it is—then our beliefs and teachings are authoritative only to the extent that they both "rest on the truth of the Gospel" and "nurture and cultivate relatively free human beings who then may encounter a benevolent transcendence through the images and symbols which make up the nurturing matrix."[34] In other words, our beliefs and teachings are authoritative to the extent that they make creative use of the harmonies, tensions, and even conflicts among such diverse sources as scripture, tradition, reason, and experience. And our beliefs and teachings are authoritative to the extent that they encourage and enable generative relationships with those who differ from us, relationships that are characterized by mutuality and also by enjoyment and delight in difference.

Indeed, when our shared life is itself diverse and when it is set in an irreducibly pluralistic context, we need actually to engage in discourse that recognizes that truth (and so the good) is to some extent intersubjective, to be discovered or disclosed by mutual questioning and exploration; and that *any* claim to truth must be subjected to further critical exploration. In this view, it is important to ask by whom, concretely, authority is held and exercised, and how persons (or groups) are granted or denied authority.

Our understanding of truth and its discernment and the way it shapes action must reflect our understanding of experience—including experience of truth—as plural, that is, as diverse but connected. This requires a critical examination of our customary modes of discourse, the grounds of our notions of who is qualified (and allowed) to speak, and the issues we choose to address. And we need to look, as always, at the theological, ethical, and other presuppositions and claims that are related to our common speech and life.

As Sharon D. Welch recently argued, commonly held notions of responsibility assume that agency is synonymous with observable effectiveness: "What counts as 'responsible action' . . . assume[s] that to be responsible means that one can ensure that the aim of one's action will be carried out." Yet in situations where authority and power are dispersed, no individual agent can rest on such an assurance. Instead, Welch argues, responsible action entails "not the certain achievement of desired ends but the creation of a matrix in which further actions are possible, the creation of the conditions of possibility for desired changes" in the present and the future. Such action "is sustained and enabled by participation in an extensive community" where difference is seen as generative rather than threatening, and where difference is sought out rather than merely tolerated when it appears.[35] Concretely, this suggests that the church's concern with economic justice (for example) must be focused by church members' participation with the poor and marginalized in a diverse, extended community of solidarity. As Timothy Sedgwick has argued, the aim of the church's teachings and work in the area of economic life is appropriately directed not toward the achievement of an ideal of material fulfillment for all but rather toward encountering the marginalized as one would encounter Christ.

Concrete action grows out of this encounter, and is directed toward actualization of a vision of full humanity in which material and spiritual well-being are integrated. In this process, the lives of all participants are changed, both materially and spiritually, as the poor benefit from redistribution of wealth and power, and the more privileged renounce their relative comfort in favor of the compassion of the Good Samaritan. Such change entails a transformation of understandings of rights and values, so that a minimally decent standard of living and the right to self-determination are at least as fundamental as, say, the right to free speech. This transformation also involves the conversion of the church to a *communitas fidelium*, where the faithful respond collectively, "bending over the fallen victims of a life of oppression and assisting them to liberate themselves and to live more humanely and humanly."[36] The response of the faithful involves sharing the joys of those they encounter, even as it may entail alleviating their unjust suffering.

The response of the community of the faithful to other issues ought to follow a similar pattern. For example, the church's consideration of human sexuality, in this understanding, must begin with an analysis of the historical and social constructions of gender, race, class, and sexuality that inform the church's historic and current thought and practice. Such an analysis will critique the generally implicit use of the sexual experience of heterosexual male elites to provide church and society's normative view of sexuality. This view will be modified by the experience of women, of gays and lesbians, and of the victims of sexual abuse. These "others" point to the confusion of sexuality with power in Western thought (including Christianity). They also locate the discussion of sexuality with the framework of transformation of systems of patriarchal domination to more participatory systems. Also important in this discussion is the relation of family and childrearing arrangements to economic status, and to racial identity. In other words, liberation theologians insist, questions concerning sexuality must be placed within the context of overall community well-being, and teachings on sexuality must contribute to the well-being of all, particularly those who suffer from marginalization and domination.

Responsible action, then, emerges in dialogue that intends an expansion of the communities among which dialogue occurs, and an enlargement of theological, moral, and practical vision, where "more adequate understandings of what is just and how particular forms of justice may be achieved." Dialogue is characterized by the partners' being "visibly . . . informed by a sustained and even-handed process of inquiry," to say what they mean and mean what they say, "to endure necessary conflict, to change [their] mind[s] if the evidence suggests it."[37] In content, dialogue should often

> stress a kind of common law mentality in which we eschew grand statements of principle, rather trusting that moral truth will emerge in Christians' educated grapplings with problems. Consensus is not to be manufactured; it happens, and the process will not be rushed or engineered.[38]

(Stephen Sykes makes a similar point thus: "The positive nature of the authority which binds the Anglican communion together is . . . moral and spiritual, resting on the truth of the Gospel, and on a charity which is patient and willing to defer to the common mind."[39])

Dialogue has sound theological reasons to commend it as well. For dialogue presumes that

> God is present, and is seeking to speak [God's] word in the life of the church. Although one cannot claim full confidence that

the moral consensus of the church is the voice of God, nevertheless [God's] Spirit is present in human deliberation and action.[40]

The ultimate source of authority is a God who is good and just and graciously self-giving. The dispersal of authority among persons, structures, and modes of reflection and discourse works to maintain the singularity of the ultimate authority of the divine. Appropriate human exercise of authority derived from this God is exercised persuasively rather than coercively, and through dialogue that seeks to create and nurture a genuine *consensus fidelium*. Such a genuine consensus, I have suggested, cannot emerge unless and until participation in the gathering and decisionmaking of the faithful actually includes those whose voices have been ignored, silenced, and suppressed in church and society. Such participation can be enhanced through dialogue that intends the enlargement of spiritual, moral, and practical vision.

THE BIBLE AS AUTHORITATIVE TEXT

The role of the community of the faithful, in this view of authority, is of great significance. That community is itself founded, sustained, and authorized by God. It is secondarily founded and nurtured by its historical foundations, the most important of which is the scriptures. The scriptures have a unique status in that the community of the faithful considers them the norm that is itself uniquely normative: it is the scriptures and the scriptures alone that "containeth all things necessary to salvation; so that whatsoever is not read therein, nor may be proved thereby, is not to be required of any man [*sic*]."[41]

Protestant theology particularly emphasizes that God is heard and encountered—not just learned about—through the scriptures.[42] Yet those concerned with liberation and transformation are suspicious of the authority of scripture, because the text (as well as its interpretation) has so often been used to support domination. For this reason, liberation theologians grant authority to the scriptures on the basis of their ability to empower and nurture the subjugated to act.

This mode of granting authority is consistent with the manner in which *all* theologians view the authority of scripture. In his 1975 study, David Kelsey examines the ways in which scripture functions both authoritatively and normatively within theologies that assume that authority is dispersed for precisely the reasons the Lambeth Conference used. In these theologies, scripture is *normative* in that it is used specifically to authorize or warrant theological proposals. But *how* the scriptures will be used is determined by the theologian's selection of a root metaphor or pattern, an "imaginative characterization of the central reality of Christianity." That is, scripture is "*construed* in terms of a certain set of patterns found, to be sure, in the texts." Scripture, Kelsey demonstrates, "is *relevant* to the making of that imaginative judgment because it shapes the context in which it is done and provides the range of materials out of which it is made. But Scripture is not *decisive* precisely because the judgment is imaginative, free, creative." Nevertheless, precisely because scripture *is* relevant, the patterns found in the Bible "set limits to the range of ways in which it may be construed."[43]

These limits are set in at least three other ways as well. First, scripture is a function of ecclesial community: the use made of the scriptures in the life of the church "helps shape a theologian's imaginative construal of the way that use is conjoined with God's presence among the faithful." Second, the imaginative construal is also shaped by what is "seriously imaginable" in the context from which a particular theology emerges.[44] Theological proposals must then be, in some sense, appropriate to the scriptures (and to other aspects of church tradition), and intelligible and credible in the contemporary world.

A third and most important limit is set by the character of the scriptures as a web of imaginative narratives, rather than as a set of literal historical accounts or theological propositions. As recent discussions of narrative and theology have made clear, narratives contain surpluses of meaning; that is, they provoke multiple responses, and so multiple interpretations. Thus, the meaning of a narrative is produced by the encounter and dialogue between text and reader, which is similar to the dialogue between differing persons or groups. In this dialogue, the reader encounters the text as both familiar and "other"; the effect on the reader is both a participation in the world of the text and a distancing from it. For the reader, then, the text is both *manifestation* of the sacred and *proclamation about* the sacred.[45]

Thus the term *meaning* refers to "existential significance, not truth in the abstract that one remains free to engage or ignore, but truth in the concrete that by the very fact of being grasped seizes its subject."[46] The divine is encountered in experiences where the particularity of the human subject is intensified, and the sacred is experienced as overwhelmingly powerful. (This particularity is, remember, shaped by both the "inner" and "outer" life of the experiencing subject.) The reader describes the encounter in terms of disclosure or manifestation *of* the sacred, and in terms of concealment or interpretive proclamation *about* the sacred, which stands at some distance from and over against the reader. In both moments, the reader produces the expression; in other words, there is always an interpretation of the experience that arises out of the reader's reflection on it.

Further, "the existential meaning of the text is dialectically engaged with the world of the reader."[47] This means that the contexts of human experience and reflections on those experiences provide significant mediation of encounters with the divine in a manner that effectively shapes participation in and distancing from them. Thus, the very possibility of encounter with a "divine foundation of reality which is ultimately good, which does not wish evil nor create evil, but affirms and upholds our autonomous personhood"[48] is both enabled and suppressed by the conditions and particularities of human existence. As noted above, the mediating power of the context of domination in which subjugated persons encounter scriptural texts brings about an alienation and fragmentation of the relation between the subjugated and the divine. Yet this relation persists, albeit in a distorted form that both conceals and discloses the fact of that relatedness. The oppressed continue to long for wholeness; and in their explicitly liberative and transformative experience, they are enabled to break through the negative mediations of domination and discover validity and meaning in their longing for wholeness and connection.

Thus, liberated consciousness can contribute to a conversion experience: the divine is newly encountered through manifestation both as a fellow sufferer of violent suppression and degradation, and as movement and power that awakens and inspires. These manifestations, then, are expressed in a combination of images drawn both from the subjects' liberating experiences, and from the contexts in which those experiences occur and are brought to reflection. These images are ambiguous in at least two ways. First, they utilize traditional symbols that have been linked with both oppressive and liberating proclamation. Second, they both disclose and conceal the authentic novelty of the encounter, in that the use of customary symbols continues to evoke familiar responses even as it transforms them and produces new ones. Yet in the midst of this ambiguity, liberation reflection on "primal re-encounter with divine reality" and "the primary intuitions of religious experience"[49] expresses and empowers liberating action that further reduces the alienating mediations of the dominating contexts of human life and experience.

Liberation scriptural interpretations, then, are profoundly conversational, engaging past, present, and future, and locating the individual interpreter always within communities of discourse and practice. The authority this interpretive perspective may bear is dependent not only on the presence of one or more communities but also on those communities' being capable of actual dialogue. This dialogue is characterized by a "stubborn generosity toward divergent opinions."[50] And this "stubborn generosity" is present precisely because liberation theologians rely heavily on and grant authority to experience, which is recognized as being fluid, diverse, and complex. Thus, any interpretation of scripture is verified and validated by its ability to contribute to concrete corporate movements toward greater freedom for all of humanity.

The understanding of authority as authorization and empowerment is wholly consistent with liberation-theological notions of the human and of the divine and of their relationship. Liberation theologies recognize the authority of a number of sources for theological proposals. Conflicts between possible authorities—scripture and tradition, reason, and the *consensus fidelium* (including the complex and ambiguous history of their development)—are adjudicated, first, by identifying a privileged locus—a moment in history, a group, a movement—where divine authorship is most evident; this locus contains struggles for liberation and transformation. Second, the conflict itself is examined in light of the theological insights that are resident at that locus. Third, resolutions to the conflict are proposed using imagination and practice as well as critical reason; these resolutions are developed and evaluated communally, maintaining "stubborn generosity." Finally, these resolutions are submitted to the theoretical and practical wisdom of communities of discourse and practice for testing. When necessary, the resolutions are both defended and revised. Theologies of liberation thus fit the pattern described by Kelsey: they use imaginative construals based in scripture to warrant their proposals; among their communal bases are those in which the Bible is used as scripture; and their proposals are submitted to public scrutiny and critical evaluation.

Nevertheless, it should be noted that in their reconstructive approaches liberation theologies do not grant normative character to the scriptures alone. Divine activity and revelation are ongoing, and may be encountered in nonbiblical contexts with a force equivalent to that claimed for scriptural times. The multiple loci of revelation—including scripture—are deemed authoritative precisely because they are illuminated by and illuminate each other. Concretely, the force encountered in current struggles for liberation is recognizable as of divine origin and meaning (rather than as false consciousness generated by human sinfulness) precisely because it is consistent both with what has been encountered and recognized in other times and places, and with the vision of the liberated and transformed future that arises from past and present encounters with the divine.

Second, the reconstructive moment of liberation hermeneutics argues that the Bible itself is only ambiguously an expression of the normative locus. Because the canonical scriptures are of human authorship and formation and reflect the patriarchal domination of their context, they must be read and used critically so that their revelatory power may emerge. Where liberation scholarship diverges from other familiar scholarly approaches is in expanding criticism to include an exhaustive critique of the role of ideological context in forming both text and reading. Appeal to the canonical scriptures as authoritative may not be made automatically; the scriptures' authority must be discovered rather than presumed to be embodied.

Yet this principle finally holds nothing other than what theology has long maintained in asserting that the source of all authority is God. Compare the statements of Stephen Sykes regarding the 1948 Lambeth Conference discussions of authority:

> There is only one source of authority which is the freedom and love of the Triune God. In human life, in Scripture, in the creeds, in the decisions of councils, in the liturgical order and canon law, in church leadership, there is only the discovery of authority, not its embodiment. . . . Authority is not embodied, it is dispersed; and the reaching of authoritative decisions is a continuous process involving all the participators.[51]

SUMMARY

Thus, for liberation theologies, the interpretation of scripture is a process of critical appropriation of a complex, ambiguous text that has been at one and the same time a support for unjust systems and ideologies of domination, and a source for liberating transformation of those systems and ideologies. Appropriation of scripture is made possible by theologians' use of imaginative construals of the central witness of Christianity to the redemption being worked by God. In liberation theologies, this redemption is available in human history through freedom from sin (e.g., the sin of patriarchal domination) and liberation from the effects of sin (e.g., oppression and subjugation). The conviction that God is a historical liberator as well as the ultimate savior then shapes concrete experience and reflection on that experience as well as on scripture, tradition, reason, and other elements contributing to faith. The authority of these elements is discovered in their legitimation and empowerment of action and discourse that tends toward freedom for all, especially the subjugated. The appropriation of these elements, understood and interpreted in the context of struggles against domination and for transformation, comes through processes that rely on the emerging consensus of relatively free participants. This consensus is a *consensus fidelium*, for it arises in a dialogical community whose fidelity is not, primarily, to a set of doctrinal teachings, but to participation in the ongoing transformative action of God in concrete human history.

ACKNOWLEDGMENTS

This essay has been revised in light of comments and suggestions from the following persons, for whose assistance I am most grateful: James H. Evans, Jr., William R. Herzog II, A. J. van den Blink, Elizabeth P. Waller, Elizabeth A. Zivanov, Robert J. Wright, Eleanor McLaughlin, the authors of the other commissioned papers on this topic (Stephen Noll, Richard Norris, and Charles Price), and members of the Conference of Anglican Theologians.

NOTES

1. Kenneth Burke, quoted in Rebecca S. Chopp, *The Power to Speak: Feminism, Language, God* (New York: Crossroad, 1989), 133 n. 24.

2. Daniel L. Migliore, *Faith Seeking Understanding: An Introduction to Christian Theology* (Grand Rapids, Mich.: Eerdmans, 1991), 5.

3. Richard Hooker, *Of the Laws of Ecclesiastical Polity*, in *The Works of That Learned and Judicious Divine Mr. Richard Hooker with an Account of His Life and Death by Isaac Walton*, arranged by John Keble, 7th ed. (New York: Burt Franklin, 1888; rpt. 1970), book 5, chapter 56, paragraph 1 (hereafter referred to as *Laws*).

4. "[S]ith God hath deified our nature, though not by turning it into him self, yet by making it his own inseparable habitation, we cannot now conceive how God should without man either exercise divine power, or receive the glory of divine praise. For man is in both an associate of Deity" (Laws 5.54.5).

5. *Laws* 5.56.2; italics in the original.

6. John Booty, "Richard Hooker," in *The Spirit of Anglicanism*, ed. William J. Wolf (Wilton, Conn.: Morehouse-Barlow, 1979), 19.

7. Leonardo Boff, *Trinity and Society*, trans. Paul Burns (Maryknoll: Orbis Books, 1988), 4-5.

8. Ibid., 6-7.

9. Throughout this paper, I will use two terms interchangeably: *patriarchy* and *domination* (or systems of domination). According to Elisabeth Schüssler Fiorenza, "Patriarchy defines not just women as the 'other' but also subjugated peoples and races as the 'other' to be dominated. It defines women, more-over, not just as the other of men but also as subordinated to men in power. . . " Patriarchy, then, is a "pyramidal system and hierarchical structure of society in which women's oppression is specified not only in terms of race and class but also in terms of 'marital' status" (*Bread Not Stone: The Challenge of Feminist Biblical Interpretation* [Boston: Beacon Press, 1984], 5). I use the term *domination* as well as *patriarchy* to make clear that race, class, and sexual orientation are at issue as well as gender.

10. The term *womanist* refers to the liberation theology being developed by women of color, who face double or triple oppression on the basis of race, gender, and, often, class.

11. As Sandra M. Schneiders writes, by "history of effects" or "effective history" is meant "historical reality not only as initiating event but also as modified and amplified by all that the initiating event has produced . . . we Americans cannot know the Vietnam War 'as it happened' but only in terms of . . . all that the Vietnam War has come to be down to today . . . We can only understand what really happened between the first and last shot in and through and in

terms of all that the war produced and continues to produce. . . It is a reality that goes on into the present, all of whose elements are mutually interactive" (*The Revelatory Text: Interpreting the New Testament as Sacred Scripture* [San Francisco: Harper San Francisco, 1991], 159-60).

12. Because of its patriarchal character, Scripture itself requires "women to identify with a male perspective . . . in order simply to follow the story line; we must, in other words, imagine ourselves as male in order to fulfill the conventional role of reader. In the case of Scripture the underlying message is that to be addressed by God, to be a full member of the divinely created universal order, we must pretend we are male and consequently pretend that we are *not female*" (Mary Ann Tolbert, "Protestant Feminists and the Bible: On the Horns of a Dilemma," in *The Pleasure of Her Text: Feminist Readings of Biblical and Historical Texts*, ed. Alice Bach [Philadelphia: Trinity Press International, 1990], 18).

13. Mary Ann Tolbert, "Defining the Problem: The Bible and Feminist Hermeneutics," *Semeia* 28 (1983): 120; Tolbert, "Protestant Feminists and the Bible," 13.

14. Rosemary Radford Ruether, "The Future of Feminist Theology in the Academy," *Journal of American Academy of Religion* 53 (December 1985): 710-11.

15. Schüssler Fiorenza, *Bread Not Stone.*

16. Kelsey, David H. *The Uses of Scripture in Recent Theology* (Philadelphia: Fortress Press, 1975), 142.

17. Leonardo Boff, *When Theology Listens to the Poor,* trans. Robert R. Barr (San Francisco: Harper and Row, 1988), 61.

18. Tolbert, "Protestant Feminists and the Bible," 16ff.

19. Tolbert, "Defining the Problem," 126.

20. Jean Lambert, "An F Factor? The New Testament in Some White Feminist Christian Theological Construction." *Journal of Feminist Studies in Religion* 1, no. 2 (Fall 1985): 93.

21. Nannerl O. Keohane, Michelle Z. Rosaldo, and Barbara C. Gelfin, eds., *Feminist Theory: A Critique of Ideology* (Chicago: University of Chicago Press, 1982), vii.

22. Teresa de Lauretis, *Alice Doesn't: Feminism, Semiotics, Cinema* (Bloomington: Indiana University Press, 1984), 159, 182.

23. See Teresa de Lauretis, *Feminist Studies/Critical Studies* (Bloomington: Indiana University Press, 1984), 8.

24. Tolbert, "Defining the Problem," 120.

25. Stephen Lukes, "Introduction," *Power,* ed. Lukes (New York: New York University Press, 1986), 5.

26. Letty M. Russell, *Household of Freedom: Authority in Feminist Theology* (Philadelphia: Westminster Press, 1987), 21.

27. John E. Skinner, "Ideology, Authority, and Faith," in Stephen W. Sykes, ed.,

Authority in the Anglican Communion: Essays Presented to Bishop John Howe (Toronto: Anglican Book Centre, 1987), 35. The bracketed phrase comes from another sentence on the same page, and is used there to modify "nurture."

28. Richard Sennett, *Authority* (New York: Alfred A. Knopf, 1980), 22.
29. Lambert, "An F Factor?" 93; Skinner, "Ideology, Authority, and Faith."
30. Schneiders, *The Revelatory Text*, 56.
31. See "The Meaning and Unity of the Anglican Communion," printed in *The Lambeth Conference 1948* (London, 1948) and reprinted in Stephen W. Sykes, The *Integrity of Anglicanism* (London and Oxford: Mowbray, 1978), 112-14.
32. Skinner, "Ideology, Authority, and Faith," 42.
33. Quoted by H. R. McAdoo, "Authority in the Church: Spiritual Freedom and the Corporate Nature of Faith," in Sykes, ed., *Authority in the Anglican Communion*, 76.
34. Skinner, "Ideology, Authority, and Faith."
35. Sharon D. Welch, *A Feminist Ethic of Risk* (Minneapolis: Fortress Press, 1990), 3, 20, 21, 75.
36. Boff, *When Theology Listens to the Poor*, 46-47.
37. Welch, *A Feminist Ethic of Risk*, 126, 129; David H. Smith and Judith Granbois, "New Technologies for Assisted Reproduction," in *The Crisis in Moral Teaching in the Episcopal Church*, ed. Timothy Sedgwick and Philip Turner, 50; David Tracy, *Plurality and Ambiguity: Hermeneutics, Religion, Hope* (San Francisco: Harper and Row, 1987).
38. Smith and Granbois, "New Technologies for Assisted Reproduction," 51.
39. Sykes, *Integrity of Anglicanism*, 13.
40. James M. Gustafson, *The Church as Moral Decision-Maker* (Philadelphia: Pilgrim Press, 1970), 132.
41. Articles of Religion, VI.
42. Tolbert, "Protestant Feminists and the Bible," 12.
43. Kelsey, *Uses of Scripture in Recent Theology*, 142, 151, 206 and passim. Kelsey studies works by theologians representing a wide range of Protestantism, from conservative to liberal.
44. Ibid., 205, 170-75.
45. Paul Ricoeur, "Manifestation and Proclamation," *Journal of the Blaisdell Institute* 12 (Winter 1978): 13-35. See also David Tracy, *The Analogical Imagination: Christian Theology and the Culture of Pluralism* (New York: Crossroad, 1981), chaps. 5 and 9.
46. Schneiders, *The Revelatory Text*, 16.
47. Ibid.
48. Ruether, "The Future of Feminist Theology," 710-11.
49. Ibid.
50. Lambert, "An F Factor?" throughout.
51. Sykes, *The Integrity of Anglicanism*, 98-99.

ADDITIONAL READINGS

Cardenal, Ernesto. *The Gospel in Solentiname*, vol. 1. Translated by Donald D. Walsh. Maryknoll, N.Y.: Orbis, 1984.

Comstock, Gary L. "Two Types of Narrative Theology." *Journal of the American Academy of Religion* 15, no. 4 (Winter 1987): 687-720.

Cone, James. *For My People: Black Theology and the Black Church*. Maryknoll, N.Y.: Orbis, 1984.

——. *Speaking the Truth: Ecumenism, Liberation, and Black Theology*. Grand Rapids, Mich.: Eerdmans, 1986.

Croatto, Severino. *Biblical Hermeneutics: Toward a Theory of Reading as the Production of Meaning*. Translated by Robert R. Barr. Maryknoll, N.Y.: Orbis, 1987.

Evans, James H., Jr. *We Have Been Believers: An African-American Systematic Theology*. New York: Crossroad, 1992.

Felder, Cane Hope. *Troubling Biblical Waters: Race, Class, Family*. Maryknoll, N.Y.: Orbis, 1989.

Freire, Paulo. *The Pedagogy of the Oppressed*. Translated by Myra Bergman Ramos. New York: Herder and Herder, 1970.

Herzog, William R., II. "The 'Household Duties Passages': Apostolic Traditions and Contemporary Concerns." *Foundations* 24 (1981): 204-15.

Heyward, Carter. *The Redemption of God: A Theology of Mutual Relation*. Washington, D.C.: University Press of America, 1982.

——. *Speaking of Christ: A Lesbian Feminist Voice*. Edited by Ellen C. Davis. New York: Pilgrim Press, 1989.

——. *Touching Our Strength: The Erotic as Power and the Love of God*. San Francisco: Harper and Row, 1989.

Martin, Clarice J. "*The Haustafeln* (Household Codes) in African American Biblical Interpretation: 'Free Slaves' and 'Subordinate Women.'" In *Stony the Road We Trod: African American Biblical Interpretation*, edited by Cain Hope Felder, pp. 206-31. Minneapolis: Fortress Press, 1991.

Ogden, Schubert M. "The Authority of Scripture for Theology." In Ogden, *On Theology*, pp. 45-68. San Francisco: Harper and Row, 1986.

Poling, James N. *The Abuse of Power: A Theological Problem*. Nashville: Abingdon, 1991.

Ruether, Rosemary Radford. *Mary—The Feminine Face of the Church*. Philadelphia: Westminster Press, 1977.

———. *New Woman/New Earth: Sexist Ideologies and Human Liberation*. New York: Seabury, 1975.

———. *Sexism and God-Talk: Toward Feminist Theology*. Boston: Beacon Press, 1983.

Schüssler Fiorenza, Elisabeth. *In Memory of Her: A Feminist Theological Reconstruction of Christian Origins*. New York: Crossroad, 1983.

Sedgwick, Timothy S. "Moral Teachings on the Economic Order." In *The Crisis in Moral Teaching in the Episcopal Church*, edited by Timothy F. Sedgwick. Wilton, Conn.: Morehouse-Barlow, 1992.

Smith, Archie, Jr. *The Relational Self: Ethics and Therapy from a Black Church Perspective*. Nashville: Abingdon Press, 1982.

Soelle, Dorothee. *Thinking about God: An Introduction to Theology*. Philadelphia: Trinity Press International, 1990.

Sykes, Stephen W. *The Integrity of Anglicanism*. London: Mowbray, 1978.

Wilson-Kastner, Patricia. *Faith, Feminism, and the Christ*. Philadelphia: Fortress Press, 1983.

Wondra, Ellen K. "The Dispersal of Moral Authority." In *The Crisis in Moral Teaching in the Episcopal Church*, edited by Timothy F. Sedgwick. Wilton, Conn.: Morehouse-Barlow, 1992.

READING THE BIBLE AS THE WORD OF GOD

Stephen F. Noll

WORDS AND THE WORD

Biblical Interpretation in Crisis

As is now widely acknowledged, the fault lines that run through the Christian church on matters of theology and ethics, evangelism and apologetics, are manifestations of a tectonic shift in worldviews in which "hermeneutics" or biblical interpretation plays a central role.[1] To paraphrase Abraham Lincoln's Second Inaugural Address, all interpret the same Bible, but the interpretation of all cannot be equally valid or the Bible ceases to have any coherent authority. While hermeneutics since Schleiermacher has held out the dream of a path between ancient text and modern believer, it has produced instead a dense undergrowth of theories whose applicability to central Christian affirmations is confusing at best.

My goal in this essay is to argue that the classic way of reading scripture is in terms of its *literal sense* and that this approach remains normative and credible for the church today. I am aware of the danger involved in attempting to rehabilitate the word "literal," as its meaning is frequently caricatured or trivialized. Since the advent of the scientific revolution, "literal" has often been taken narrowly to mean "factual" or "empirically and historically verifiable."[2] Hence some fundamentalists have sought to "prove" the literal character of Genesis 1 by means of "creation science."[3] Some liberals, on the other hand, have attacked plain biblical teaching as mindless "literalism."[4] For all this potential confusion of terminology, "literal sense" has a long and honorable place in the history of interpretation. Its very scandalousness points to crucial issues of the faith which face the contemporary church.[5] Simply to grade the essays in this volume along a conservative-liberal-radical scale would miss the family distinctives of classical and modernist approaches to the Bible.[6]

I begin this chapter with a meditation on the Johannine presentation of Word and Spirit and its relevance for understanding the Bible as the inspired Word of God. I shall then survey the church's tradition of literal interpretation as a more or less consistent application of this apostolic understanding. Finally, I shall return to a restatement of the approach to the literal sense of the Bible which is faithful to the past yet aware of problematic issues in modern hermeneutics.

My hope and expectation is that readers will follow the argument of this position paper to the end and apply to it the classic tests of truth: its conformity to scripture and to the faith of the church. I do not see this statement as a final word but rather as an invitation to a renewed discussion of the foundations of Christian doctrine and identity.

The Word of God and the Literal Sense

The literal sense of scripture can only be rightly understood as a *reflex* of the Word of God, that is, the appropriate medium of understanding that accompanies verbal revelation and inspiration. When after each lection in the liturgy we announce "the Word of the Lord," we are attesting to the authoritative character of a particular text in all its specificity, even as we are also claiming that text as a part of the whole message of salvation received and proclaimed by the church in word and sacrament.

The prologue to John's Gospel sets *Logos* as the supreme category of understanding the revelatory activity of the Triune God in his ordering of creation, his prophetic message to Israel, his incarnate Person and work, and in the believing response of the community to his revealed glory.[7]

In the beginning was the Word and the Word was with God and the Word was God. The inner-Trinitarian love of the Father and the Son is bathed in the light of the divine speech, what Athanasius called God's "intimate locution." As Pannenberg says: "The way in which Jesus speaks of the Father is the only access to knowledge of the Father, but also of the Son, for only through the Father is Jesus known as the Son (Matt. 11:27)."[8]

By Him all things were made . . . God's Word upholds the cosmos in its orderliness, and humanity in God's image participates *mirabile dictu* in created rationality. The Word of God not only forms us after himself but makes room for our free response. Psalm 19 captures the manifold wisdom of God's Word: "The heavens are telling the glory of God . . . the law of the Lord is perfect, reviving the soul . . . may the words of my mouth and the meditation of my heart be acceptable in thy sight." God's word is embedded in the creation, revealed in his law, and returned to him in the praises of his saints.

He came to his own, but his own received him not. The Word of God entered into the space-time matrix of historic Israel, the bearer of the oracles of God. And although the Old Testament forms of the Word were shadows and types, in Israel, too, "the Word of God was mediated in such a way that a divinely prepared form of obedient response was included within it."[9] Israel's response was above all embodied in the hymns and psalms of the Royal Servant who must suffer rejection by Israel, his most intimate enemy (Ps. 41:9; Isa. 53:3; Zech. 13:7).

And the Word became flesh and dwelt among us, full of grace and truth . . . The Word of God, fragmented in creation and history, becomes united once for all in the God-Man Jesus Christ. In him the Word not only takes on human garb but is crucified for our sake, and the gospel becomes forever "the word of the Cross," which is folly to worldly wisdom but grace and truth to those who believe. In his incarnate and risen glory he makes known ("exegetes") the hidden Father.

. . . and we beheld his glory, glory as of the only Son from the Father. The incarnation of the Word is not left without witness. The apostolic "we" is included in the revelation of his glory. In the incarnate I AM, being and knowing are united and offered as light and life to those who are born of his Spirit. And the proper mode of knowing the in-breaking truth of the gospel is faith in the name of Jesus Christ the only-begotten Son (John 20:30-31; Acts 4:12).

In what way can we draw an analogy between the Incarnate Word and the written words of the Bible? In one sense scripture is not identical with the Divine Word or an object rivaling him in glory or calling for worship (Rev. 19:10-11). Jesus Christ is both the Form and Object of the biblical witness; his royal image is the stamp impressed in the substance of scripture. In this age the written words are the mirror in which we see him; when the perfect comes, we shall see him face to face (1 Cor. 13:12).[10] But there is no getting behind (or in front of) the verbal testimony of scripture. The Divine Essence in its Personal relations is "Logical," and his revelation comes in words and in deeds interpreted by words (John 14:11). This revelation is received by his rational creatures, irrationally rejected, and finally enfleshed in the Person of the Son, whose grace calls forth a new people with ears to hear his gospel.

As the literal sense of scripture is the reflex of the saving Word entering our world, so also it is the *inspired letter* of God, the work of the Holy Spirit (2 Tim. 3:16; 2 Pet. 1:20-21). Thus the Prayer Book Catechism says that we call the scriptures the Word of God "because

---

God inspired their human authors and still speaks to us through the Bible." Once again, John emphasizes the Trinitarian context of the inspiration of scripture.

These things I have spoken to you while I am still with you. But the Counselor, the Holy Spirit, whom the Father will send in my name, he will teach you all things and bring to your remembrance all that I have said to you (John 14:25-26). The words of the incarnate Son, his commandments, are the substance of scripture; it is the role of the Spirit to recall and exegete these words. The Spirit brings no new revelation but speaks through the apostolic word: *He will bear witness to me, and you also are witnesses* . . . (John 15:26-27). At the crisis point of history, the Lord Jesus promises that the Spirit will come and reveal the truth of his words and work through the gospel.

When he comes, he will convict the world . . . (John 16:8). The gap between appearance and reality—Koheleth's chase after wind, the flickering shadows of Socrates' cave—is closed by the Spirit of Truth, who no longer speaks in figures but transparently of the Father (John 16:12-13, 25-30). The Spirit, who is Author of the created forms of human speech, now opens these categories to the incarnate Truth of God, evoking faith as the only way of knowing.

The epistemological role of the Spirit is crucial to understanding scripture as literal truth. Paul's rhetorical contrast of letter and Spirit in 2 Corinthians 3-4 has often been misunderstood in this regard. In an elaborate midrash on Exodus 34, Paul identifies the "letter" with the Mosaic Torah, which despite its divine origin operates within the sign-world of human command (2 Cor. 3:7-11). By contrast the apostolic "statement of the truth" (4:2) breaks forth as new light from the Creator God, and this unveiled gospel is received not by compulsion but in a receptive freedom which is itself a work of the Spirit (3:17-18). Paul's denigration of the letter is not about the mode of verbal revelation; on the contrary, he sees an enhanced role of the inspired word in converting hardened hearts. Thus the word of God can now be called the "sword of the Spirit" (Eph. 6:17; Heb. 4:12).

The Literal Sense and the Tradition of Interpretation
In coming to his own, the Word of God emerges from, yet transcends, the tradition of Israel and the church. The very idea of tradition itself presupposes a determinate sense of scripture, since tradition by definition passes on something other than itself. Jewish interpreters, for all their exegetical virtuosity, regarded the letter of scrip-

ture as normative for life in the covenant and in the age to come.[11] Early Christian apologetics toward Judaism assumed a common sky under which the truth of God could be disputed.

The great challenge faced by the apostles was to reconcile the interpretation of the Old Testament with the fulfilling revelatory event of Jesus Christ. In one of the earliest records of apostolic tradition, Paul states that Jesus' saving death and resurrection happened "according to the Scriptures" (1 Cor. 15:1-11). Paul's tradition undoubtedly employed specific Old Testament *testimonia*, an exegetical method fully at home in the Jewish milieu.[12] At the same time, the gospel was proclaimed as a new covenant of the Spirit that could not be simply poured out from the carnal wineskins of Jewish exegesis.

Gnosticism proved to be a snare to early Christians because it appeared to carry the common distinction between carnal and spiritual senses to its logical conclusion. However, the Gnostics radically reinterpreted the New Testament sense of flesh and spirit. Gnostics rewrote scripture in such a way that its literal referents (God, creation, and law) were seen to be essentially demonic.[13] As can be seen by contrast with Christian gnostic texts, the apostolic development of historical allegory, or typology, was not a departure from literal interpretation but a reorientation of the corpus of scripture from the perspective of the gospel (1 Pet. 1:10-12), a move that would lead inevitably to the twofold testament of the Christian Bible.

The Rule of Faith, that summary of doctrine that the Fathers used in their combat with heresy, presupposes a literal meaning of scripture.[14] At the same time the Rule of Faith gave a "theological" focus to Christian hermeneutics which could embrace such diverse exegetes as Origen and Theodore of Mopsuestia.[15] The debate between the schools of Alexandria and Antioch temporarily restricted the literal sense to the "carnal" and "narrative" dimension of scripture.[16] Augustine, however, restored the normative balance of the letter as a key to the spiritual meaning of the text.[17] The Augustinian synthesis soon unraveled, however, into the medieval distinction of levels of meaning. Thus the literal sense once again was seen as being *transcended* in allegory or *supplemented* in the scholastic distinction of a "double literal sense."[18]

The outbreak of exegetical theology in the sixteenth century worked to restore the fullness of the literal sense of scripture. The Reformers' use of typology or "figural reading" was not a quaint holdover of medieval allegory but a vigorous reassertion of the unity of the testaments and of the narrative and doctrinal dimensions of scripture. Although the Reformers were united in their basic approach, each emphasized particular elements of scripture as the inspired Word. Luther saw the gospel of Christ as the hermeneutical focus of both testaments, in its role as promise to be received by faith.[19] For Calvin the key to scriptural interpretation was the activity of the Holy Spirit, who inspired the words and gave inner testimony to the believer.[20] Richard Hooker emphasized the role of "right reason" in correlating the truths of nature and biblical revelation with regard to the proper ends of each, the latter being eternal salvation in Christ.[21]

The modern grammatical-historical approach, or "higher criticism," represents both continuity and crisis for the literal sense. The Reformation attention to the grammar and logic of the text was developed through painstaking application of the emerging disciplines of philology and the social sciences. At the same time exegesis of a text focused on the reconstructed intention of an original author whose life-setting and aims were often seen as radically discontinuous with those of later redactors. The schism of canonical text and original author was a kind of Cartesian stake driven into the heart of the literal sense. While a boon to research in ancient Near Eastern and Greco-Roman culture, the historical method presents immense difficulties for reading and preaching the Bible in the faith community.[22] It would be fair to say that all subsequent theories of interpretation have had to grapple with the loss of innocence in literal reading caused by higher criticism.

In reacting to historical criticism, with its distancing of author, text, and reader, "romantic" hermeneutics has attempted to recover the power of the biblical word by abandoning the notion of literal reference.[23] The interpreter begins with the grammar of the text and then makes an intuitive leap into the consciousness of the author (Schleiermacher), or is called to authentic existence by the "Word" (Bultmann), or identifies with a paradigmatic experience of oppression (liberation theology), or enters into the "world of the text" (Ricoeur). Contemporary hermeneutics descending from Schleiermacher is founded on the dogma of historicism and its corollary, the "hermeneutical circle," which teach that human consciousness cannot transcend its own time-bound milieu.[24] Hence *experience* replaces literal content as the locus of biblical authority.[25] Philosophically, this position has never been able to escape the charge of logical absurdity: "Historicism thrives on the fact that it inconsistently exempts itself from its own verdict about all human thought."[26] Historicists insist that their theory—and theirs alone—be taken literally and for all time. Historicism thus wrongly absolutizes the difficulty of human communication from person to person and age to age.[27]

Another attempt to reestablish the literal sense of the Bible without ignoring the work of higher criticism is the "canonical approach" of Brevard Childs. Childs's project is a massive one: providing new forms of biblical introduction, critical commentary, and integrative biblical theology. What is sometimes overlooked is his call to recover a form of the literal sense of scripture as a necessary aspect of the canon.[28] "Canonical intentionality" is that cooperative inspiring work of the Holy Spirit and traditioning work of the community of faith which produces a final text of scripture normative for all future generations of believers. The aim of literal interpretation in the postcritical age will be the same as that of previous generations but with a greater consciousness of the diachronic witness of the biblical text. Childs, along with other conservative postmodern theologians, seeks to reestablish the "grammar" of the faith tradition of the church.[29] Whether he does justice to the referentiality of the text is another matter.

The reaction to the higher critical method among evangelicals has been ongoing since the eighteenth century and has focused on defending the literal sense of the Bible in terms of verbal inerrancy. This defense is often philosophically rigorous and exegetically sensitive to the variety of genres found in scripture.[30] While affirming the variety of biblical forms and imagery, J. I. Packer nevertheless emphasizes that the Bible is a "corpus of God-given instruction relating to Jesus Christ." For Packer, scripture is accommodated divine speech: "God has put His words into the mouths, and caused them to be written in the writings, of persons whose individuality, as people of their time, was in no way lessened by the fact of their being thus overruled."[31]

Other evangelicals would question the paradigm of "divine speaking" as the key to the literal sense. They would emphasize the freedom, under the overarching sovereignty of God, of the authors and editors to respond to God's revelatory deeds and oracles.[32] For them, inerrancy, if the term is retained, is not an architectonic principle of inspiration, but "simply means that the Bible can be trusted in what it teaches and affirms."[33] If the inerrancy view is overly deterministic, this latter view may be in danger of introducing the dichotomy between verbal revelation and experiential inspiration that has been the bane of modern hermeneutics.[34]

All exegetes and theologians have had the task of "rightly dividing the word of truth," of moving from the letter of the biblical text to its sense or meaning. Thus interpretation is inevitably dialectical, involving text (words), reference (Word), and reader (significance). Dialectic, like a dance, requires a lead partner. In classic hermeneutics, the literal sense of the Word leads the dance of interpretation; in modern (and gnostic) views, the consciousness of the interpreter or interpreting community governs the final sense of scripture.[35]

A Preliminary Definition

The literal sense is that meaning appropriate to the nature of the Bible as the Word of God in the words of men. As the Word of God, scripture is imprinted by the gospel, that obedient movement of the divine Son Jesus Christ from the transcendent Father to his own sinful people and back to him to the praise of his glory (Phil. 2:1, 6-11).[36] As an inspired human word, it participates in natural forms of speech and the historical traditions of the communities of Israel and the church, even as it summons people to faith and new life in Christ.

Three implications follow from this definition. The first is the *referentiality* of the text. Scripture "means what it says," and the "what" must refer to something else outside the text. Hence translation and exegesis necessarily accompany exposition and homiletics. It is a basic misunderstanding of the literal sense to miss the organic link between literal sign and the "thing signified." Fundamentalists often treat the words of scripture as "steno-symbols," having one and only one reference, but this move is defensive and rationalistic. Since the referent can be something visible or invisible, or both, the literal sense is the natural basis for figuration, allegory, and ambiguity.[37] Ironically, when language is seen to be essentially metaphorical, as it is in many contemporary theories, it can no longer mean anything in particular and becomes a kind of verbal black hole.[38]

The second implication of the literal sense is the existence of an *authorial purpose*. When I first wrote these words, I hoped to convey to the Episcopal bishops a particular meaning. In this version I have rephrased my argument in order to respond to criticism and to address a wider audience.[39] I have chosen to speak of authorial purpose rather than "intentionality" because *intention* is often confused with a state of mind, whereas *purpose* looks to the end or design of a writing. Purpose also leaves open the possibility that an author's design could be further elaborated by others.

The divine inspiration of scripture raises a special set of questions. Who is the true author of a particular book of the Bible? Is it possible for the human author to mean one thing and God something totally different? While the idea of human and divine authors working at cross-purposes may be accepted as theoretically possible (Gen. 50:20), it goes against God's character as truthful (2 Tim. 3:16). Like iconographers, biblical writers and editors experienced inspiration within a tradition. Prophets who claim to be direct recipients of revelation present their new word by a creative synthesis of tradition, and their disciples reorder their oracles into a shape consonant with the overall shape of the faith.[40] Jesus defined his mission by appropriating in unexpected ways the figures of the Suffering Servant and the Son of Man (Mark 10:45). Thus the *sensus plenior* of scripture is a function of God speaking "at many times and in many ways" through the partial purposes of his agents and gathering them together into one great canonical Design. It is in this sense that one can speak of a "canonical intentionality."[41]

The final implication of the literal sense is the *clarity* of scripture. While the Bible declares the mysteries of God, it does not do so esoterically. Traditionally theologians have distinguished between the external and internal clarity of the Bible. Meir Sternberg refers to the Bible's particular external clarity as that of "foolproof composition":

> Biblical narrative is virtually impossible to counterread. The essentials are made transparent to all comers: the story line, the world order, the value system. The old and new controversies among exegetes, spreading to every possible topic, must not blind us (as it usually does them) to the measure of agreement in this regard. The bedrock agreement is neither accidental nor self-evident. Not accidental, because it derives from the Bible's overarching principle of composition, its strategy of strategies, maneuvering between the truth and the whole truth; nor self-evident, because such a principle does not often govern literature operating at the Bible's level of sophistication and interpretive drama.[42]

The relevance of biblical clarity is especially important given the global context of the church's mission. The diversity of language, culture, and education among those who hear the gospel demands a plain sense of the biblical offer of salvation. American Episcopalians, with their perception of the overwhelming difficulty of cross-cultural communication, can learn something from the "naive" confidence of African, Hispanic, and Asian Anglican evangelists and catechists that the Word of God can go out to all the earth.

The Bible's external clarity does not mean that all who read will obey.[43] Internal clarity is the work of the Triune God, evoking faith in the heart: "For it is the God who said, 'Let light shine out of darkness,' who has shone in our hearts to give the light of the knowledge of the glory of God in the face of Christ" (2 Cor. 4:6). The focusing of the rays of God's word in the gospel of Christ is a new creative act, "what eye hath not seen nor ear heard," and this act marvelously includes those who are being saved and bestows on his saints "hearing with faith" (1 Cor. 1:18, 2:9; Gal. 3:2). There is no ground for boasting about our knowledge of God's word because "no one comprehends the thoughts of God except the Spirit of God" (1 Cor. 2:11).

THE FULLNESS OF SCRIPTURE AS GOD'S WORD

Three Dimensions of Scripture

Contrary to the opinion that literalism involves a narrowing of biblical meaning, a proper literal sense is rich and complex, reflecting the very character of God, out of whose fullness we have received grace upon grace. A literal sense actually guarantees the *possibility* of multiple meanings (or "allegories" in the broadest sense). One might draw a limited analogy to a dictionary entry, in which one word has a number of distinct though overlapping senses. Meaning, of course, is not only lexical but syntactic, which further enriches the tapestry. Finally, biblical language claims to be a vehicle of revelation, by which words can come to say something new in the service of the in-breaking Word of God.

The inspired letter of scripture, far from being flat, is spacious, encompassing poetic, truth, and salvation-historical dimensions. Like the threefold cord that is not easily broken (Eccles. 4:12), any biblical text will reflect its own particular configuration of these dimensions.[44]

The poetic dimension of the Bible—I am using "poetic" in the broadest sense of human artistry—is the self-effacing activity of the Word of God coming to us in fully human words. When God speaks, he lisps in human language forms, and the Spirit guides the biblical writers in speaking of him (2 Pet. 1:21). Literal interpretation thus requires careful attention to the syntax of a biblical passage: word usage, grammatical structure, literary devices, and genre. Since the Bible is ancient literature, it is important to employ historical tools of comparative linguistics and higher criticism along with literary analysis of the text itself.

Literal sense is "genre-related." We must constantly ask: what kind of writing is this? Form and genre criticism have heightened our awareness of the diversity of biblical revelation as it comes to us through legend, novella, chronicle, testament, hymn and lament, admonition and proverb, dialogue and love song, judgment and salvation oracle, gospel, epistle and apocalypse. The distinctness of biblical literary forms is a witness to God's involvement in the whole life of his people and also in the various affections of the individual soul.[45] The whole Bible is thus a resource book for the believer, "a mass of strange delights," as the poet George Herbert describes it, "where we may wish and take." Put another way, scripture is like a musical score: only as the words and melody are performed do we hear the creation of the Author.[46]

The truth dimension of scripture refers to its claim to participate in the speech of God. Truth, which derives from the universal sovereignty of God, is the basis for the authority of the biblical word that stands firm even if heaven and earth should pass away (Mark 13:31; Rom. 3:4). At the same time, truth is apprehended not by mystical absorption into God but through the structures of reality, things visible and invisible, and through the analogical nature of language (Ps. 33:4-9).

Truth is attested to in both propositional and representational form. As propositions, the words of scripture can also be called God's "commandments" (Deut. 4:2-9; John 14:21-24). Like the two tables of the Law, these commandments include matters of belief about God and obedience to his moral will. The primacy of Torah ("teaching") reminds us of explicit doctrines and commands to be heeded. While the teaching of Jesus transforms the commandments of the Mosaic Torah, it retains their normative form: discipleship involves single-minded adherence to his words (Matt. 5:17-20, 7:24).

Representational truth, or *mimesis*, operates by verisimilitude, or truth-likeness.[47] Mimesis is not thereby artificial or purely formal: it is Lady Wisdom, the force of truth, of nature, drawing the soul to understanding.[48] Mimetic truth operates differently from propositional. It is grasped by the imagination, and it draws on common experience and creates new experience.[49] It is the fruit of a conversation in which no "answer" is given but a relationship affirmed. When God proudly displays to Job his creature Leviathan, who is "king over all the sons of pride" (Job 41:34), Job is satisfied, knowing himself even in his quandary to be loved as a royal son.

It is a mistake to identify biblical truth with either propositions or mimesis exclusively, as in the reduction of scripture by fundamentalists to a set of lessons or by liberals to "the play of metaphor." A proposition such as "the LORD reigns" can be represented narratively by means of the "omniscient" viewpoint of the biblical narrator and in the "omnipotent" outworking of God's will, as when Hushai bests the counsel of Ahitophel (2 Sam. 17:14).[50] On the other hand, a well-chosen proof-text or allusion can summarize a wealth of biblical experience and imagery, as in Peter's appeal:

> Come to him, to that living stone, rejected by men but in God's sight chosen and precious; and like living stones be yourselves built into a spiritual house, to be a holy priesthood, to offer spiritual sacrifices acceptable to God through Jesus Christ. (1 Pet. 2:4)

The interplay of propositional and mimetic truth accounts for the Bible's "history-like" character, which has been at the center of the knotty question: Is biblical narrative history or fiction?[51] Propositional truth asserts the actuality of an event, mimesis only its plausibility. Several years ago, when I wrote a brief commentary on the Book of Esther, the editors wished me to assert the essential historicity of the events it describes, but I found it impossible to separate with any certainty the elements of history, liturgy, and fiction.[52] While our modern sensibility insists on deciding the issue, biblical writers seemed confident that fact and fiction can be mixed and remain a witness to a transcendent order not of our own making.

In speaking of the third or *salvation-historical dimension*, I am using "historical" in the theological sense of God's sovereign revelatory activity with its insistent eschatological thrust. A corollary to this historicality is the scandal of particularity: as Wesley says, "'Tis mystery all, the Immortal dies." The saving activity of God is a mystery that cannot be deduced from the truth of God or the laws of history (Eph. 1:9-10). The literal word, historically considered, breaks in as the preaching of Christ and forms faith in the hearer (Rom. 10:17). Christology thus becomes the lens through which the special history of Israel and the church is read.

What role then does historic Israel play in this scenario? Philosophical hermeneutics, from Origen to Bultmann, have foundered on the "problem of Israel." It was the genius of Luther to recover from Pauline theology a "literal-prophetic" sense of God's word of promise which united the hopes of Israel with the faith of the church.[53] Typology is the characteristic interpretative activity that honors the original situation of the oracles of God while pressing on to enunciate their fulfillment in Christ.

The "historicity" or background of the Bible, both in matters of natural and human history, is the context, the home, into which the Word comes. Higher criticism has given a wealth of data to illuminate this history, although its direct relevance to the text of scripture has at times been overstated.[54] Unfortunately, skeptics and defenders of orthodoxy have chosen to skirmish in the historical underbrush. By asking a different set of questions of the biblical data ("Did it really happen that way?"), they have obscured the more eschatological concern of biblical narrators ("Where is it all headed?"—Luke 24:13-27). On the other hand, some postmodern literary critics, in recovering the literary unity of the biblical text, have neglected the historical context that is an accidental property of God's revelatory activity.[55]

The salvation-historical dimension of scripture works to unify not only events but genres, as can be seen in the grouping of biblical books under the authorship of Moses, David, Solomon, or Paul, and beyond that in the equating of "all scripture" with prophecy (Luke 24:44). Implicitly, the biblical authors assume the position of omniscient access to God's will and purposes in creation and history.[56] Whereas higher critics have excelled in dissecting the text into its formal units, premodern commentators, with their focus on its inspired unity, often saw it as of one genre: hence the different typographic conventions of King James and modern versions. The mosaic unity of the Bible, as Northrop Frye calls it, constitutes the "world of the text" that recent critics have rediscovered.[57]

Likewise propositional and mimetic truth are ultimately reconciled by eschatological hope. In the same breath, the Psalmist proclaims that the Lord reigns and cries out, "How long, O Lord?" Even after the deepest probing of the mysteries of life, the sages return to affirm God's ways (Job 42:1-8; Eccles. 12:13).[58] To set our mind on things above and let the word of Christ dwell richly within us gives a perspective from which to enter into the problems and ambiguities of living in fallen structures of society (Colossians 3-4). The world awaits the coming of the Lamb to reveal its purpose, and when he opens "the scroll written within and without," its rationality is not destroyed but redeemed by a reordering of its priorities (Revelation 4-5).[59]

The unifying movement of salvation history is never simply complete. As the short ending of Mark suggests, the essential work of the Son of God is done, but the story breaks off so that the reader may paint himself into the picture. It is in this sense that one can speak of scripture as an "open parable":[60] the church down to the end of the age is called on to participate in the divine plan of salvation (Eph. 2:9-10).

An Example: The Parable of the Wicked Tenants (Mark 12:1-12) In this section I hope to consider how a literal exegesis of a well-known parable of Jesus might be done.[61] In no way can this be a comprehensive presentation. Neither do I claim special originality, since most competent biblical criticism includes serious attention to the literal sense. In pursuing the three dimensions of meaning, however, my exegesis will take a different final shape than that found in many standard commentaries and studies.

The Poetic Dimension

Modern form criticism has discovered much about the distinctive nature of Jesus' parables.[62] Clearly they are patterned after the form of the wisdom similitude (*mashal*). What is not so commonly noticed is that the *mashal* is explicitly used by the Prophets to communicate the end-time mysteries of God's judgment and salvation (Num. 23:7 passim; Ps. 78:2; Ezek. 17:2; Hab. 2:6). The prophetic use of the parable fits the setting of conflict with the Jewish leaders but also Jesus' use of a prophetic proof-text to clinch the argument (Mark 12:10-11/Ps. 118:22-23).

Since the writings of Jülicher, Dodd, and Jeremias, it has been commonly accepted that Jesus' parables are realistic stories that make one existential point and that any additional allegorical details are the work of church redactors. To be sure, the parables in their original telling were intentionally opaque, crying out for interpretation (Mark 4:11-12). The parable works by tricking the hearers and confronting them with their stubbornness. In Mark 12, Jesus lures the chief priests and scribes, wealthy men all, into identifying with the landowner, only later realizing that *they* are the villains of the piece (cf. Matt. 21:45). Confronting sinners does not necessarily exhaust Jesus' purpose in telling parables, however. Craig Blomberg has argued that Jesus' parables are "rhetorical allegories" in which several referents are possible.[63] As one might expect in a form borrowed from wisdom literature, the parable is a special teaching device adapted to the role of Jesus as eschatological mediator of the kingdom of God.

The synoptic gospels set this parable at the climax of Jesus' entry into Jerusalem. Having foreseen his own betrayal and death at the hands of the chief priests and scribes (Mark 10:33), Jesus and the Jewish leaders proceed in the Passion narrative to act out the parable, much like Hamlet's play within a play. One wonders retrospectively whether the framing of Jesus' and John the Baptist's ministry and death, especially in Mark, does not reflect the influence of this parable (e.g., 9:13).

Mark has placed the parable in a catena of conflict pericopes following the Temple cleansing (A/11:27-33; B/12:1-12; C/12:13-17;

B'/12:18-27; A'/12:28-34).[64] This series of confrontations begins with the question: "By what authority are you doing these things?"; and it ends with Jesus' magisterial claim: "You are not far from the kingdom of God." The question about God and Caesar is the centerpiece of the series. When we connect the parable of the tenants to this pericope, we see that Jesus is interpreting Israel's history from the viewpoint of "two kingdoms." The tenants refuse to recognize the heavenly reign of God and his messiah and will try to kill him in order to grasp their earthly inheritance. Just as they cannot understand the resurrection life (12:27), so they are hardened in unbelief when the rejected stone becomes head of the corner (12:12).

The Truth Dimension

If we grant that the interpretation of allegories can yield determinate meanings, what then does this passage teach? First, in the landowner we come to see God as a patient Lord over his people. Yet he also requires his just due, and his patience comes to an end in sudden and final judgment. Whether or not the absentee landowner's behavior in sending his son is to be considered conventional by first-century standards, he certainly miscalculates and endures the final humiliation of rejection by his own tenants. Thus the enigma of the merciful yet exacting landlord points to a resolution that goes beyond the boundaries of the story in the amazing event of resurrection when God makes the rejected stone head of the corner.

The citation of Isaiah 5:1-7 connects the vineyard with Israel. The logic of the parable, however, discourages a direct identification of the vineyard with either the land or the people of Israel. Rather the vineyard is called an "inheritance" by the tenants (12:7), and in Matthew, Jesus refers to it as the "reign of God." The vineyard thus represents the claim of God to rule over his people, a claim channeled through Israel but for the sake of all the nations. Thus the wicked tenants are the leaders of Israel, a type of those who had previously led Israel into sin and exile (e.g., Micah 3). The people themselves are the audience, called on to adjudicate the dispute between the owner's party and the tenants. Luke especially holds out hope for a faithful response to Jesus from the Jewish people. He places the parable in the setting of Jesus' teaching and evangelizing the people (20:1); and while the leaders harden their hearts, the people's "God forbid!" suggests a shock reminiscent of the day of Pentecost (20:16; Acts 2:37).

The messengers in the parable refer to God's prophets sent repeatedly so that Israel would never lack the word of God, but also that

Israel, except for a remnant who live by faith, would harden itself to that word. Matthew extends the allegory by speaking of two groups of prophets, probably the "former" and "latter" prophets of canonical scripture. The prophets not only spoke the word but suffered for it, thus foreshadowing the ministry of the Son. The accompanying psalm citation includes David in the goodly fellowship of prophets and may suggest David as a type of royal sufferer (Ps. 118:10-18; 132:1).

The son in the parable and the stone in the psalm proof-text both refer to Jesus himself. Many commentators admit that Jesus identified himself in some way with the son and that this was a messianic claim (cf. Mark 12:35-37).[65] Although Jesus' or Mark's reasons for secrecy about his identity are debated, there is no doubt about Mark's final understanding of Jesus' identity: he is the Son of God (1:1; 15:39). Likewise he is the founder of a new community of disciples.

The Salvation-Historical Dimension

What is the significance of the introduction: "And he began to speak to them in parables"? Read straightforwardly, the text transmits the *ipsissima verba Jesu*, the very words of Jesus. Yet comparison of the synoptic gospels shows that, in all probability, Matthew and Luke did not hesitate to alter Mark (e.g., Mark says that the tenants killed the son and cast him out of the vineyard, while Matthew and Luke apparently updated the parable in the light of the crucifixion and have the son cast out first and then killed). By analogy, could Mark not have altered the actual Jesus tradition? We have already noted that "historicality" does not demand exact "historicity" to authenticate its claim to be a genuine witness to history. Even the minimal version of the parable in the *Gospel of Thomas* would preserve a common core of meaning.[66]

Unfortunately, the higher-critical concern for historical reconstruction has often obscured other legitimate historical features of the passage. The voice of Jesus in this parable claims an imperial authority in interpreting the end of history. He recounts the entire history of Israel as the response to an offer of an inheritance (the vineyard). If the stone citation includes an allusion to Daniel 2:44/7:27, the inheritance received by the son is a universal and eschatological kingdom. The dispute between the owner and the tenants runs parallel to Jesus' disputes with the chief priests and scribes. By absenting himself, the owner opened himself to ambiguous legal determinations as to right of possession. To enter into disputes about the Law, according to Jesus, was to misunderstand its purpose; but it was that very this-worldly claim to "ownership of meaning" that blinded the tenants to the fact that the kingdom of God had drawn near (Mark 12:28-34).

The sending of the son to receive the inheritance is the climax of the parable. While not denying the veiled form of the parable, I would join those who see an astounding identification of the owner (God) with the son (Jesus). Whereas the messengers (the prophets) only remind Israel of the aim of its election, the son by his arrival claims to realize that aim. The tragic denouement is that in recognizing his claim, the tenants attempt to nullify it by killing him. Much like the Deuteronomic and Danielic histories, the parable thus ends on a note of judgment and exile. God's determination to begin again with a new set of tenants would satisfy justice but not answer the question of "Who is worthy?" to bring the cycles of sinful history to an end.

The citation of the "stone" texts resolves the tension caused by the parable itself. Whether or not Jesus intended a word-play on son/stone (ben/'eben), the rejection of the stone is clearly meant to interpret the killing of the son in the parable. The stone texts go further than the parable by pointing to a miraculous act of God, breaking through the natural and historical cycles and leading to the exaltation of the rejected stone. The new people of God are not just another historical nation but those who confess about God's new act in Christ: "It is marvelous in our eyes." The true end of history, then, is the fulfillment of God's saving purposes in the apparently tragic death and the miraculous exaltation of Jesus the Son.

Historical criticism cannot prove or disprove how far the "historical Jesus" understood the outworking of this parable. The precise arbitration of who said what between Jesus and the church is not crucial to establish the historical dimension of the passage. Such a quest, while not illegitimate in itself, can distract us from the powerful crisis of response which the parable conveys. The Gospels not only report what Jesus said and did, but they confront us, like the original hearers, with the challenge: Who do you say that I am? Bultmann was absolutely right to sense this dimension of the Bible, but he was wrong in attempting to separate it from the truth dimension of the scripture as the Word of God.

Let me add an unscholarly footnote to this study. As I pondered the letter of the text, I found myself drawn into the vortex of the parable: who is this owner and his son? and who is this Jesus who speaks the word with such authority? And from this center, I could not help but wanting to preach the passage and relate it to the current debate over biblical authority. Are we not in this churchly exercise disputing the ownership of meaning? Does not the parable itself call into question the exclusive right of the priestly and scholarly guild to interpret the meaning of scripture? But is it really possible to avoid hermeneutical authoritarianism or pluralism? I take the parable to say yes, there is a coherent message in Israel's history and scripture, and yes, it is received by those who, under the spell of the gospel, look again at the letter and say, "It is marvelous in our eyes!"

AUTHORITY: TAKING GOD AT HIS WORD

The Primacy of Scripture

Anglicanism has gladly joined with the Reformation in its affirmation of the scripture principle—the primacy and sufficiency of the Bible—as its norm in matters of doctrine, discipline, and devotion.[67] This primacy is acknowledged explicitly in the Anglican formularies, such as the *Thirty-nine Articles of Religion*:

Article 6: Of the Sufficiency of the Holy Scriptures for Salvation.

Holy Scripture containeth all things necessary to salvation: so that whatsoever is not read therein, nor may be proved thereby, is not to be required of any man, that it should be believed as an article of the Faith, or be thought requisite or necessary to salvation.

Article 20: Of the Authority of the Church.

The Church hath power to decree Rites and Ceremonies, and authority in Controversies of Faith: and yet it is not lawful for the Church to ordain any thing that is contrary to God's Word written, neither may it so expound one place of Scripture, that it be repugnant to another.

While some may question the authority of the *Thirty-nine Articles* in the American church, J. Robert Wright has demonstrated that they are the theological basis for the Episcopal ordination oath: "I do believe the Holy Scriptures of the Old and New Testament to be the Word of God, and to contain all things necessary to salvation."[68] The portrait one gets in these formularies is of a church and clergy reading, expounding, and believing scripture as "God's word written." This view is also implicit in the assignment of scripture reading in every service of the Prayer Book.[69]

The classic stance of Anglicanism has not gone without question or qualification. Many Anglicans, fearing bibliolatry, see an absolute disjunction between Christ as the Word and scripture as the witness to the Word.[70] Another current view sees scripture as the "repository of the Church's symbols of life and faith,"[71] from which the church draws new light in every age, a view that I would less politely call the "grab-bag approach." Finally, among many Anglican writers the perspective of the Knower (reader) has come to take priority over the determinacy of the Known (literal text), so that the "inerrant truth" of the Bible now becomes the "experience" that we share with religious people of all ages.[72]

I have argued that literal sense remains the most credible approach to interpreting the Bible. I likewise maintain that only in the light of its referentiality, purposiveness, and clarity can scripture function as prime authority in the church. In accordance with Jesus' teaching that "man cannot serve two masters," approaches that treat scripture as one authority among others inevitably end up granting autonomy to the individual conscience or the collective conscience of the church.[73]

The appropriate response to biblical primacy is hermeneutical submissiveness. The church and the individual are to receive the gospel in the spirit of the Blessed Virgin: "Behold the handmaid of the Lord; let it be to me according to your word." In the fascinating liberal-evangelical dialogue between David Edwards and John Stott, the extent of this submission to scripture is the central issue.[74] Edwards argues that

> for all Christians the Bible, in some sense, is or becomes or conveys "the word of God." Its history is, in some sense, "salvation history." Its great images are signs pointing to our salvation, from the Garden of Eden to the final City of God. That seems— to understate its value for our salvation—sufficient. (pp. 43-44)

Edwards defines the term *sufficient* to mean "minimally necessary," thus creating a vast space in which his reason can pick and choose as to which biblical teachings are authoritative. Stott's reply focuses on whether such minimalism is finally coherent:

> Sometimes you seem anxious to demonstrate that your position is more biblical than mine. I wonder why? I mean, if you could prove this to me, I would want to change my mind and position at once. But if I could show you that my position is more biblical than yours, would you be willing to change? . . . In later chapters you reject traditional Christian teaching about the atonement, miracles, homosexual partnerships, and the awful reality of hell, not only on the ground that you consider them unbiblical, but because on other grounds you find it unacceptable. Does this not mean that in the end you accord supremacy to your reason rather than to Scripture? (pp. 104-5)

"Searching the scriptures" requires both access to the whole Bible and willingness to follow wherever it leads (Acts 17:11; John 5:39). In what I have called the grab-bag approach, scripture is seen as a resource from which we choose the correct and omit the incorrect elements in preaching and theology. This view, mentioned above, is implicit in the 1979 Prayer Book Lectionary, and explicit in any sample of Episcopal preaching. When the grab-bag method is used, the choice and use of the texts usually ends up conforming to the priorities of the late twentieth-century enlightened consciousness. I do not deny that every interpreter brings a certain bias, or that there is a legitimate canonical focus on central texts, or that different kinds of scripture function authoritatively in different ways.[75] Nevertheless, the Christian who reads the Bible literally must be attentive to every text, comparing scripture with scripture as a check against one-sided reading.

Transformed by the Word

Before addressing the specific assigned topics for application, let me begin with a meditation on the means of spiritual transformation inherent in a literal reading of the Bible. The meditation follows the lines of Cranmer's collect: "Blessed Lord, who hast caused all holy Scriptures to be written for our learning . . . "

Grant us to hear and read them: The first aim for the church's disciplines of preaching and teaching, worship and prayer, is a literate congregation of believers (Matt. 28:20; Acts 2:42). In the apostolic church, this was done through public reading and preaching and memorization; since the print revolution, private Bible reading has become a major devotion for Christian discipleship. The disappearance of reading in the twentieth century is not simply due to lack of time but reflects the hermeneutical crisis of Western thought.[76] Even if they have never heard of the deconstructionist theory that texts are self-immolating, people are daunted by the welter of experts advocating opposite opinions on every subject. With its classic approach to literal and plain sense, the church has a compelling reason to promote literacy among its own and in the society at large.

. . . *mark and learn them*: Reading must be accompanied by critical analysis and synthesis. It is characteristic of the Bible that it invites exegesis.[77] The advent of higher criticism has greatly increased our awareness of the genre differences and the diachronic character of the biblical text. What has often been lost, on layperson and scholar alike, is the theological unity of scripture, which is a key assumption of its authority (Ps. 119:160; Article 20). I would like to commend the lost art of proof-texting as a remedy to the fragmentation of the biblical text.[78] Good proof-texting is a foundation not only for biblical theology but for systematic theology and preaching as well, as it forces one to ponder the literal sense of a passage and its intertextual connections with other passages. Just as one would wish to understand the thought of a politician, writer, or philosopher by apt quotations from his works and accurate footnotes, so proof-texting seeks to justify generalizations and applications of the word of God by means of literary reference.

. . . and inwardly digest them: A further step in this process is the drawing of analogies between the biblical texts and our context. While there are appropriate rules for contextualization, the process of reading and marking the words of scripture is an activity of the Spirit forming a Christian personality and worldview.[79] Classic African-American preaching, for instance, assumes the authority of the Bible as a whole but exhibits a freedom of movement from text to text with a creative retelling of the story, interpreting the experience of slavery and racism in a "Bibleistic way."[80] Truly digesting the word is difficult for modern readers because we have all imbibed the "hermeneutics of suspicion" in regarding all argument as propaganda. We need to learn not only to approve those judgments of scripture that confirm our views but to expect judgments that find us guilty, trusting that in those judgments we will find our true life (Mark 8:34-38; John 6:68).[81] It has never been easy to emulate the prophet who ate the scroll of God's word and found it sweet to the tongue but bitter in the stomach (Ezek. 3:3; Rev. 10:10).

Resurrection and Virgin Birth

A mind formed by the literal sense of scripture finds denial of Jesus' bodily resurrection and virgin birth unthinkable. Virtually all responsible biblical exegetes would admit that *as a whole and in its final form* the New Testament proclaims that Jesus rose bodily from the dead and reigns eternally in heaven; that he is uniquely Son of man and Son of God; and that these things are in accordance with the prophetic sense of the Old Testament scriptures. All those writings that purport to narrate Jesus' life refer to the empty tomb, and other texts (e.g., Acts 2:23-24, 31-32; 13:29-30; 1 Tim. 3:16; Heb. 12:2; 1 Pet. 3:18-19) are more consistent with the empty tomb than with any other hypothesis. Likewise the two Gospels that relate Jesus' human origin say that he was born of a virgin, and no other New Testament Christological statement presumes some other form of birth. Working from the canon therefore, we can appreciate the "cultural-linguistic" framework from which the credal affirmation of the virgin birth developed.

The perceived problem of the resurrection and virgin birth has to do not with whether the Bible attests to them but whether they are true, either as historical events or as necessary doctrines. At one level, this involves a philosophical debate about the possibility of miracles.[82] Even granting that miracles are possible, which is clearly the assumption underlying the literal sense of scripture, higher criticism has attempted to unwind the threefold cord by identifying earlier and later forms of tradition, different literary forms of the Gospel accounts, and the influence of the church's faith in articulating the event. This exercise has made clear the difficulty, if not the impossibility, of simply harmonizing the various infancy and resurrection accounts and has sensitized us to the kerygmatic character of the Gospel narratives.[83] But it also has obscured the integrity of the biblical witness to the truth of these mighty acts of God and the evangelical power and normative imprint of the text in shaping the believer and the church.[84]

In reporting historical events, biblical authors often *assume* that their words will be accepted as they intend them. Only occasionally do they state their canonical purpose explicitly as John does when he writes: "Now Jesus did many other signs which are not written in this book; but these are written that you may believe that Jesus is the Christ and believing you may have life in his name" (20:30-31). John is claiming contact with factual events that "Jesus did," especially the resurrection. At the same time these events have revelatory power to bring people like Thomas to faith.

In doctrinal matters as well, the truth dimension of scripture is usually tacit; but when challenged, biblical writers do make clear normative claims. When Paul confronts those who said there was no resurrection of the dead in 1 Corinthians 15, he is uncompromising in his retort. He recites the apostolic tradition that he received as absolutely reliable (15:1-11). Then he argues that this tradition has two and only two logical outcomes: either its truth confirms the coming general resurrection of the dead, or its falsity means that the gospel is blasphemy and Christians are fools and knaves (15:12-20).

With regard to the incarnation, John is equally uncompromising: "Every spirit which confesses that Jesus Christ has come in the flesh is of God, and every spirit which does not confess Jesus is not of God" (1 John 4:2-3). John is not simply asserting the existence of the historical Jesus but the divine Sonship against those who are scandalized by the particularity of God in the flesh. In one sense the virgin birth is analogous to the empty tomb in the order of teaching, that is, it is not part of the earliest kerygma (Acts 10:38-41; Rom. 1:3). However, since the virgin birth is the perfect narrative complement to New Testament teaching on the nature of Christ,[85] and since no other explanations of Jesus' birth are seriously considered by New Testament authors,[86] the incorporation of the virgin birth as an item of credal orthodoxy appears a natural deduction from scripture itself.[87]

Sexual Morality

I hardly need mention that sexual morality is the worldview battleground in late twentieth-century America, with such issues as divorce, abortion, and homosexuality featured in the media and politics. This has led in the church to a corresponding battle for the Bible, with some calling for an abandonment of biblical teaching as oppressive and others for radical reinterpretation of traditional texts. In the latter category, I would include the influential book by William Countryman on sexual ethics.[88]

Countryman's avowed method is "to read the texts as literally as possible" (p. 2), and he does indeed engage in exegesis of a wide range of biblical texts. Because the worldview of ancient texts is, for him, so obviously irretrievable, literal reading serves to "relativize the present" and so open us to adapting our sexual ethics to new, evolving norms of modern individualism (pp. 237-40). Countryman goes to great length to show that none of the New Testament writers literally intended to proscribe physical fornication and homosexuality (p. 141), but given his approach, what difference would it make if they did? Using Jesus' declaring all foods clean (Mark 7:19) as an interpretative fulcrum, he allegorizes Jesus' specific condemnation of "fornication, adultery, and licentiousness" in the verses immediately following (pp. 84-86). Countryman's attempt to drive a wedge between "metaphorical purity" and specific moral behavior is possible only because he overlooks the foundational role of the doctrine of creation.[89] This leads to an odd kind of spiritualizing of the literal sense in a gnostic direction.

By contrast, I would suggest Mark 10:2-9 as a more central text in gaining access to Jesus' understanding of sexual morality. The pericope is the first of a series of "hard sayings" about discipleship in chapter 10. For the sake of the kingdom of God, the disciple will be utterly faithful in marriage, will manifest childlike openness to God's will, will be ready to sell all possessions, will abandon family status and property, will drink the cup of suffering and death, and will become servant of all. All of these sayings involve a reversal of worldly expectations, giving up the normal social honors. What then does the disciple give up in marriage? Jesus' answer seems to be, divorce!

Why should giving up divorce further the aims of the kingdom? Jesus does not say directly. His argument, however, is reminiscent of the Wicked Tenants' parable. Jesus places his teaching above that of Moses and claims to reveal a primal design of God from the beginning. This design involves a uniting of two in one flesh and a call for utter faithfulness between them. This faithfulness, he implies, is not possible by human will because of the hardness of the human heart; but "with God all things are possible" (10:27). Grace reverses the Law and perfects nature in this parable of the New Covenant between God and his people. But grace comes at a price: sacrificing one's right to leave. Paul, who likewise speaks of marriage as a "mystery," calls for mutual submission of husband and wife; and John in the wedding of Cana links the cup of joy with the cup of sorrow. Matthew adds another hard saying of the Lord to suggest that the celibate life is an equivalent dedication to the kingdom (19:11-12).

Jesus places on the legal ordinance of marriage the honor and weight of representing his new relationship as Bridegroom with his church. The specific outworkings of this new institution in the life of the church have been somewhat variable.[90] In equating remarriage with adultery, it is not completely clear whether he intends to rule out every conceivable case or rather to challenge disciples dramatically to single-minded obedience. It is clear that he affirms the natural basis of marriage as good, but beyond that identifies marriage (and celibacy) with his own work of atoning sacrifice. Jesus may have widened the menu of food choices, but his teaching on sexual relations is narrow. Thus people, then and now, have wondered: Who can stand it? (Matt. 19:10). The church has no authority to reconfigure marriage but calls men and women to offer their fallen human sexuality within marriage and in "single"-minded service of the gospel.

To know Christ's word is not to do it, but it is the first step to grace and hope. Richard Hays, who has made an especially clear exposition of Paul's understanding of homosexuality in the Epistle to the Romans,[91] has written elsewhere a moving account of a man named Gary, who was wrestling with the word:[92]

> Gary came to New Haven in the summer of 1989 to say a proper farewell. My best friend from undergraduate years at Yale was

dying of AIDS . . . For more than 20 years Gary had grappled with his homosexuality, experiencing it as a compulsion and an affliction. Now, as he faced death, he wanted to talk it all through again from the beginning, because he knew my love for him and trusted me to speak without dissembling. For Gary, there was no time to dance around the hard questions. As Dylan had urged, "Let us not talk falsely now; the hour is getting late."

In particular Gary wanted to discuss the biblical passages that deal with homosexual acts. Among Gary's many gifts was his skill as a reader of texts . . . The more we talked the more we found our perspectives interlocking. Both of us had serious misgivings about the mounting pressure for the church to recognize homosexuality as a legitimate Christian lifestyle. As a New Testament scholar, I was concerned about certain questionable exegetical and theological strategies of the gay apologists. Gary, as a homosexual Christian, believed that their writings did justice neither to the biblical texts nor to the depressing reality of the gay subculture that he had moved in and out of for 20 years . . .

Gary wrote urgently of the imperatives of discipleship: "Are homosexuals to be excluded from the community of faith? Certainly not. But anyone who joins such a community should know that it is a place of transformation, of discipline, of learning, and not merely a place to be comforted or indulged." . . .

In the midst of a culture that worships self-gratification, and a church that preaches a false Jesus who panders to our desires, those who seek the narrow way of obedience have a powerful word to speak. Just as Paul saw in pagan homosexuality a symbol of human fallenness, so I saw conversely in Gary, as I have seen in other homosexual friends and colleagues, a symbol of God's power made perfect in weakness (2 Corinthians 12:9) . . .

That seems to be the spiritual condition Gary reached near the end of his life. He wrote this in his last letter: "Since All Saints Day I have felt myself being transformed. I no longer consider myself a homosexual. Many would say, big deal, you're 42 . . . and are dying of AIDS. Big sacrifice. No, I didn't do this of my will, of an effort to improve myself, to make myself acceptable to God. No, he did this for me. I feel a great weight has been lifted off me."

Gary and his friend Richard, it seems to me, are examples of what it means to be servants of the Word. Gary was truthful about his own life experience but also stubbornly honest in acknowledging the possibility that scripture might judge rather than endorse that experience. His friend acted as the good pastor-teacher in sympathetically listening to him and searching the scriptures with him. The beginning of wisdom for Gary was a weighing of words which claim the authority of the Word; the end, however, was the work of the Spirit, applying the forgiveness of sins and new life in Christ from which nothing in heaven and earth can separate us.[93]

The church's submission to the word of God in scripture is nothing more than trusting in God's power and God's way of salvation on behalf of all the lost sheep of Christ's fold. When we let God be God and let God speak, then we will come to know that his word to us is not Yes and No, but finally and forever Yes in the Son of God, Jesus Christ (2 Cor. 1:18-20).

> O God, whose glory it is always to have mercy: Be gracious to all who have gone astray from your ways, and bring them again with penitent hearts and steadfast faith to embrace and hold fast the unchangeable truth of your Word, Jesus Christ your Son; who with you and the Holy Spirit lives and reigns, one God, for ever and ever. Amen.

ACKNOWLEDGMENTS

I would like to thank those whose conversation and written comments helped me to formulate my views even when we saw things differently: my mentor in biblical studies, Prof. Francis Andersen of New College, Berkeley; Prof. John Koenig of the General Theological Seminary; Prof. Moisés Silva of Westminster Theological Seminary; Prof. Bonnie Thurston of Wheeling Jesuit College; fellow members of Scholarly Engagement in Anglican Doctrine, including Prof. Elizabeth Koenig, the Reverend Joseph Trigg, the Reverend Alison Barfoot, and the Reverend Sara Chandler; and colleagues on the faculty at Trinity Episcopal School for Ministry. Finally, I am grateful to my wife Peggy for continuing to supply me with excellent proofreading and steady encouragement in the Lord.

NOTES

1. In his recent worldview analysis, *Culture Wars: The Struggle to Define America* (New York: Basic Books, 1991), 44-45, James Davison Hunter distinguishes two main views of authority. "Orthodoxy" involves the "*commitment on the part of adherents to an external, definable, and transcendent authority.*" "Progressives," by contrast, share the "*tendency to resymbolize historic faiths according to the prevailing assumptions of contemporary life.*" As an example of the latter strategy, see John Shelby Spong, *Born of a Woman: A Bishop Rethinks the Birth of Jesus* (San Francisco: Harper, 1992), 173: "Like all theological statements, the creeds are filled with symbolic words and time-distorted meanings. . . . The only way to keep symbols alive forever is to crack them open periodically so that they can be filled with new meanings."

2. See the general cultural analysis of George Steiner, "The Retreat from the Word," in *George Steiner: A Reader* (New York: Oxford University Press, 1984), 283-304.

3. For the background of fundamentalism in Baconian science, see George Marsden, *Fundamentalism and American Culture: The Shaping of Twentieth-century Evangelicalism 1870-1925* (Oxford: Oxford University Press, 1980), 55-62.

4. I have been sent numerous articles in Episcopal publications attacking what Bishop Spong refers to as the "beast of literalism" in *Rescuing the Bible from Fundamentalism* (San Francisco: Harper, 1991), 215. The tip-off to caricature is the use of "-ism," which reminds me of the epigram that "tradition is the living faith of the dead, traditionalism is the dead faith of the living."

5. Many theological friends warned me against using the term *literal* to define a distinct hermeneutical position. When I asked them for an adequate substitute, they could not agree on one. So I followed the advice of Jean Cocteau when he said, "Listen carefully to first criticisms made of your work. Note just what it is about your work that critics don't like—then cultivate it. That's the only part of your work that's individual and worth keeping."

6. I argue in my responses to Price, Norris, and Wondra that they share common presuppositions of biblical meaning as ineffable and hence governable by human consciousness, over against my view that the Divine Logos determines the "logic" of the literal sense of scripture, which in turn governs the response of the believer.

7. See the fine meditation on John 1:1-18 in T. F. Torrance, "The Word of God and the Response of Man," in *God and Rationality* (London: Oxford University Press, 1971), 137-53.

8. Wolfhart Pannenberg, *Systematic Theology* (Grand Rapids, Mich.: Eerdmans, 1991), 1:308.

9. Torrance, "Word of God," 149.

10. Augustine, *On Christian Doctrine* 1.39.43; Calvin, *Institutes* 1.6.1.

11. J. L. Kugel, "Early Interpretation: The Common Background of Late Forms of Biblical Exegesis," in *Early Biblical Interpretation*, ed. J. L. Kugel and R. A. Greer (Philadelphia: Westminster, 1986), 70-71.

12. Luke 24:44-49. Cf. C. H. Dodd, *According to the Scriptures: The Sub-Structure of New Testament Theology* (London: Nisbet, 1952), 28-60.

13. B. A. Pierson, "Use, Authority and Exegesis of Mikra in Gnostic Literature," *Mikra: Text, Translation, Reading and Interpretation of the Hebrew Bible in Ancient Judaism and Early Christianity*, CRINT 2.1 (Assen: Van Gorcum, 1988), 635-52.

14. R. P. C. Hanson, *Tradition in the Early Church* (Philadelphia: Westminster, 1962), 124-29.

15. R. A. Greer, "The Christian Bible and Its Interpretation," in Kugel and Greer, *Early Biblical Interpretation*, 184-85.

16. Maurice Wiles's comment on Origen is revealing: "Despite the great range of his intellectual gifts, Origen was totally lacking in poetic sensitivity. The literal sense of scripture is for him the literally literal meaning of the words." See "Origen as Biblical Scholar" in *The Cambridge History of the Bible* (Cambridge: Cambridge University Press, 1970), 1:470. The Antiochenes in reacting against allegory likewise tended to restrict the meaning of Scripture to its "narrative sense" (*historia*).

17. The starting point of Augustine's doctrine of scripture is the clarity of the canonical text: "Anyone who understands in the Scriptures something other than that intended by them is deceived, although they do not lie" (*On Christian Doctrine* 1.36.41). At times he can refer to this intentional reading as the "literal sense." He can also make a distinction between "literal" and "figurative" signs; the literal signs have a primary verbal referent ("ox" = the animal), while figures refer to something else, as in 1 Cor. 9:9 (*On Christian Doctrine* 2.10.15). In most cases figures turn out to be Old Testament types.

18. Cf. Raymond Brown's case for sensus plenior as a second meaning of the text, in "What the Biblical Word Meant and What It Means," *The Critical Meaning of the Bible* (New York: Paulist, 1981), 23-44.

19. See J. A. Preus, *From Shadow to Promise: Old Testament Interpretation from Augustine to the Young Luther* (Cambridge: Harvard University Press, 1969), 267-68.

20. "For as God alone is a fit witness of himself in his Word, so also the Word will not find acceptance in men's hearts before it is sealed by the inward testimony of the Spirit." *Institutes* 1.7.4.

21. See esp. *Laws of Ecclesiastical Polity* 1.14, 2.8, 3.8, and 5.59.2; E. Grislis, "The Hermeneutical Problem in Hooker," in *Studies in Richard Hooker* (Cleveland: Case Western, 1972), 193-96.

22. See survey and evaluation in B. S. Childs, *Introduction to the Old Testament as Scripture* (Philadelphia: Fortress, 1979), 34-41.

23. A. C. Thiselton, *New Horizons in Hermeneutics* (Grand Rapids, Mich.: Zondervan, 1992), 209-16, limits "romantic" hermeneutics to Schleiermacher and his contemporaries; however, he does show how Schleiermacher has set the agenda for all subsequent "post-modern" hermeneutics.

24. Thiselton, *New Horizons*, 226-27, credits Schleiermacher's attention to the semantic aspect of a text. Nevertheless, for Schleiermaicher it is possible to understand a text better than the author because the author's historical perspective is particular and primitive, while the interpreter brings a mature and universal modern consciousness.

25. "Historicist experience" is fundamentally opaque, whereas in classical thought common-sense experience or opinion is the beginning of true insight (Aristotle, *Nichomachean Ethics* 1.4). This is why "experience" is such a loaded term in current discussions about authority.

26. Leo Strauss, *Natural Right and History* (Chicago: University of Chicago Press, 1953), 25.

27. Note the wry comment of Oliver O'Donovan in *Resurrection and Moral Order* (Grand Rapids, Mich.: Eerdmans, 1986), 161: "Cultural foreignness, which we meet in our contemporaries daily, is not a final barrier to understanding, but a warning against shallow understandings."

28. "The Sensus Literalis of Scripture: An Ancient and Modern Problem," in H. Donner et al., eds., *Beiträge zur Alttestamentlichen Theologie* (FS Zimmerli; Göttingen: Vandenhoeck und Ruprecht, 1977), 80-93.

29. Childs, "The Canonical Approach and the 'New Yale Theology' in *The New Testament as Canon* (Philadelphia: Fortress, 1984), 541-46; E. V. McKnight, *Post-Modern Use of the Bible* (Nashville: Abingdon, 1988), 74-79.

30. See, e.g., the philosophical theology of Carl F. H. Henry, *God, Revelation, and Authority* (Waco: Word, 1976); and the hermeneutical essays in *Hermeneutics, Authority, and Canon*, ed. D. A. Carson and J. D. Woodbridge (Grand Rapids, Mich.: Zondervan, 1986).

31. "The Centrality of Hermeneutics Today," in D. A. Carson and J. D. Woodbridge, ed., *Scripture and Truth* (Grand Rapids, Mich.: Zondervan, 1983), 333, 349-50.

32. William J. Abraham, *The Divine Inspiration of Holy Scripture* (Oxford: Oxford University Press, 1981), 67. This family debate demonstrates the ongoing vitality of the Calvinist-Arminian strands of classic Protestantism.

33. Clark H. Pinnock, *The Scripture Principle* (San Francisco: Harper, 1984), 78.

34. Abraham, *Divine Inspiration*, 106, explains New Testament references to the whole Old Testament as the Word of God in this way: "Recognizing that God has spoken his word [on occasion] and that this is recorded in the Old Testament they happily talk of all of it being the Word of God." I think he

mistakes the mode of verbal revelation (e.g., God speaking to prophets) with the character of all scripture as verbally inspired.

35. Postmodernism claims to be a third way but has not really demonstrated its coherence as a worldview except by negation.

36. Pannenberg, *Systematic Theology*, 1:313, sees the essential intratrinitarian relations as the "handing over" of lordship by the Father to the Son and the Son's "handing back" of that lordship.

37. Older commentators observed a necessary link between the literal and figurative senses. So Patrick Fairbairn writes: "All languages are more or less figurative; for the mind of man is essentially analogical . . . and in regard to things lying beyond the reach of sense or time, it is *obliged* to resort to figurative terms . . . " *Hermeneutical Manual: Introduction to the Exegetical Study* (Philadelphia: Smith, English, 1859), 158.

38. Cf. Northrop Frye in *The Great Code: The Bible and Literature* (New York: Harcourt Brace Jovanovich, 1982), 61-62: "The Bible means literally just what it says, but it can mean it only without primary reference to a correspondence of what it says to something outside what it says."

39. E. D. Hirsch quips in *The Aims of Interpretation* (Chicago: University of Chicago Press, 1976), 6: "Whenever I am told by a Heideggerian that I have misunderstood Heidegger, my still unrebutted response is that I will readily (if uneasily) concede that point, since the concession in itself implies a more important point, namely that Heidegger's text *can* be interpreted correctly, and has been so by my accuser."

40. Gerhard von Rad, *Old Testament Theology* (New York: Harper, 1965), 2:319-35; and Austin Farrer, *The Rebirth of Images: The Making of St. John's Apocalypse* (Westminster: Dacre, 1949), 13-22.

41. Childs, *Introduction*, 78-79; Douglas Moo, "The Problem of Sensus Plenior," *Hermeneutics, Authority, and Canon*, ed. Carson and Woodbridge, 204-9.

42. *The Poetics of Biblical Narrative: Ideological Literature and the Drama of Reading* (Bloomington: Indiana University Press, 1985), 50-51. Note the attack on "foolproof composition" by D. N. Fewell and D. M. Gunn, "Tipping the Balance: Sternberg's Reader and the Rape of Dinah," *JBL* 110 (1991): 193-211; and his rebuttal, "Biblical Poetics and Sexual Politics: From Reading to Counter-Reading," *JBL* 111 (1992): 463-88.

43. K. J. Vanhoozer, "The Semantics of Biblical Literature: Truth and the Scripture's Diverse Literary Forms," in *Hermeneutics, Authority, and Canon*, ed. Carson and Woodbridge, 99-100, points out that "illocutionary speech" is effective "simply in the hearer understanding the utterance of the speaker." Sinful human beings, apart from God's grace, can reject a clear message of scripture.

44. Both Origen and John Cassian supported the threefold distinction among the sense of scripture by references to Prov. 22:20 (LXX): "Write these things triply

in your heart . . . " Among modern commentators, Sternberg, *Poetics*, 41, makes a triple distinction among ideological, historiographic, and aesthetic principles of biblical narrative.

45. Thiselton, *New Horizons*, 597-99, points out a major distinction in speech acts between promises and authorizations, which communicate commitments on the part of the author, and prayers and confessions, which call for a commitment on the part of the readers.

46. The power of Handel's *Messiah* derives from a similar synthesis of texts and music. Cf. Hans Urs von Balthasar, *Truth Is Symphonic: Aspects of Christian Pluralism* (San Francisco: Ignatius, 1987), 7-9.

47. The classic description of mimesis in the Bible is that of Erich Auerbach, *Mimesis: The Representation of Reality in Western Literature* (Princeton: Princeton University Press, 1953). I am indebted to a development of Auerbach's case by A. D. Nuttall, *A New Mimesis: Shakespeare and the Nature of Reality* (London: Methuen, 1983).

48. Nuttall, *New Mimesis*, 181-93.

49. Cf. Stephen Prickett, *Words and the Word: Language, Poetics and Biblical Interpretation* (Cambridge: Cambridge University Press, 1986), 4-36.

50. On the use of literary omniscience and omnipotence, see Sternberg, *Poetics*, 100.

51. See David L. Bartlett, *The Shape of Biblical Authority* (Philadelphia: Fortress, 1983), 43-81.

52. *Evangelical Commentary on the Bible* ed. W. A. Elwell (Grand Rapids, Mich.: Baker, 1989), 326-28. Cf. C. S. Lewis's letter to E. J. Carnell (4/4/53): "In what sense does the Bible 'present' the Jonah story 'as historical'? Of course, it doesn't say 'This is fiction' but then neither does our Lord say that the Unjust Judge, Good Samaritan, or Prodigal Son are fiction. (I would put *Esther* in the same category as Jonah for the same reason.) How does a denial, a doubt of their historicity lead logically to a similar denial of New Testament miracles?"

53. See, for instance, his 1535 commentary on Galatians 3:2: "all the patriarchs, prophets, and devout kings of the Old Testament were righteous, having received the Holy Spirit secretly on account of their faith in the coming Christ."

54. W. G. Dever, "Archaeology," *IDBSup* (1976): 51.

55. See critiques by Sternberg, Poetics, 2-35; and Baruch Halpern, *The First Historians: The Hebrew Bible and History* (San Francisco: Harper, 1988), 3-32.

56. Sternberg, *Poetics*, 34: "Omniscience in modern narrative attends and signals fictionality, while in the ancient tradition it not only accommodates but also guarantees authenticity."

57. Frye, *Great Code*, 206.

58. It may be objected that the conclusions of Job and Ecclesiastes are pious deflections of the skeptical questions within the books. Even if this were true,

the canonical framing sets the books within the larger wisdom tradition, without denying their radical thrust. Similarly, Shakespeare can bring Fortinbras on stage to restore the kingdom of Denmark without undoing the radical disorder that Hamlet's questioning has caused.

59. O'Donovan, *Resurrection and Moral Order*, 25: "Only God expresses love by conferring order upon the absolutely orderless, and he has contented himself with doing it but once."

60. For the term, see Frederick H. Borsch, *Many Things in Parables: Extravagant Stories of New Community* (Philadelphia: Fortress, 1988), 12-13.

61. Cf. now B. S. Childs, *Biblical Theology of the Old and New Testaments: Theological Reflection on the Christian Bible* (Minneapolis: Fortress, 1992), 337-47.

62. For an overview, see Grant R. Osborne, *The Hermeneutical Spiral: A Comprehensive Introduction to Biblical Interpretation* (Downers Grove: IVP, 1991), 235-51.

63. *Interpreting the Parables* (Downers Grove: IVP, 1990), 29-69.

64. I am indebted for this insight to my colleague, Stephen M. Smith. See also J. D. Kingsbury, *Conflict in Mark: Jesus, Authorities, Disciples* (Minneapolis: Fortress, 1989), 65-88.

65. J. Jeremias, *The Parables of Jesus* (London: SCM, 1963), 72-73. For a survey of Christological options, see Blomberg, *Interpreting the Parables*, 313-23.

66. The case for *Gospel of Thomas* as secondary is stronger than the reverse; see K. Snodgrass, "The Parable of the Wicked Husbandmen: Is the Gospel of Thomas Version the Original?" *NTS* 20 (1974): 142-44.

67. See R. H. Fuller, "Scripture," in *The Study of Anglicanism*, ed. S. Sykes and J. H. Booty (London: SPCK, 1988), 79-91.

68. "The 'Official Position' of the Episcopal Church on the Authority of Scripture. Part I: Present Teaching and Historical Development," ATR 74 (1992): 350.

69. Oliver O'Donovan, *On the Thirty-nine Articles: A Conversation with Tudor Christianity* (Exeter: Paternoster, 1986), 51, notes that *reading* of the Bible in the Tudor church took logical priority over exposition because "the way of knowing any given thing is dictated in large measure by *what the thing is*, and not only (or mainly) by the situation of the person who has come to know it."

70. As Wright notes ("Official Position," 355-56), the 1983 statement of the Episcopal House of Bishops apparently intended (!) to espouse this view by omitting the familiar phrase "to be the Word of God" in alluding to the Oath and by adding the statement that "God's Word is a Person, not a book." This view is apparently also behind the revising of the 1982 Hymnal (see esp. the revisions to Hymn 632 and the new hymns 629 and 630).

71. Anglican Church of Canada, *Book of Alternative Services* (1985), 9. I find curious Robert Wright's comment ("Official Position," 350) that the ordination oath does not "expressly deny the existence of some further Word or word(s) of

God beyond or above the Sacred Page." If he means to extend this higher authority of other Word/words to matters of salvation, how can scripture contain all things necessary to it?

72. The Episcopal Church's Teaching Series claims: "What we mean by calling the Scriptures authoritative is simply that we know that the church has experienced the presence and power of God through the Bible." R. A. Bennett and O. C. Edwards, *The Bible for Today's Church* (New York: Seabury, 1979), 72. For Philip Culbertson, "Known, Knower, and Knowing: The Authority of Scripture in the Episcopal Church," *ATR* 74 (1992): 172, the common experience is the "constancy of change." For Bishop Spong, *Rescuing the Bible*, 243, it is the call "to love, to live, and to be."

73. Note how the orthodox intention of Charles Gore in the original *Lux Mundi* in asserting the inspiration of the church alongside the inspiration of scripture has become radicalized in the identification of the Holy Spirit and "experience" in the centenary update of his position. D. N. Power, "The Holy Spirit: Scripture, Tradition, and Interpretation," *Keeping the Faith: Essays to Mark the Centenary of Lux Mundi* (Philadelphia: Fortress, 1988), 153.

74. *Evangelical Essentials: A Liberal-Evangelical Dialogue* (Downers Grove: IVP, 1988).

75. Cf. Bartlett, *Shape of Scriptural Authority*, 131-54.

76. Robert Alter points out that not only have ordinary people given up reading, but students of literature have as well. See *The Pleasures of Reading in an Ideological Age* (New York: Simon and Schuster, 1989), 11.

77. St. Augustine (*Confessions* 3.5.9) describes scripture as "a text lowly to the beginner but, on further reading, of mountainous difficulty and enveloped in mysteries." Sternberg's *Poetics* is a tour de force in demonstrating the "key strategy" of biblical discourse: "the art of indirection or, from the interpreter's side, the drama of reading" (pp. 43-44).

78. Richard B. Hays, *Echoes of Scripture in the Letters of Paul* (New Haven: Yale University Press, 1989), 178-92, has shown how this method underlies Paul's reading of the Old Testament in the light of Christ. George Herbert enunciates the classic Reformation principle, based on 1 Cor. 2:13, in his second sonnet on "The Holy Scriptures": "This verse marks that, and both do make a motion/Unto a third, that ten leaves off doth lie."

79. Cranmer's sense of "digesting" scripture surely reflects the precritical assumption, as explained by Hans Frei, *The Eclipse of Biblical Narrative: A Study in Eighteenth and Nineteenth Century Hermeneutics* (New Haven: Yale University Press, 1974), 3, that "since the world truly rendered by combining biblical narratives into one was indeed the one and only real world, it must in principle embrace the experience of any present age and reader." In like fashion, Herbert can go on to say in his scripture sonnet: "Such are thy secrets, which my life makes good,/And comments on thee: for in ev'rything/Thy

words do find me out, and parallels bring . . . "

80. Cf. David T. Shannon, "'An Ante-Bellum Sermon': A Resource for an African American Hermeneutic," in *Stony the Road We Trod: African American Biblical Interpretation*, ed. C. H. Felder (Minneapolis: Fortress, 1991), 98-123.

81. I know of no more convincing demonstration of this truth than Chana Bloch's eloquent exposition of George Herbert's poetics in *Spelling the Word: George Herbert and the Bible* (Berkeley: University of California Press, 1984), 30-31:
> Writing about Scripture, Herbert sets before us the mind and heart of the Christian who reads and interprets. Precisely where we might expect to find the self humbled and subordinated, we find it instead vigorously at work and conscious of its own motions in bringing the text to life. . . . The delighted play of the mind, so characteristic of *The Temple*, belies Stanley Fish's picture of Herbert, martyrlike, building his poetry into a pyre of self-immolation. In Herbert's poetry the self is not effaced but improved.

82. See Colin Brown, *Miracles and the Critical Mind* (Grand Rapids, Mich.: Eerdmans, 1984); and Gary Habermas and Anthony Flew, *Did Jesus Rise from the Dead? The Resurrection Debate* (San Francisco: Harper, 1987).

83. Raymond Brown's *The Virginal Conception and Bodily Resurrection of Jesus* (New York: Paulist, 1973), sums up the evidence from historical criticism.

84. See Childs, *The New Testament as Canon*, 157-65.

85. Karl Barth, *CD* 2.1.207; P. E. Hughes, *The True Image: The Origin and Destiny of Man in Christ* (Grand Rapids, Mich.: Eerdmans, 1989), 213-23.

86. The charge of illegitimacy was of course raised by Jesus' opponents (John 8:41). See the tendentious revival of this case argued by Jane Schaberg in *The Illegitimacy of Jesus: A Feminist Theological Interpretation of the Infancy Narratives* (San Francisco: Harper, 1987).

87. Cf. Bishop Spong, *Rescuing the Bible*, 217, for the *ex cathedra* pronouncement of the new orthodoxy: "The virgin birth tradition of the New Testament is not literally true. It should not be literally believed."

88. *Dirt, Greed, and Sex: Sexual Ethics in the New Testament and Their Implications for Today* (Philadelphia: Fortress, 1988).

89. Ibid., 265: "The few pertinent verses in Genesis 1 and 2, for example, are brief and allusive in their language, which leaves them open to a variety of speculative interpretations." By not beginning in the beginning, he fails to see the natural law logic behind the purity code and behind Hebrew marriage and family law, a logic that Mary Douglas calls "keeping distinct the categories *of creation*" (my italics); *Purity and Danger: An Analysis of Concepts of Pollution and Taboo* (London: Routledge, 1966), 53.

90. Cf. H. W. House, ed., *Divorce and Remarriage: Four Christian Views* (Downers Grove: IVP, 1990).

91. "Relations Natural and Unnatural: A Response to John Boswell's Exegesis of

Romans 1," *Journal of Religious Ethics* 14 (1986): 184-215.

92. "Awaiting the Redemption of Our Bodies," *Sojourners* (July 1991): 17-21.

93. Cf. *Issues in Human Sexuality: A Statement by the House of Bishops of the General Synod of the Church of England, December 1991* (Harrisburg, Pa.: Morehouse, 1991). This report certainly takes the first step in identifying the "ultimate biblical consensus" about monogamy and celibacy (p. 18), and it refuses to grant homosexual practice the status of a "parallel or alternative form of human sexuality" (p. 40). Where the report falters (p. 41) is in granting autonomy to individual conscience over the clear teaching of scripture, thus selling short the transforming power of grace.

THE SCRIPTURES IN THE LIFE OF THE CHURCH

Richard A. Norris, Jr.

1. The writings or "scriptures" collected in the Old and New Testaments have a pre-eminent place in the life of the church. They are called simply "*the* books" (*ta biblia*, whence the English "Bible"); and this phraseology quite deliberately sets them apart from all other books. They are *the* books because they can be trusted to evoke, nurture, and structure the life of faith—the life in which, through the power of the Spirit, people discover themselves "in Christ" as children of God. They are seen to provide, and indeed to constitute, "an entry into [God's] heavenly Kingdom."[1]

Naturally enough, then, the scriptures stand at the center of the ordinary, day-to-day, and week-to-week life of the church. They—and normally they alone—are read out in Lord's Day assemblies of the church, and not merely read out but also, where preachers understand their calling, expounded. They are the subjects of intense study, both in academic and in congregational settings. They may even be read and pondered privately in the home, by individuals or by familial groups, though this is a custom less commonly observed than it once was.

The perception of the scriptures and their significance that is embodied in such practices has traditionally been expressed in a series of powerful metaphors. The scriptures are designated "Word of God."[2] They are described as "in-breathed," inspired, by the Holy Spirit.[3] They are said to have God as their Author.[4] "The Books," then, are experienced and conceived as *media through which God communicates with believers*; and in this respect, perhaps, they are not unlike sacraments, with the difference that the "sign" (*sacramentum*), in the case of the scriptures, is constituted solely by written words.

2. One might suppose, given these traditional practices and beliefs, that most questions about the status and use of the scriptures had long since been settled. In fact, of course, that is not—and, it might be added, never has been—the case. Differences about the canonical *status* of the various books of the Bible began in the church with the very process by which the canon was formed, and they have

continued without intermission up to the present day. Issues concerning the use and interpretation of the scriptures are, by the same token, as old as the writings of the New Testament itself.[5] They have been argued at great length in every age,[6] and they have arisen in concrete and practical form in connection with every controversy, doctrinal or moral, in which Christians have engaged. Christians, it seems, have always agreed that the scriptures are authoritative and just as regularly disagreed about how to read and how to render them.

On reflection, however, this circumstance is neither odd nor even paradoxical. The passion and zealous precision with which believers have argued over the meaning(s) of the scriptures represent not a denial but an affirmation of the Bible's authority, just as the authority of the Constitution of the United States of America is not questioned but established in the unending debates about *how* it should be read and *what* its deliverances imply for present practice. In both cases, such debates presuppose, even while they obscure, the existence of a society or community whose understanding of itself and its world—of "the way things work"—is and has been shaped by the "mind" embodied in its foundational document or documents. To be sure, internalization of this sort is always a matter of degree. Each new issue that arises elicits doubts about the seriousness or fidelity with which church or commonwealth has appropriated the "truth" about itself and its identity that is represented by Bible or by Constitution. Such doubts, however, and the acerbic debates they evoke reflect and in the end confirm the normative status of the writing or writings in question.

In this brief essay, accordingly, I will not concern myself with the question whether the scriptures of the Old and New Testaments ought to have authority in the churches of Christ. I assume that such a question is pointless. I assume that scripture and church are strictly correlative in the sense (a) that the Bible exists, as a set of scriptures called "sacred," only in and for the church, and (b) that the church is recognizable as church only through its engagement with, and responsiveness to, the message that the scriptures definitively convey. This is not to say that the scriptures cannot be read or understood outside the church, or that the truth embodied in the scriptures cannot be otherwise conveyed (else why are there preachers and commentaries, not to mention a whole corps of systematic theologians?). It is merely to say that Bible and church produce each other—that, historically speaking, the emergence of the church and the emergence of its scriptures go hand in hand. One cannot say what the church is apart from reference to the Bible, and one cannot say what the Bible is apart from reference to the church: they are to each other as chicken and egg.

The problem to be addressed here, then, is a secondary one. Granted that the scriptures are foundational for the church (and vice versa), how are we to understand the way in which "the Books" *function* in the life of Christian communities? By phrasing the question in this way, I mean to set aside the method of arguing by way of deduction from traditional confessional statements—for example, "The Bible is the Word of God," or "The scriptures are divinely inspired." As a way of evolving a theory of scriptural authority, this method has not proved very successful in the past, and for good reason. Such confessional propositions are not only rich and ambiguous in meaning (as all serious metaphors are); they are also derivative. They do not represent the starting points, or premises, of reflection on the status and function of the scriptures. Rather, they represent established transcriptions of the fruit of such reflection: useful because they are summary catchwords. As centuries of argumentation have clearly enough shown, however, when such confessional statements are asserted in splendid dogmatic isolation, their implication is neither clear nor distinct. What they signify can only be gathered by reference to their contextual matrix, that is, to the experience and the practice out of which they have grown. One must begin, then, by asking *what* the scriptures are, *how* they function in the church, and *in what way* their burden is conveyed and received.

3. The first of these questions—that of *what the scriptures are*—is at heart a question about the genre of the Bible, and it turns out to be a puzzling one to answer. Where the Constitution of the United States is concerned, it is easy enough to identify what it is: a legal document that dictates fundamental procedures and rules for the government of a federal commonwealth. In the case of the Christian scriptures, no such quick response is available. One can say with assurance that they have habitually been read as the bearers of "revelation" from God, but this cannot be taken as an account of their genre. The New Testament, for example, contains only one book that explicitly claims to convey a revelation—the Apocalypse of John;[7] and its claim to a place in the canon was long disputed on doctrinal grounds.

3.1. The nature of the problem here becomes manifest when one recalls something I have already noted: that the term "Bible" is an unfortunate English rendering of the Greek phrase *ta biblia*—unfortunate because it conceals the fact that *biblia* is a plural noun. The phrase in question means "the books" (maybe even "the bibles"). The fact that since the advent of the printing press these books have usually been bound together in a single volume should not be allowed to obscure the fact that the Bible is not a single work, like the Koran, but a *collection* of books, a small, relatively convenient library. The widespread, though often unconscious, assumption that "the Bible" is a single book (and, one might add, a single book that speaks in *our language*) must therefore be set aside consciously and deliberately. The scriptures in the translated form in which we normally read them are attempts to *interpret*, in a language different from that in which they are written, approximately sixty-six distinct writings.[8]

Taken precisely as a collection of books, these writings answer to a fairly wide range of interests, as any decent library must. The ordinary reader who comes upon this small but select collection finds not only some first-class fiction, but also songs, love poetry, letters, law-codes, large swathes of tendentious history, a great deal of historically based legend, political tracts, preaching—and more. The books that make up the Bible, in other words, are not of one genre: they represent many different kinds of writing, which answer to many different needs and tastes; and some of these genres— prophetic oracles, for example, and gospels—are otherwise unfamiliar to modern readers.

What is more, the writings this library contains were set down, as far as one can tell, over a period of a millennium or more. They respond, therefore, to a wide variety of problems and circumstances, from many different points of view. Thus they reflect a broad spectrum of history and of experience. Their variety lies not only in their literary forms but also in the concrete situations and experiences that they presuppose, interpret, and address. Naturally enough, then, these works not infrequently differ, at once in the assumptions they make and in the outlooks, teachings, and values they convey. James is not entirely at one with Paul on the subject of the value of "works." John differs from Mark about the chronology of Jesus' last days. The laws of Leviticus breathe a somewhat different spirit from those of Deuteronomy. The poem of Job deliberately questions some of the fundamental beliefs expressed in Proverbs.

3.2. It is pointless, then, to ask about the genre of the Bible if by "Bible" one means "book" in the singular. The question is not "What kind of book?" but "What kind of library?" And when the question is put in this form, one can begin to see more clearly what sort of thing the scriptures are.

To begin with, it is plain that the collection itself, whether in its Jewish or its Christian form, has a certain *skopos*, as early Christian exegetes regularly insisted: a certain logic, a certain aim, and hence a certain dominant subject-matter. One evidence of this is the fact that from beginning to end these writings build on, comment on, revise, criticize, and generally echo one another. Chronicles redoes Kings. Paul presents a critical rereading of the Abraham epic, in the interests of his Gentile mission,[9] and in this he follows the examples of Isaiah and Ezekiel, both of whom had recalled the story of Abraham, though to quite inconsistent ends.[10] The gospels of Matthew and Luke in effect comment on Mark and set about the business of improving on it. All these writings are part of an ongoing conversation, then, a conversation spanning many generations, in which new circumstances compel thoughtful folk ever and again to rehearse and reinterpret its earlier stages.

Nor is this a merely desultory or unfocused conversation. It has a clear and persistent theme: the relationship of a continuing community or communities to the divine Agent who calls and gathers them. The focal interest of these writings is a people's engagement with the God of Abraham, Isaac, and Jacob—the very God who, in "the fulness of time," not only "sent forth his Son" (Gal. 4:4), but "glorified his child Jesus" (Acts 3:13) by raising him from the dead. Their burden, their *skopos*, is in this sense *theological*.

The scriptures then may well be, on the one hand, almost bafflingly *various*—in their literary forms, in their locations in time and space, in the particular problems and circumstances they address, and in the points of view they adopt; but on the other hand, they maintain a singular unity of purpose in their concern to *attest* and to *interpret* the experiences, events, and persons through which God has called, led, judged, graced, and saved a community of faith. The person who reads them may well—and quite naturally— become fascinated by one or more of the trees that constitute this little forest: by the narrative structures of the stories in Genesis, say, or by the odd personality of the prophet Ezekiel or the apostle Paul, or by the historical problems that the gospels raise. The forest, however, cannot be ignored. The collection as a whole, and not just its individual parts, stands as an invitation to read one's own life in the light of the scriptures' witness: that is, to join, as a reader and interpreter, the conversation with God and about God that they embody, and in doing so to accept its premises. Thus one becomes a part of the broad community of faith that their message generates.

3.3. It will not do, however, to speak in these merely general terms about the genre of the scriptures. This library exists only because there were specific communities that found its books uniquely rewarding for their understanding of themselves and their problems. It was in the communities that repeatedly and habitually referred to these writings that the books were treasured and transmitted. Moreover, such was their sense of the value of these testimonies that—not unlike people who refinish a treasured piece of furniture or redo such a film as *Casablanca* in color—they also occasionally annotated them with precious comments, and here and there rewrote, re-edited, or supplemented them to bring them up to date. In some cases, they supplied them with what amount to interpretative introductions or appendices. And by the time all this was done, it was no great problem to make, as it were, catalogues of the best-sellers, and even to classify them in a regular order, so that every local assembly of the people might be perfectly clear what books were at once essential for its library and suitable for public reading and exposition. This centuries-long process—in which editing, explicating, and canonizing[11] blend into a single continuum—gave the scriptures a specific logic as well as a general theme. The conversation, one might say, went somewhere, as generation after generation made its contribution; and one cannot say what the scriptures are without noticing where this conversation went.

3.3.1. When New Testament writers refer to "the scriptures," what they mean is of course the library normally treated as authoritative in early Judaism, whose contents were catalogued under the headings of Law, Prophets, and Writings. In the time of Jesus and Paul, the contents (if not always the text) of the first two of these three subcollections were already fixed, by a consensus that had grown up over a period of four centuries or so. The texts in question, then, were texts that had already established themselves, through long usage and devout interpretation, as rich and reliable sources for Israel's understanding of itself and its relation to God. What the process of canonization ultimately effected was, from one point of view, simply a prohibition against the further incorporation of commentary on the texts into the texts themselves. It was this prohibition that established them as books which "defile the hands,"[12] and as an unchanging witness to God's historical way with Israel.

The early Christians, most of whom, to start with, were Jews anyhow, were not aware that they were in the business of founding a new religion. To them, the Law, the Prophets, and the Writings attested the ways and the will of the same God who had brought them to faith in Christ; and in the second-century controversy occasioned by the teaching of Marcion, they explicitly reaffirmed this stance. What distinguished them from other followers of the God of Abraham was that they took the ministry, death, and resurrection of Christ as a definitive, because divine, comment on the Law and the Prophets. That is to say, they took their own experience of God in Christ as the hermeneutical key to the scriptures. Hence they treated the Mosaic covenant as prefatory to, or anticipatory of, the new covenant with God which they had entered at baptism. It is also true, of course, that they tended to follow the practice of Hellenistic synagogues and to read the scriptures in the Greek translation of the Septuagint, which they, like many Jews, regarded as inspired in its own right; and for this reason, the canon of the Mosaic covenant came in Christian circles to differ from the Hebrew scriptures both in its ordering[13] and, though marginally, in its content.[14] More important for our present purposes, however, is the fact that it came to differ in its *function*, and thus to become, as "the Old Testament," a different *sort* of collection—that is, to do a different job.

3.3.2. What that job was—and is—is defined by the New Testament, the collection in which the churches of the second and later centuries discerned the authentic distillation of what I have called "their own experience of God in Christ," and which, for them, defined the logic of the entire library called "scripture."

It is not our business here to rehearse the long and complex story of how the official collections of local Christian communities came more and more to coincide. The important thing is to see what such a library of the New Covenant was meant to do; and the fullest answer to that question comes from Irenaeus of Lyon, one of the first writers to accord certain Christian writings a status approximating that of the Law and the Prophets. Irenaeus's "New Testament"[15] included as a central core the Four Gospels (though this list was still a matter of debate), the Pauline corpus,[16] and the Acts of the Apostles.[17] He judged that these books were uniquely valuable because they contained *in written form* the testimony of the apostles or their immediate disciples. These apostolic persons,[18] he insisted, are the sole authentic source of "the teaching of the Son of God," which is "the Gospel," "the Truth," "the divine scheme [*oikonomia*] of our salvation."[19] The books of the New Covenant, then, are marked off by their *subject matter* ("the Gospel," "the scheme of salvation") and by their *source* (the apostles or their immediate disciples). Furthermore, Irenaeus thinks that since the original bearers of the kerygma did not preach or write until after the church had received the gift of the Spirit at Pentecost, they were "inspired" by the same Spirit that now dwells in the church.

Clearly, then, one of the functions of this library of "apostolic" writings was *to guarantee the authenticity of the church's teaching,* that is, to assure that the message conveyed in the church's catechesis was the original Gospel on which the community of the New Covenant is founded, and not some other. For that reason, the list of writings that emerged was not a list of "inspired" books: if anything is clear it is that the early church regarded many works as inspired which it could not count as apostolic. Furthermore, it is not a list simply of writings that in some fashion convey the Gospel (Irenaeus, e.g., thought his own writings, not to mention the apostolic "Rule of Truth," did that). Rather it is a collection of the written forms of teaching traditions that were rooted in, and emerged out of, the life of the first-century communities and were in that sense "apostolic." The library thus incorporated a variety of traditions, and in consequence of that fact did not speak with a single voice. The churches even admitted that there were four differing versions of the apostolic Gospel—those "according to" Matthew, Mark, Luke, and John; and this in spite of the fact that they understood the Gospel to be one. The list that ultimately emerged, therefore, presented a broad and variegated spectrum of witness and teaching, and required in effect that the several traditions be read side by side, and so as complementing and correcting each other. The late R.P.C. Hanson was entirely justified in his judgment that "the New Testament constitutes, *as a collection,* [a] unique historical witness to the life and career of Christ and to the earliest, primitive Christianity";[20] but it needs to be added that this witness, like that of the Jewish scriptures, comes in the form of a *conversation* and not of a straightforward, perfectly self-consistent declaration—and indeed that it comes as a contribution to, and a comment on, that earlier conversation to which it is subjoined as conveying the substance of a *new* covenant.

3.4. The Christian scriptures, then, are a diversified library with a long and complex literary history, whose contents reflect a people's conversation with God and about God as that conversation was conducted in a variety of different places and times. Furthermore, the conversation it reflects has a direction and an issue: it goes somewhere or, better, arrives somewhere. And the "where" that it attains is the good news embodied in the ministry, death, and resurrection of Jesus Christ, as attested in four "gospels," the letters treasured by the "schools" of Paul and John, and other such writings. It is from the vantage-point, then, of this Gospel that the churches read and pondered the records of the conversation's earlier stages. They envisaged what they called the scriptures of the *Old* Covenant as showing, so to speak, how things got to the point of Christ—how God brought the conversation along to the point where the divine contribution to it, the divine Word, became flesh. They were, to be sure, visibly embarrassed by some of the stories and characterizations of God in the Jewish scriptures: Marcionite polemic was not, after all, without a certain plausibility. They also thought much of the legislation in the books of Moses superfluous or transitory ("ceremonial" prescriptions, for example, or moral pronouncements they considered dubious, like "an eye for an eye"[21]). But they also judged that the Old Testament reflected a people's engagement with the very same God who had raised Jesus Christ from the dead; and therefore they looked to it to illumine their experience of Christ, even as they took Christ to be the key to an understanding of it.[22] Taken as a whole, then, the Christian scriptures are by their history and form just what Martin Luther, in a nice figure, asserted them to be: the cradle of Christ.

4. With this account in mind, we can begin to approach our second question: that of *how* the scriptures function—or, to put it in slightly different terms, how they convey their message. Clearly, they do so by the use of words or language. But human language works in many different ways and to many different ends. We have to ask, therefore, in what mode or modes the language of the scriptures operates; and to answer this question, there are some preliminary matters that demand attention.

4.1. The late F. D. Maurice was wont to argue that far too many people mistook the true character of Christian faith by confusing faith with assent to a set of ideas. In fact he was given to accusing some of his contemporaries of derailing the church by substituting theologies or doctrines—"systems," as he put it—for God. This conviction was almost an obsession with him, and no doubt he let his mind dwell upon it with too exclusive a passion; but his insight was an important one in his own time and is, I suspect, an equally important one for ours. Christian faith and life can be, as we say, "accessed" by inspecting people's beliefs; but they *consist* in a concrete relationship to God, a relationship enabled and determined by God in Christ and actualized through the power of the Spirit. Inasfar, then, as the scriptures in the providence of God serve this relationship and nourish it, inasfar as their message is constitutive and foundational in the life of the church, they must in the first instance be conceived as a *medium* through which this relationship can occur.

They may in the process tell people useful things *about* God, but that is not their primary job. The scriptures are not a theological, moral, or even historical databank, but a *medium of communication* between two parties.

This distinction is a crucial one. By using the image of a "conversation," I have already suggested that what is going on in the scriptures is what one might call a many-sided *communicative exchange*, in the course of which change of mind and of life occur (a thing that not infrequently happens in conversations); and while this is no doubt very much a *human* conversation, there is, undergirding and evoking this human talk, a relationship in which God too appears as one who has something to say—in which God is objectified as a *word for us*. This word, reflected in human accounts of it and responses to it, initiates and sustains the conversation.

Now plainly there is, in this image of conversation or communicative exchange, a possible clue to the way in which the scriptures count as "revelation," or as "Word of God." This image, however, which stresses the communicative function of words and language, has, in the mind of every individual who has been schooled in a modern Western culture, a serious rival. That rival image does not question the assertion that language occurs, as it were, between people or that its function is to convey meaning from one speaker to another; and in that sense, it does not deny that language is communicative. But the rival image is not much *interested* in what goes on between people. It is interested almost exclusively in the relationship between what is said and "the world" that is, "the object-world." Language is envisaged solely from the point of view of what it tells (someone) *about* something; and it is valued exclusively for its "accuracy."[23] Speaker and hearer quietly fade from the picture (even though, as we know from experience, the truth of a statement can depend on who is talking and who is listening). And anyone who, consciously or unconsciously, thinks of language in these terms will see the scriptures as "revelatory" precisely to the degree that they convey freestanding "correct information" *about* something.

The trouble with this rival view, as I have called it, is not that it is wrong but that it is narrow in the sense of being specialized. As an ideal of language, it has been fostered by the interest of modern science in the prediction and control of nature (not excluding human nature). As such, however, it is not well suited to the needs of theology, since on the one hand God—and this, surely, explains one of the principal factors in modern "atheism"—is *ex hypothesi* not an "object" open to human prediction and control, and, on the other hand, God graces human beings with responsive freedom in their relationship to their creator and redeemer.[24] Our language *about* God, then, must be understood in the broader context of what I have called "communicative exchange." Just as one might be told a great deal *about* a person, but would not claim to *know* the person until one had, as we say, "met" her, so the scriptures, whatever they may tell us or enable us to infer *about* God, become revelatory of God inasfar as they enable us to be *engaged* with God. They convey what they convey by being a medium of communication.

4.2. It becomes important, then, to understand, if only in a superficial and preliminary way, what goes on and how language functions in a situation of communicative exchange—a situation in which, by engaging one another, people share themselves with and reveal themselves to one another.

The first thing to say in this connection is that communicative exchange is a matter of more than words. For the most part, when people hear "language," they think "words"; and this is surely not incorrect. On the other hand, from time to time we catch ourselves saying, in high metaphorical style, that "actions speak louder than words," and we concede therewith that human beings use media other than words to tell about themselves—that "language" names a category which includes more than speech. Furthermore, it is not only people's observable deeds that reveal them, it is also their gestures and expressions and posture: what we have learned to call "body-language." In any engagement or exchange between two people, it is always their *bodies* that convey who they are and what they mean; for even words and deeds are, in the end, a kind of body-language. There can be no such thing as a "disembodied" communicative exchange.

For meaning to be communicated, however, a second element is required. Communicative exchange, when it happens, comes about in and through a delicate and complex process of *interpretation*. Suppose that *A* says to *B*, "It is raining outside." This is a piece of objective information. In a communicative exchange, however, it will almost certainly convey, and thus mean, much more than it says. For example, what *B hears* may be a proposal ("Let's not go out after all"), or a reminder ("Don't forget your umbrella"), or even a demand ("You owe me five dollars"—with tacit allusion to a bet made the day before). Since each of these interpretations is possible in the abstract, *B* in effect has to *render* the words spoken in the light of a whole host of other contextual factors, not excluding past circumstances (e.g., the bet that was made, or the speaker's known phobia about getting wet) or past conversations. If the interpretation *B* arrives at fits, though, something more than information ("It is raining outside") has been shared: *B* knows *A* better and shares *A*'s world more fully. Indeed, should *B*, a day or so later, report this exchange to *C*, the report might well run like this: "*A* is so afraid of getting wet that he wouldn't go to the movies with me yesterday." This of course is not an *accurate* account of what was said (namely, "It is raining outside"), for the account incorporates the interpretation; but it may well be a *true* account of what transpired—though, to be sure, only from *B*'s point of view. A third party might well wonder whether *B* was correct, since what was seen and heard did not necessitate this interpretation but merely evoked it.

On the other hand, *B* may misinterpret the situation: *A* may just have been thinking out loud, with no particular intention of conveying anything to *B* or to anyone else (although people who dreamily think out loud are surely revealing themselves in that act). And this risk of misinterpretation is real, not merely because people are not infallible in the assessments they make of others' language, but also because *A*'s words and behavior are genuinely susceptible of being taken in more than one way. Fortunately, however, it is often possible to resolve such ambiguity, or to compensate for one's limitations as an assessor, by recollection of past experience of the same person; or alternatively, by *continuing* the conversation in order to clarify what *A* was trying to get across ("Are you saying . . . ?"). By the same token, appeal might be made to the common wisdom distilled from others' experience of *A* ("That nut will sacrifice *anything* to keep from getting wet!"). "Getting with" someone through his or her "language" is a chancy business, then, but we manage it with reasonable success most of the time. The odd thing is that in such a conversational process even mistakes can become vehicles of better and deeper understanding, since the engagement is real even when the language is partially misinterpreted. *A*'s words, after all, were *meant* for *B* (and not for a neutral third party), and thus they inevitably embodied and reflected *A*'s understanding of *B*: interpretation is a two-way street.

For present purposes, though, the point of all this is to underscore how language—in the broad sense I defined just above—works in situations of communicative exchange. Taking a lead from some suggestions of Karl Rahner,[25] we can say that language in such instances functions as a *symbol*, which is to be distinguished from a mere sign. A mere sign simply points to what it designates, like a Social Security number or a description. "Symbol," as Rahner understood it, means rather a sign that is constituted by an act of self-expression: that is to say, a sign through which an agent is *present,* or which is an agent's "putting" of itself. It *bodies* the agent *forth* (Rahner sees the human body as, in this sense, the self's symbol[26]) and is the mode of its presence, its accessibility. There is, then, a certain identity between the symbol and the reality it conveys: to deal with the one is to deal with the other. On the other hand, there is a real difference between them: the symbol is the presence of something that also exceeds and escapes it. And the fact that there is a difference of this sort means that *the symbol does not convey its reality automatically.* One can get it wrong.

Indeed—and this point is not an unimportant one—a person can very well doubt whether something that is seen or heard or touched, something that "occurs" within the range of someone's awareness, really *is* a symbol in this sense, that is, the communicative act of an agent who is "bodied forth" in this occurrence. The behaviorist school in psychology, for example, in effect denies that the behavior of the human body can be taken as symbolic. Classical psychoanalysis, on the other hand, has vigorously affirmed this proposition. Even psychoanalysis, though, acknowledges that there is a way—in its case a long and devious way[27]—to be traveled from the symbol to the reality it conveys. Human language—that is, human behavior, verbal and nonverbal— reveals the self only to the degree that it is engaged, through dialogue, in a process that opens it up for interpretation. In other words, the symbol functions as symbol only in extended and reiterated conversation, where it interprets even as it is interpreted. In such a situation, however, the symbol conveys its reality *even though, at any specifiable point in the dialogue, the process of interpretation is incomplete.*

4.3. If, then, the scriptures are to be conceived primarily as a medium of communication, as I have suggested, and if their human language works in its normal way, then that language must be taken as *symbolic* in the sense I have just indicated. "Symbolic" here is not, I must add instantly, opposed to "literal," or intended to convey that all the language of the Bible is figurative or poetic, which is simply false. Rather it characterizes the way in which *any* language, literal or figurative, verbal or nonverbal, functions in a situation of communicative exchange: namely, as rendering present or conveying, but always through an ongoing process of interpretation, a reality that shapes and informs it but with which it is not simply identical. It remains to see what this may imply for an understanding of the particular case of the scriptures.

4.3.1. In that connection, the very first thing to be said amounts to no more than a statement of something obvious—but so obvious that it tends, in discussions of the role of the scriptures, to be forgotten. *The primary medium of believers' engagement with God is Christ.* This, I take it, is what was in the back of Luther's mind when he called the scriptures the cradle of Christ; and the Apostle conveys the same idea by characterizing "Christ Jesus the human person" as the "one mediator between God and human beings" (1 Tim. 2:5). To put the same thing in other terms: believers' engagement with God, within the covenant created in baptism, comes about in and through Christ; for "grace and truth," as John says, are conveyed through the "flesh" that the Word of God has become.[28]

This Johannine proposition invites us to regard Jesus, as "rendered" in things he did, things he said, and things that happened to him, as the primary *language*—and thus as the primary *symbol*—in which the Word of God is present for us. It may be true, as *The Thirty-Nine Articles of Religion* aver, that God is "without body";[29] but God makes Jesus of Nazareth in his life, death, and resurrection a "body" in and through which our humanity engages its creator and redeemer—makes him, that is, the Mediator, the focal medium of divine revelation. The incarnation, viewed from this angle, is a divine act of symbolization. No doubt there are, and have been, other such acts: the liberation of the Hebrews from their Egyptian bondage; the oracles of the prophets; the sacraments of the New Covenant—even, perhaps, on occasion, certain sermons. When, therefore, the church describes the scriptures as "Word of God," this means that they too—the human writings that constitute the church's official library—are a *symbol* in this sense. It must be clear, however, that they, like the sacraments or the individual prophetic oracles they contain, are symbols of the second order: symbols that give access to the primary symbol of Christian faith, Christ. It is, then, *not alongside Christ but as bodying Christ forth* that these other symbols are recognized and encountered as such. It is as their language brings into focus the mystery of humankind with God in Christ that the scriptures are "Word of God." They are, to employ an ancient terminology, the *letter* (= symbol) of which that mystery is the *spirit* (= reality).

4.3.2. It must be made clear, however, what the point of the metaphor "Word of God" is. It does not intend to say that God "wrote" the words of the Bible, or even "dictated" them, if those expressions are taken either (a) to deny that the scriptures must be read as documents composed in the ordinary fashion by human beings, or (b) to assert that to understand the letter is automatically to grasp (and be grasped by) the spirit.

In the first place, since the activity of God is not empirically accessible, there is and there can be no evidence to show that anyone but a human being composed any book of the Bible. That, I take it, is the explanation of Calvin's insistence that "they who strive to build up firm faith in scripture through disputation are doing things backwards."[30] The symbol that the scriptures constitute is a set of human writings. One cannot *show* that they body forth the Word of God, any more than one can *show* that human utterance in general, or some particular human gesture, has the nature of a symbol. That fact, if it is a fact, is discerned only *in* a certain kind of interpretative engagement: or, to use Calvin's language, it takes "pure eyes and upright senses" and the interior "testimony of the Spirit" to see the scriptures as the medium of divine revelation. One has to be engaged in the conversation that the scriptures record; and it is always possible, and not unreasonable, to read the scriptures without actually being engaged in that conversation.

In the second place, if "what is revealed" is God-in-Christ or God-with-us, it is absurd to suggest that there can be a simple identity between that revelation and the lexical meaning of any particular set of words. The mystery of God cannot be reduced to human words; it can only be rendered accessible through them, that is, conveyed symbolically by them. People, as we know, often have a hard time getting each other straight, for the good enough reason that their words and gestures are inadequate to what they convey; one can hardly suppose, therefore, that the case would be different with the Word and Wisdom of God. As the record of a human conversation about God and a reflection of human engagement with God, the scriptures are a "glass" in which people "see" indeed, but "darkly" for all that—even if the glass be assiduously cleaned and polished.[31]

The fact is, then, that the expression "Word of God," when applied to these writings, is a metaphor.[32] And the function of this metaphor is to invite and enable us to *see* the scriptures as *symbol,* and not only as symbol but as a symbol in and through which people can enter into a communicative exchange with God through Christ. Similarly, if the church speaks of the scriptures as divinely inspired, that is because it comes to share God's presence and God's "world" in them and through them—because it experiences them as a means by which God opens out, and includes us in, the divine *oikonomia.*

The problem here is really not much different from the analogous one I noted above in connection with human communication. It is not immediately obvious that the gestures, sounds, and postures of a body other than my own are symbolic: that is, that they are self-expressive acts which serve, or can serve, the purpose of communication. The self that is alleged to be communicating symbolically in these acts is not directly given nor even inferred by strictly logical processes. By the same token one cannot *show* that "the heavens declare the glory of God" (i.e., that they are symbols expressive of their Creator); or that the humanity of Christ is a bodying-forth of the divine Wisdom (i.e., God's saving gesture to us-wards); or that the writings contained in the Bible are a divine self-communication. These things are *apperceived,* as I have said, in a certain kind of interpretative engagement. It is perfectly possible to look at the sky, or to find out some things about Jesus, or to read the Bible, and *not* to perceive them as symbolic realities that open a way from God to us and from us to God. The empirical phenomena do not *require* such interpretation; they are merely open to it. And what this means is that the symbol is never simply identical with what it conveys: the Word of God is *more* than the scriptures.

5. From all this it is, or should be, plain that our third question—about the way in which the burden of the scriptures is conveyed and received—can be answered in a single phrase: by interpretation. In order to see the point of that answer, however, one must dispense with any notion that interpretation means "making something" of what has already been understood. People do not hear or read something, grasp its meaning, and then "interpret" it. Interpretation refers to the whole process by which one comes to understand something that functions as an expressive symbol: whether that be an utterance heard, a text read, a piece of clothing worn, or a set of socially institutionalized forms of behavior. This is the reason why interpretation, under the label "hermeneutics," has become a central concern—perhaps even *the* central concern—of contemporary philosophy, social science, and literary criticism. "Interpretation" names the activity in which human persons construe their world and themselves in relation to it—in which they model themselves and others in the process of communicative exchange.

It goes without saying, then, that there is no space here for any fundamental discussion of the broad theme of interpretation in general. That would require a good deal more than a brief essay. The best that can be done is to comment on certain issues about *biblical* interpretation in the light of our characterization of the scriptures as the *record of a conversation that functions as symbol of God's Word.*

5.1. The first, and perhaps the most important, of these issues has to do with the matter of *context*. By now it should be plain that interpretation is always contextual: to understand something is to make sense of it in the light of its setting. The statement "The cat descended on Robert's back" is, if taken in isolation, ambiguous. "Cat" might refer either to a pet Siamese or to a certain species of whip, and the sense of the statement will appear only when one knows which of these meanings fits either the literary context in which the statement occurs or the other circumstances of the situation it describes. To understand something—in this case a statement—is to *see* how it fits in with what is, or is going on, around it.

Now the scriptures are *writings*; and written words differ from spoken words in two very crucial ways. First, writings completely lack the auditory, tactile, and visual accompaniments of spoken discourse, and I cannot appeal to tone of voice, gesture, or facial expression as clues to their meaning. Second, every written text taken as a whole is continually being displaced and thus has more than one context in time and space. It may have been written (for example) in the fifth century before Christ in a community of exiles in Babylonia, whereas I am reading or translating it in New York City in 1993. How then am I to understand it? Shall I read it *as it speaks to me*—that is, as fitting in with the circumstances, assumptions, values, problems, and hopes that are common to people in my place and time? Or shall I read it *as it spoke to its original readers*? I might, of course, decide that neither of these alternatives is correct, and that I ought to understand the text as it might have made sense to a monk in eleventh-century France. Written texts suffer, then, from a severe case of multiple contextual location, and they are hard to understand—to interpret—for just that reason. In any literary work, the only stable context of any sentence is other sentences in the same text.

To be sure, this problem is not universally felt or experienced. Most people read, and have traditionally read, the scriptures (and not only the scriptures) as if they had come hot off the press just the day before yesterday. Modern readers, then, will understand the Gospels on the tacit assumption that they are rather like obituaries in the *New York Times*, and the opening of Genesis they will take as a contribution to current discussions of the "big bang." In the end, though, this approach breeds difficulties, for the expectations brought to the text are not met. The Gospels seem far too imaginative and inconsistent to qualify as good obituaries; and Genesis does not appear to address, or even to understand, the issues currently being canvassed by astrophysicists.

The ancient solution to this sort of problem was to allegorize the scriptures: to read them as "saying something else." The modern solution, by contrast, consists in acknowledging that the original context of these writings was radically different from the present, and in making a serious effort to understand them as they would have been taken in the settings in which they were first read. This, of course, is the enterprise that is commonly labeled "historical criticism." This discipline, in its several branches and forms, concerned itself first with the historical location of the scriptural writings (date, authorship, purpose) and with the history of their literary composition. In the process it shocked many of the pious by raising questions about the authorship of certain writings and by being blunt about inconsistencies and inaccuracies in the Bible. It went on, further, both to employ the Bible as a source for the reconstruction of ancient history and to employ the cultural, social, and intellectual history of the ancient world as a resource for understanding the texts of the several scriptural writings. Historical criticism, in short, recontextualized the scriptures—reconstrued them as ancient documents.

This process, though, created difficulties of its own. The most serious of them was not the discomfort occasioned by the discovery that historical (or for that matter scientific[33]) accuracy is not the scriptures' strongest suit. Rather it was—and still is—what I would call the *alienation* of the scriptures—a phenomenon that has two dimensions. One effect of historical criticism, with its relocation of the scriptures in the past, is to set the Bible as it were at arm's length, to render its contents difficult of access and the people who speak or figure in its pages foreign. The historical critic's Bible can often evoke in students what amounts to a reaction of xenophobia: "It doesn't speak our language"—an observation that is of course quite true, in spite of the plethora of new, and sometimes tendentious, translations into up-to-date English.

But this is not all. The sense of alienation is also fostered by the historical "method" itself. Any method is like a net. It is designed with the deliberate aim of capturing data that will answer a particular sort of question in a relatively reliable way; but to do this, it allows other sorts of data, relevant to other sorts of questions, to escape through its meshes. Historical method is not equipped to treat mathematical, philosophical, or chemical questions, and neither is it designed to respond to theological questions. This means, though, that historical-critical study of the scriptures must deliberately ignore the very issues with which the scriptures themselves are centrally concerned; and that is more or less exactly what it has done, with the inevitable result that it has seemed to silence the Bible on the very matters in which it (not to mention most of its readers) is directly interested. In this way the scriptures become not merely foreign but religiously irrelevant. They are reduced to the letter, and the spirit is ignored: the symbol is illuminated, but the reality disappears from the student's purview.

5.2. In the very statement of this problem, though, there is the suggestion of a solution, if one takes seriously the characterization of the scriptures as a *conversation*. Extended conversations have *stages*, after all; and what is going on at one stage may reflect circumstances and beliefs that are not operative at another. The historical critic's distancing of the scriptures is not in itself, therefore, the source of the dilemma. Indeed it corresponds to the very character of the scriptures. It is only in virtue of such historical distancing that the scriptures can speak with a voice of their own and thus function in a situation of communicative exchange: one can only *engage* what is truly "other." Naive and uncritical reading of the scriptures, which simply assumes that they say what we expect and want or, if they do not, discards them, is therefore unlikely to let one learn anything from them. The tension between the modern reader's context and that of the original readers is, therefore, a requisite for any communicative function the scriptures may perform.

This tension, however, does not *necessarily* amount to an alienation; and the reason, I suggest, can be found in the fact, which I have deliberately stressed here, that the library of the church's books is the record of *a conversation whose subject matter is common to all the successive participants in it.* The connection between today and yesterday, profoundly different as they may be, lies in the historical course of the conversation itself: in the fact that my questions today, and indeed many of my assumptions, grow out of the way in which that conversation has developed. Its earlier stages, therefore, are not alien to me; and the reconstruction of them by critical methods—a process which is itself a dialogue between present and past—can create, as it were, a common "world" in which the testimony of an Isaiah or of a tale like that of Jonah alters my way of seeing things (including myself) even as it takes on a new dimension of meaning by entering my present. It is when this happens that "interpretation" comes to its (temporary) conclusion. That conclusion does not consist simply in the historical knowledge I have acquired about the symbol, but in my apperception, acknowledgment, and appropriation, through participation in the conversation, of the reality the symbol intends and intimates. The difficulty about historical—and perhaps even literary—criticism is not that it reconstructs the conversation or some phase of it by its own methods and in that way distances it; but that its methods do not encourage its practitioners to join the conversation: that is, to have a concern (perhaps even an ultimate concern) for the subject matter of this communicative exchange.

5.3. What does it mean, though, to characterize this conversation, continued as it is in the very process of interpretation, as "symbol"? Here there may be help to be found in a brief discussion of the problem of interpreting the so-called resurrection narratives in the Gospels. Historical critics, I think, have been much maligned on this score. They have been accused of denying or questioning the resurrection by casting doubt on the accuracy of these narratives. The great majority of them, however, have done no such thing. They have merely called attention to the character of these narratives: that is, to the character of the symbol we are called upon to understand and interpret. And in doing so, whether intentionally or not, they have illuminated the way in which these narratives work.

Two things, in fact, are striking about the resurrection narratives in the Gospels. The first, of course, is their inconsistency, which needs no illustration here, but which requires explanation. The second and more interesting thing is that they are in fact not resurrection narratives at all. None of the Gospels describes, or gives an account of, the resurrection of Jesus. (Indeed if "on the third day in accordance with the Scriptures"[34] is taken as an allusion to Hos. 6:2, the resurrection was probably not, at first, even dated.) What the Gospels provide is differing versions of a tradition that reported encounters between Jesus and his disciples after his death. The earliest form of this tradition is found at 1 Cor. 15:4-8 (which means that its credentials are very early, especially since Paul says that it was *handed down* to him); and Paul's language makes it plain that these encounters were experienced as *revelations*. There is no reason to doubt, then, either that these revelation experiences occurred, or that they were, like most such experiences, at once wonderful and profoundly puzzling.

Given these circumstances, it seems plain that the essential experiential basis of the proclamation, "God raised him from the dead," was not the ambiguous emptiness of a tomb—an *absence*—but the experience of Christ as *living*. Yet "living" in this case meant something a bit different from what it signifies in ordinary usage; and the gospels convey this in two ways. First, they convey it by the paradoxical character of the "appearances" they narrate. Jesus is not around in the ordinary way: rather he is "manifested" from time to time, and rather spookily at that. On the other hand he is portrayed as absolutely real: as tangible and audible, even if hard to recognize at first. D. H. Lawrence, then, when he speculated in a story that the "resurrected" Jesus traveled to Egypt and there married a priestess of Isis and lived contentedly on, was missing the point: the gospel stories do not pretend that Jesus was resuscitated in such wise as to continue leading an ordinary human life. They insist that he, the Jesus they had known, is alive and real, but quite plainly *not* in the same sense or in the same way that one's next-door neighbor is alive and real. And this same point is conveyed in a second, and perhaps clearer, way by the very use of such expressions as "God raised him," or "resurrection." For this language refers to what we may call "eschatological" life: the life of "heaven" or of the Kingdom of God that Jesus had proclaimed.[35]

What then do we mean when we ask whether the resurrection was "physical" or not? What the gospels suggest—and take a great deal of trouble to suggest—is that the life to which Jesus is raised does not fit our normal notions of life. It is not, to use Pauline language, the life of "flesh and blood," but the life of the Spirit, of a "spiritual body."[36] Does this mean then that the resurrection was "spiritual," in the normal modern sense of that term? No; for "spiritual," to us, implies "notional," "quasi-real," whereas for Paul and his friends it connoted reality and power. Well, then, was the resurrection "physical"? No; for that would allow one to infer that it occurred as an event in and of the natural[37] (flesh-and-blood) order, and the Reign of God is not such an event and cannot be described in "secular" terms (i.e., in terms derived from the life of "the present age"). The truth seems to be, then, that the alternative "physical"/"spiritual" itself falsifies the reality that the gospels, with their narratives about the appearances of Jesus, are trying to convey. What they want to say is that in the crucified and risen Jesus the Age to Come has already been actualized: that he is the present reality of the future God is bringing. And this is not an easy thing to convey.

This analysis may suggest—even if it errs at particular points—how the critical *distancing* of a scriptural text can serve the useful purpose of allowing it to "speak," or, as I would prefer to put it, to talk back. More than that, however, it may provide some hints about reading and understanding the Gospels. These books are narratives; and as far as we moderns are concerned, the business of narratives (to put the matter crudely) is to recite *the sorts of things that a CNN camera might have recorded* in the order in which they occurred.

"Interpretation" we want to find elsewhere, perhaps on the op-ed page. The truth is, though, that narratives *are* interpretations: they *show* what something means (as distinct from *telling* what it means) by the way in which they set the story out. The peculiarity of the gospels from a contemporary point of view is that *their normal way of explaining or interpreting is to retell or to vary a story.* To their authors or editors, this meant that the truth, or some aspect of it, was being more fully or more pointedly conveyed. To us, on the contrary, it suggests that consistency, and with it accuracy, are being violated. This may explain why some moderns prefer, on the whole, to read Paul rather than to read the gospels: we prefer to take our editorializing in the form of expository rather than of narrative prose. While the gospels do in fact provide a good deal of useful information, their stories are told to evoke a recognition of *what it all means*: "These are written that you may believe that Jesus is the Christ, the Son of God, and that believing you may have life in his name" (John 20:31).

In the case of the gospels, then, the symbol with which interpretation deals is a conversation about the significance of Jesus conducted by means of theologically framed narrative. Criticism distances these narratives—and it may, of course, use them for purposes other than those for which they were written: for example, for what they can tell us, indirectly and at a significant remove, about life in first-century Palestine. In distancing them, however, it cannot obscure what they convey. This is, to be sure, something that no CNN camera could capture (what would a videotape of "the resurrection" show?); but then there is a great deal that CNN cameras cannot capture, and this is no doubt why their films are always accompanied by what is interestingly called "commentary." The interpreter's business is to *see* the picture of things that the text as symbol opens out: and the final step in that process is to see oneself *in* that picture, which is exactly what John means by the words "that you may believe."

5.4. Understood in this way, the interpretation of the scriptures is a process that never concludes. The conversation that they record is *canonical*—normative and constitutional—in the sense that it is by joining *this* conversation that the Christian community enters into the mystery of humanity-in-Christ—the mystery that the scriptures body forth as symbol. Nevertheless, the process of interpretation *continues* the conversation, and what transpires in this continuation is relevant and indeed necessary to any grasp of the scriptures' burden. The Bible, in other words, does not "speak" in a vacuum. It conveys its message in and through the ongoing life of communities that understand themselves through their rendering of the scriptures. Hence the church reads its Books both in the light of its own established tradition of interpretation, and, at the same time, in the light of fresh problems that arise in the course of its life. The questions and interests that inform the community's reading of the Bible derive, then, from its settled manner of "taking" the scriptures on the one hand, and, on the other, from conflicts engendered in one of two ways: either by dissonances *within* the tradition or, just as frequently, by dissonances between that tradition and the changing cultural and social world that the church inhabits. Such conflicts, moreover, have regularly brought about "turns" in the churches' dialogue with the scriptures—that is, they have compelled reassessments or reappropriations of earlier understandings.

Such a turn occurred, for example, in the whole series of doctrinal controversies set off by Arius in the fourth century—controversies that turned in part on the theological sensibilities of persons formed by a late-antique worldview and in part on the interpretation of such texts as Proverbs 8:22-23. It was through these controversies that the churches explicitly *discerned* and categorically *formulated* their trinitarian account of the God whom believers confess, and with whom they are joined, in the paschal mystery of baptism. In a similar way, Augustine of Hippo's studies of Paul overturned, at least in the West, traditional ways of understanding the apostle's letters and themselves generated a whole "school" of Pauline exegesis, whose approach is a matter of debate even today. In a more contemporary vein, the movement labeled "liberation theology" has reread not only the Exodus narrative, but the prophets and the gospels as well, from the angle of groups whose lack of economic and political power renders them perpetual victims of exploitation in the modern world; and it has found in these scriptural sources a message that summons the churches to bear active witness to God's commitment to justice for those whom "the system" systematically abuses.

Much the same sort of movement can be discerned in Christian interpretation of behavioral injunctions in the scriptures. To be sure, there has always been a regular, almost unvarying bass rhythm in Christian renderings of biblical ethical injunctions. The church has always treasured the Ten Commandments (in spite of its scant respect for Sabbath observance and its regular use of pictures and statues). Indeed it has tended from early on to take them as a particular promulgation of certain elements of "natural law."[38] Similarly, the double commandment of love for God and for neighbor has, especially in the light of Pauline and Johannine emphasis on the centrality of *agapé* in Christian life, provided the basis and the *Leitmotiv* of the churches' ethical teaching. These two foundational commitments, however, have allowed for a not inconsiderable variety in regard to particular issues and in regard to the degree of respect accorded particular biblical admonitions.

For one thing, Christian communities have usually set a high value on the settled (i.e., undebated) customs and "high" moralities of the cultures or subcultures within which they have lived; and they have accordingly tended to take the scriptures as confirming these norms. Monogamy, for example, was more emphatically enjoined in the ancient world by the practice of both Jews and pagans than it was by any scriptural injunction; and the notion that sexual intercourse has procreation as its sole justification derives not from the Bible but from Stoic teaching. By the same token, the early Christians made much—as modern Christians on the whole do not—of scriptural advices in favor of sexual continence and of contempt for property and possessions; and they were generally at home—as, again, modern Christians are not—with Paul's uneasy toleration of the institution of slavery and with the structures of the strict patriarchal household.

Furthermore, in the light of cultural and social circumstance, the church has allowed itself to debate, or to ignore, a variety of the scriptures' moral judgments: on the matter of usury, for example; or on the propriety of believers' allowing their disputes to be adjudicated by secular courts; or on the necessity for bishops to be (once-) married householders. It has also, in the light of teaching that emerges in the New Testament, tended, at one time or another, to pass negative judgment on commandments explicitly stated in the Old: the principle of "the right of the first-born,"[39] for example, or divine injunctions that have seemed to encourage genocide.

None of this is odd, or even very startling. The "mind" with which Christians read the scriptures is inevitably formed by the customs and prepossessions of their culture; conversations *do* take new turns; and reflection on the meaning of the scriptures' conversation taken as a whole is bound to call in question, from time to time, the permanent value of particular moments in it—or to lead, in certain circumstances, to fresh appreciation of their relevance. The point is, though, that it is precisely *the meaning of the scriptures' conversation taken as a whole* that must in the end govern Christian moral reflection. Otherwise, no judgment could be made regarding the many issues to which the scriptures scarcely accord a passing glance, or of which they are ignorant: problems of war and peace, for example; or the sorts of questions raised by contemporary advances in medicine and biology. In focusing its ethical teaching on the Ten Commandments treated as embodying the elements of a "natural" ethic, and on the fundamental injunction of love for God and neighbor, the church has identified an intrascriptural basis for evolving ethical judgments in new situations and for formulating the essential moral content of the new life in Christ in a world where, plainly enough, circumstances *do* alter cases.

5.5. It is perhaps a misfortune that the scriptures deliver the truth with which they seek to involve us only through our own participation in an ongoing process of interpretation. Certainly it is the case that many folk would prefer to treat them as a work of reference in which one can "look up" the answer to any and every question. The trouble is, though, that works of reference, quite apart from the fact that they, too, can be misunderstood, tend to get out of date and to need revision. Indeed it is precisely the habit of reading the scriptures in this manner that makes them *look* out of date.

Fortunately, though, the scriptures do not provide a "system" either of doctrine or of morals. They are a medium of communication, and what they communicate is "God with us" in Christ. Accordingly, the process of interpreting them has as its goal the church's entrance into "the mind of Christ"—that is, a transformation of the way in which Christians see themselves and their world. It is out of the perceptions thus engendered that systems of morals and of doctrine arise.[40] Read in this way, moreover, the scriptures update themselves as they speak their message in ever-changing contexts. The wisdom of the past and the puzzles of the present, in their (often conflicted) dialogue with each other, become focusing devices through which the lineaments of the Word of God can be discerned anew; and to this process the "distancing" work of the critic makes an essential contribution.

The practical problem that churches face in regard to the interpretation of the scriptures comes down to this: they have no institutionalized way of coming to grips with the scriptures *as communities.* The isolated scholar at her desk is no proper model for *ecclesial* interpretation of the scriptures, any more than is the preacher who makes every text a pretext for *his* personal message. To understand in practice what interpretation of the Bible means, the church must find ways of fomenting communal, dialogical—and withal informed— study of the scriptures: and, it might be added, study that is motivated by something deeper than a desire to "find an answer" to the latest burning issue. The best scripturally grounded responses to burning issues will come out of communities that have learned to involve the diverse talents, experiences, and perspectives of a variety of people in regular, ongoing, open-ended study of "the Books," not for the sake of some instant "fix," but for the sake of the Wisdom they attest.

No doubt such a process of interpretation will involve—as it always has, and as it does in its intrascriptural form—moments of disagreement, of reappropriation and reinterpretation, of doubt and puzzlement. There is, as in any relationship of communicative exchange, always more to be learned, and "what we have always said" may on occasion seem merely partial or inadequate. But then the function of the scriptures is not to answer every question ahead of time with perfect clarity and adequacy (the fact that the scriptures "contain all things necessary to salvation" does not imply that they are omnicompetent: rather the contrary). It is to open the believer up to the depths of the mystery of Christ—which in the end *raises* as many questions for us as it answers. "Now we see through a glass darkly," and "then" is yet to come. But at least one knows where to keep looking and who it is with whom one is dealing.

NOTES

1. *Geneva Catechism*, 300.
2. See *The Book of Common Prayer* (1979), 526, 853. Calvin (*Institutes* 1.6.1) presses the metaphor and speaks of scripture as "a special gift, where God, to instruct the church . . . opens his own most hallowed lips."
3. *The Book of Common Prayer* (1979), 853: "under the inspiration of the Holy Spirit." Cf. 2 Tim. 3:16 (*theopneustos*: "God-breathed"), with reference to the Jewish scriptures; and Origen, *On First Principles* 1.*praef*.8 ("The Scriptures were written through the Spirit of God").
4. See, e.g., *The Westminster Confession of Faith* 1.4; and Calvin, *Institutes* 1.7.1.
5. See, e.g., Mark 2:23ff., 7:1-13; 1 Cor. 10:11.
6. See—to take account only of a few well-known works of the relatively distant past—Justin Martyr, *Dialogue with Trypho*; Origen, *On First Principles* 4.1-3; Augustine, *On Christian Instruction*; Hugh of St Victor, *On the Sacraments*; Huldreich Zwingli, *On the Clarity and Certainty of the Word of God.*
7. The apostle Paul also claims to have received at least two revelations (Gal. 1:12; 2 Cor. 12:2-4), but his letters are not accounts of them.
8. This is a minimal reckoning: it excludes books counted as deuterocanonical by Article VI of *The Thirty-nine Articles of Religion.*
9. See Romans 4 and Gal. 3:6-9, 15-18; and contrast Luke 3:8.
10. See Isa. 51:1-3, and Ezek. 33:23ff.
11. It should be noted that where the scriptures are concerned the basic meaning of *kanôn* was "list," to which the connotation of normativity is added. To "canonize" a book was to add it to the list of the books every church *should* have a copy of and read publicly.
12. This is a traditional rabbinic expression used to designate canonical texts.
13. Our English Bibles follow roughly the order of the Septuagint, which did not follow the Hebrew classification into Law, Prophets, and Writings. The Septuagint, however, places the Minor Prophets before Isaiah, Jeremiah, and Ezekiel.
14. For one thing, this meant that early Christians worked with a different *text* of the scriptures than did the rabbis, who not unreasonably insisted upon the Hebrew as they knew it. The difference was not due merely to translation from Hebrew into Greek (as at Isa. 7:14), but also to the fact that in many passages the Septuagint translates from a Hebrew text that differs to some degree from the text that became the basis for the standard Hebrew Bible. In the second place, it meant that their "list" came to differ from that of the Jewish scriptures, since the Septuagint contained a number of works which the rabbis, around the turn of the second century c.e., ignored in their final and definitive list of the Writings: most notably, perhaps, *The Wisdom of Solomon* and *1 and*

2 Maccabees, both of which profoundly influenced early Christian thinking. In this way Christians came to employ a scriptural canon that acknowledged as part of the scriptures—though later in the West, under the influence of Jerome and the Protestant Reformers, only as "deutero-canonical" or as marginal pretenders to canonical status—some or all of the so-called Apocrypha. The Septuagint is still the official Old Testament of Orthodox churches.

15. The quotation marks signify that Irenaeus did not use this phrase to refer to a collection of writings, but to the "covenant" that God had made with humanity in Christ.

16. The Pauline corpus for Irenaeus probably did not include Hebrews, but it did include Ephesians, Colossians, and the the so-called Pastoral Epistles. He does not cite Philemon, but this fact signifies little.

17. It is uncertain which of the "Catholic Epistles" Irenaeus counted in the church's library: 1 John almost certainly, and 1 Peter. The Apocalypse of John, whose inclusion in the canon was for a long time a matter of dispute, was a favorite of his. It seems likely that he would also have counted Hermas's *Shepherd* as authoritative (because inspired), but not as "apostolic."

18. Some such phrase as this is necessary to convey the rather vague denotation of the word *apostles* in early Christian usage. It had since at least the time of the Lucan Acts come to include "the Twelve"; but it also included Paul and probably, in principle, such persons as Barnabas, not to mention the disciples of such apostles. Generally speaking, it is best taken to mean something like "the original guardians and bearers of the Gospel message."

19. See *Against Heresies* 3.pref.-3.1.1.

20. *The Attractiveness of God* (London, 1973), 34.

21. Exod. 21:24; cf. Matt. 5:38. In the light of the "punitive damages" frequently awarded these days by American courts, one might be tempted to revise this judgment. The *lex talionis* after all forbids one to take more than an eye for an eye.

22. See 2 Tim. 3:15.

23. No one can study the history of modern philosophy without becoming conscious of its obsession with so-called epistemological questions, that is, questions about what can be objectively and accurately known.

24. On this subject, see my paper, "Human Being," in G. Wainwright, ed., *Keeping the Faith* (Philadelphia, 1988).

25. For what follows, see Rahner's "The Theology of the Symbol," in *Theological Investigations* (Baltimore, 1966), 4:221-52. I need not say that what follows here is an appropriation and not an exposition of Rahner's ideas.

26. A corpse, then, is a symbol that has ceased to function as such and has become a mere sign.

27. Psychoanalysis is concerned with situations in which communication—of the self with itself and of the self with others—is inhibited because the process of

symbolization is distorted.

28. See John 1:14.
29. Article I.
30. *Institutes* 1.7.4.
31. See 1 Cor. 13:12.
32. Indeed it is a metaphor that is based on a metaphor, since the statement "God speaks" is a shocker just in itself, considering that God is not thought to have vocal cords. It should be said that by "metaphor" here I understand, following Paul Ricoeur, a statement whose meaning lies precisely in the conflict between a literal interpretation that produces absurdity and an "expanded" interpretation—developed in response to this absurdity—that generates fresh insight. See P. Ricoeur, *Interpretation Theory* (Fort Worth, Tex., 1976).
33. Here I refer to "modern" science. It is doubtful of course whether the scriptures were scientifically accurate even in the days of Paul. The cosmos contemplated by Genesis 1 cannot be reconciled any more easily with that described in Plato's *Timaeus* or Aristotle's *Physics* than it can with the cosmos as conceived by Carl Sagan.
34. See 1 Cor. 15:4.
35. In this connection, see Luke 20:35-36, where "resurrection" and "the age to come" are synonymous and "sons of the resurrection" are said to be "equal to angels and . . . sons of God."
36. See 1 Cor. 15:50, 44.
37. It is worth reflecting that *phusikos*, "physical," means "natural," as in the old expression "physical sciences."
38. See Irenaeus, *Against Heresies* 4.13.1, 4.15.2.
39. See Deut. 21:15-17.
40. It was William Temple who wisely remarked, somewhere in the course of his *Nature, Man, and God*, that there are no revealed truths, but only truths of revelation.

RESPONSE TO PAPERS

Each author's response to the other

CHARLES P. PRICE: RESPONSE TO OTHER PAPERS

A thread which in one form or another runs through all the papers is the need for "dialogue" or "conversation" between the scriptural text and the interpreting church. One thing which differentiates the four papers is their different understandings of the status of the partners in the dialogue. Professor Noll speaks of the need for "submissiveness" as the proper response to scripture as God's Word. Professor Wondra, on the other hand, argues for a "hermeneutics of suspicion," a position which might be taken as the opposite end of a spectrum. Professor Norris and I find ourselves some place between these limits. Professor Norris speaks of interpretation as a "two-way street" and recognizes that the conversation is undertaken as a work of faith. I have used the word *love* in this connection, hoping to have implied that in such a conversation there is a kind of *mutual* submissiveness. In an analogous sense to Jesus' own self-humbling, scriptural words do not resist the apparent violence which new interpretations sometimes require; but the interpreter must also be humble and even submissive before the text.

I find Professor Norris's paper most congenial to my own thought. His term *conversation* functions much as *dialogue* and *dialectic* do for me. I am in agreement that interpretation is a "two-way street," that Word of God is a metaphor implying no identity between revelation and lexical meaning, and that scripture and church are strictly correlative terms. I appreciate his insistence that controversy about Scripture is a sign of this authority.

If there is disagreement between us, it lies in what seems to me a curious silence about the role of the Holy Spirit in both the creation and interpretation of the texts, and also in establishing Jesus Christ as the norm of interpretation—precisely through the conversation.

The element of dialogue is also essential for Professor Wondra. I respond positively to her insistence that scripture is granted authority on the basis of its ability to empower, and I appreciate her representation of the liberation theologians' insight that the voice of the "other" or the "oppressed" often functions as the voice of Christ. I should want to add" . . . as a first approximation."

I find myself in disagreement with Professor Wondra mostly in her refusal to grant scripture exclusive normative character. I interpret that move on her part as providing an undoubtedly necessary distance between the text and the concerns of liberation theologians. Her paper becomes, then, an expression of an important contemporary stage in the ongoing dialogue between emergent humanity and the scriptural text. I miss the recognition that scripture has had its role in causing that emergence, and also that in interpreting scripture in this fashion, one is also interpreted by scripture.

Professor Noll's paper is both suggestive and confusing in its definition of the "literal sense" of scripture as "that meaning *appropriate* to the nature of the Bible as the Word of God in the words of men." The definition is suggestive in that it opens the literal sense to meanings far beyond what Professor Norris calls the "lexical" sense. On the other hand it is confusing in that the norm of appropriateness is not easy to grasp. Professor Noll's tests for discovering the literal sense are (1) referentiality; (2) "authorial purpose"; and (3) "clarity." Since referentiality means that the text refers to something outside itself, either seen or unseen, the literal sense is "the natural basis for figuration, allegory and *ambiguity*" (emphasis added). Authorial purpose has to be discovered by the readers. Clarity claims "foolproof composition" in a way that many texts seem to me openly to contradict.

Of course, this opening of the meaning of the literal sense to further discussion can only be a healthy development in a conversation within the church about biblical interpretation; but when the meaning of "literal sense" is spelled out in this way, it does not seem to be significantly more committed to the historical accuracy of the text as it stands than the other approaches.

All of these positions are sufficiently in touch with each other to encourage further clarifying discussions.

ELLEN K. WONDRA: RESPONSE TO OTHER PAPERS

As Professor Norris says, "Christians, it seems, have always agreed that the scriptures are authoritative, and just as regularly disagreed about how to read and how to render them." And, as Professor

Norris notes further, this disagreement is itself an affirmation of the Bible's authority. This pattern continues among the four authors of these essays. Nevertheless, there are here significant areas of agreement, which I will state in very brief form before moving on to some areas of difference I find significant.

First, and most important, all of us agree that the source of all authority is God. The authority of scripture is derived from the authority of God, and is secondary to it.

Second, all of us agree that, *by itself*, the Bible is not scripture. Professors Noll and Price put it explicitly that the work of the Holy Spirit in and through the texts as they are formed, read, and received is necessary for the Bible to be *holy* writing.

Third, all of us agree that the Bible is scripture—holy writing—in its relation to the people of God, the church: the scriptures and the church co-constitute each other in an ongoing dialectical process.

Fourth, all of us agree that scripture is normative for Christian teaching and practice, but that it is not the only source. Beyond this, there is substantial divergence on this point, to which I shall return.

Fifth, we all agree that the scriptures issue an invitation to readers to participate in a particular world; and this purpose of engagement is more primary than the subsidiary purposes of doctrinal or moral instruction. Again, beyond this there is considerable divergence.

Finally, we all agree in practice that scripture is heard, read, understood, and used in conjunction with certain fundamental theological precepts that are based in scripture but also in the life and work of those engaged in theological reflection. It is important to mention this, because doing so helps illustrate how various dimensions of hearing, reading, understanding, and appropriating scripture are brought to bear in discussing the authority and use of scripture. Further, what these precepts are significantly shapes our particular view of scripture, as I have noted in my discussion of the work of David Kelsey.

One of the areas of divergence among the four of us is precisely what it means to say that scripture is normative, whether it is *the* primary source and norm for Christian theological reflection, or *a* primary source and norm. Another area is what sort of world scripture invites us to enter. There are two issues underlying these divergences to which I will direct my attention in this response. The first is the significance of the human reader in relation to the scriptures (or the question of dialogue or conversation) and the second is the significance of historical context in forming both the scriptures and the reader (or the question of the nature of interpretation).

First, conversation: while all four of us recognize that the Bible is scripture because of its relationship with a community (the church), three of us (Professors Price and Norris, and myself) devote considerable attention to the processes of that relationship, and hence to the nature and role of the reader and of language. This is the case because we understand revelation as conversational or dialectical, something that requires more than one active participant. God may be self-revealing; but there are also recipients of and respondents to that revelation, and how they receive and respond is part of the revelatory process. But conversation—the term we have used to describe the revelation-response pattern—has its drawbacks: inherent to it is the possibility of differences of understanding, and of misunderstandings (willful or not, conscious or not). So the choice of the metaphor of conversation brings with it the theological problem of the power of God and its relation to human limitation and freedom. If human beings are finite and free partners in this conversation, what is the relation between what God reveals and how we respond?

Each of the four of us deals with this theological problem in different ways. Professor Noll writes that Christ is a uniting of the fragmented presence of God in the world; and scriptures are the mirror of Christ. Christ is the Word of God; the scriptures are "the Word of God in the words of men." The Word of God and the words of scripture thus are fairly unmistakable; and, especially given the work of the Holy Spirit, we are therefore fairly likely to understand God's meaning, unless our own sinfulness interferes. This being the case, the obedience to the Word for which Professor Noll calls is likely to be consenting rather than coerced; human freedom is not curtailed but rather directed.

I, however, am less convinced than Professor Noll both that the Word of God is this unmistakable, or that the Word of God and the words of scripture are so closely identifiable. The reasons for my hesitancy here are clear from my essay. In a world where unjust suffering is widespread, there are significant problems with claiming that what God is doing is clear to us. Further, in a church whose history in relation to this suffering is ambiguous at best, identifying any human words with the Word of God must be done very carefully indeed, lest we claim divine sanction for human sinfulness.

So I find myself on these points in greater accord with Professors Price and Norris. Professor Price carefully distinguishes between the Incarnate Word of God, Christ, and the Word of God in the scriptures: God the Word seeks entry into minds formed by words, and the utterance of the Word is the response of some. This is a very helpful way of putting it, I think, because it establishes both continuity among various words (in scripture and elsewhere) and God the Word, while still accounting both for real differences in understanding within the household of faith, and the possibility of error.

Even more helpful, I think, is Professor Norris's discussion of the nature of language, communicative exchange, and symbol. Professor Norris makes more explicit than does Professor Price the ambiguous character of symbol or metaphor: figural speech is at the same time both true and false. That is, it points to the resemblance between two things, but it often does so by concealing or even apparently denying the difference(s). Metaphors deliberately make mistakes; but those mistakes are in significant ways generative, even if they are also at times misleading and confusing. All religious speech is finally metaphorical or symbolic: God is, after all, more than any of us can ever imagine, let alone say. Recognizing this is, I think, an indispensable component of any discussion of scripture as a primary and normative source for such speech, lest we confuse words with the Word. And it is very difficult to recognize this symbolic character while still speaking of the primacy of the "literal sense"—even in such careful terms as Professor Noll employs.

Second, interpretation: All of us agree that interpretation of scripture is unavoidable, and that the context out of which any interpretation comes helps to form that interpretation. But beyond that, there is great difference among us. Professor Noll's notion of the literal sense of scripture puts limitations on the range of interpretation possible: we are to read scripture as it was intended to be read. However, Professor Noll does not elaborate this point, so it is hard to tell exactly what this statement means; and without more content, it is not possible to assess its adequacy. Professor Price likewise limits the range of interpretation: interpretations are to begin with the literal sense, and to be in continuity with the overall tradition of the church while still bringing a "fresh" understanding. But interpretations that are "genuinely new" go too far, reconstituting both the church and the scriptures. Professor Norris states that there is more involved: we interpret the scriptures in light of the church traditions, certainly, but also in light of our own context and situation. Conflicts within and between these may lead the conversation to a new turn. My view goes beyond Professor Norris's in this regard: I am convinced that the context of the interpreter plays a very significant role, and may quite legitimately diverge from the church's traditions, even as those traditions are canonized in the scriptures.

This, I think, is a key point, and it has to do with at least two things. One is the sort of dialectical or conversational relation that takes place between the scriptures and the communities that view them as scriptures. The second of these concerns the purposes for which scripture was intended. While all of us recognize that scriptures are designated as such by the believing community, my colleagues appear to be less concerned than I with the social-contextual nature of those designating communities and the role of social context in forming the scriptures.

After all, these communities do more than designate certain writings as holy. They also are engaged in the struggles of daily life in particular times and places; and this is directly connected to how they understand the presence of the holy in those lives. In turn, the purposes of the scriptures are not limited to engaging members of that community in a relationship with God. Scriptures are also intended to form human beings into communities. And those communities reflect not only direct experience with God, which is, in any event, mediated by the context in which it occurs. They also reflect the world in which they are set, and in which human social arrangements may and historically have fostered domination as much as they do the full humanity which is part of the Good News.

Therefore, I find it vitally important to examine the scriptures themselves—as well as the history of their use—in light of the contradiction between domination and full humanity. My colleagues appear to find both the scriptures and church traditions less vexatious than I do in this regard. I would contend, however, that our shared claim that scriptures and church co-constitute each other makes it imperative that critical social theory be used to facilitate our conversation with scripture with the same rigor as the more customary critical literary, rhetorical, and canonical theories that all three of my colleagues use. This is completely consistent with the conviction that all four of us hold (in varying ways) that the scriptures are no more removed from history than is the God embodied in Christ.

Another way of putting this is that revelation is ongoing. While I agree with Professor Price that all claims to revelation or inspiration must be weighed alongside scripture, I do think that there are instances in which such claims may outweigh aspects of the scriptures. Indeed, Professor Price suggests himself that the demands of *agapé* may render scripture less than revelatory in certain regards, such as slavery. Indeed, if the constituting conversation involves scripture, the community of faith, *and* the Word of God who continues to be present to the community (as Professor Price suggests), then such a possibility must be allowed. This is not to say that new revelations will contradict or overturn the overall thrust of scripture in regard to the way in which God is involved with God's own creation; but it is to suggest that not every word is a word from God, even if it is a word in the Bible.

But about that reasonable persons may reasonably disagree. I take these disagreements as part of the ongoing conversation, initiated by God and nurtured by the scriptures in the believing community, and intended for our greater growth in the love of God and of our neighbor.

STEPHEN F. NOLL: RESPONSE TO OTHER PAPERS

Review of Charles Price's Paper
Charles Price's essay, "Holy Book, Holy People," might seem to be a moderate version of my defense of "literal sense," since he identifies himself as a liberal evangelical convinced that the words of scripture attest to the Incarnate Word and that these words are, when inspired, both powerful and normative. I will argue here, however, that Price's view shares the "romantic" presuppositions of the other papers. If I read him correctly, the Word that the words of scripture mediate is essentially nonverbal and experiential, and its "normativity" is governed by the priorities of modern consciousness rather than biblical theology.

I hope to get at Price's understanding of scripture by working backward from his application to the specific issue of homosexuality. The Christian church throughout its history has held that homosexuality is a sign of a disordered soul and society and that homosexual intercourse is a sin. The church based this moral stance on specific texts of the Bible (such as Genesis 19; Lev. 18:22; Rom. 1:26-27; 1 Cor. 6:9), which were based on the more general creation principle that God intended sexual love for male and female partners in the context of marriage and children (Gen. 2:24). While granting that God's love redeems a fallen moral order, interpreters could not conceive an *agapé* principle that contradicted the will of the Creator or the specific teaching of Jesus. Jesus himself had said, "If you love me, keep my commandments." It followed that any love that violated God's express laws and purposes was a false love.

How is it then that Price can conclude that homosexual practice is in accordance with the Word of God? His case runs something like this:

1. The Bible is not a textbook of doctrine, and specific texts must never be read apart from their context. While Price seems to agree that the literal sense of the relevant texts is "largely negative" toward homosexuality, he never goes on to wrestle with them. Presumably Christians in the past encountered them as "Word" but not so now. (Is there any chance these might become Word again in the future? Or continue to be authoritative, i.e., "life-enhancing," for some Christian communities now? Or for some Episcopalians now and not for others?)

2. The Word behind the specific moral texts of the Bible is what Price calls the "*agapé* principle" of mutual self-giving, exemplified in the Trinitarian relations and by Jesus' self-giving life. He does not investigate whether a *creation principle* might also undergird the biblical texts, or whether the *agapé* principle might possibly call for a nonsexual friendship or companionship in the gospel.

3. He argues that all relationships, heterosexual and homosexual, are capable of sinful exploitation, but equally all can be redeemed by life-long faithful mutuality. He seals this point with a proof-text: "God has bound all men to disobedience so that he may have mercy on them all" (Rom. 11:32). This text is not only taken out of context, but its application runs counter to Paul's own understanding of the nature of homosexuality in chapter 1. Was Paul purposely inconsistent, or can the mind of Christ utterly overturn the mind of Paul?

4. Price's conclusion is vintage situation ethics. More ominously, the logic of progressive revelation, which he applies to class and gender, should eventually lead him to demand for all forms of voluntary relationship, including homosexuality, that "*the church cannot be at rest until this vision of heavenly reality is translated into rules and laws and precepts for governing the life of both the church and its society here on earth*" (his italics). Ellen Wondra, of course, has already pressed this logic to its proper end.

I focus on this case because it raises a very great dilemma for ordinary Christians. They read the Bible and think they know what it says, only to have an expert tell them that they are hermeneutically naive. Presto! Change-o! The Bible comes out commending the very norms that it seemed to proscribe and that 2000 years of exposition took as clear and authoritative.

A literal interpretation, while it does not solve all difficulties of discerning God's will by any means, is not counterintuitive. The moral mandates of the Word, taken literally, cannot be understood apart from the specifics of Jesus' and the apostles' teaching. This teaching may be challenging in its rigor, and it may call for reasonable application in a modern context. But it is not finally at odds with itself.

Those who insist on an epistemological chasm between the words of the Bible and its meaning (Word) are, it seems to me, like Adam and Eve after the Fall: they hear the sound of the LORD God walking in the Garden, and they hide lest his voice should be speaking oracles of judgment. While I respect Charles Price's intention to present the Word of God in the light of modern sensibilities, I believe he is, finally, scandalized by the very words which are not only the medium but the message of the gospel.

Review of Richard Norris's Paper

According to Richard Norris, the scriptures are "not a theological and moral databank, but a medium through which people can enter into communication *(koinonia)* with God-in-Christ." With his emphasis on medium over message he is in basic agreement with Price and Wondra (all heirs of Schleiermacher, the great veil-maker of modern hermeneutics). Norris's contribution to the discussion lies in his proposal of *conversation* as a root metaphor for the interpretation and authority of the Bible: "The Christian Scriptures are the record of a human conversation, prolonged over more than a millennium, with and about God." I will attempt below to exposit this proposition about scripture as conversation, with accompanying commentary:

1. *Conversation is relational.* According to Norris, the Bible records and invites readers to respond to a conversation, not a declaration. He speaks of two rival images of conversation: one is oriented toward communicating things ("I-it" language), whereas the other is interested in the relationship created by conversation ("I-Thou"). The latter is the essential function of the Bible.

The question is, as I see it, what kind of relationship does the Bible convey? Norris's image of conversation is two friends in overstuffed chairs in front of a cozy fire, but biblical conversation starts with "take off your shoes for you are on holy ground!" Not only does God initiate conversation, his objective commandments are the non-negotiable framework for any further discussion. When God says "Come now, let us reason together" (Isa. 1:18), he follows it with specific promises and threats. The New Testament gospel is no different: while Saint Paul shared his life with his congregations, he was adamant that the message takes priority of the messenger (Gal. 1:9). Norris sets up a false dichotomy between objective and relational knowledge and reverses the biblical order of declaration and conversation.

2. *Conversation is a human activity.* The Bible, Norris says, records a human conversation, not a divine-human conversation. God did not and does not speak verbally (since he does not have a voice-box), and thus his role in the biblical conversation is not that of a normal interlocutor. Presumably God provides the ground, *koinonia*, and inspiration in which the human partners, the writers and readers of the Bible, can converse.

I agree that there is a rich intertextual conversation among the biblical writers, *but because God has spoken verbally*. It is because they claim to be reporting and passing on a revealed word that cannot return empty that they find freedom to reconfigure it, scripture interpreting scripture. Norris again sets up a reductionistic dichotomy when he says that "since the activity of God is not empirically accessible, there is and there can be no evidence to show that anyone but a human being composed any book of the Bible." Surely if conversation with God is possible, it will be *sui generis*; and that is exactly what the prophets mean by their insistent "Thus saith the Lord."

3. *Conversation overcomes historical distance.* In Norris's view, the millennium-long process that led to the production of the Bible builds cultural strangeness and diversity into the biblical library of texts. Our awareness of this strangeness and diversity, which has been highlighted by the development of modern biblical criticism, can be overcome by the canon's focusing the conversation on the agenda of theology.

I agree that the historical distances within the Bible, and between it and us, should warn us to enter carefully into what Karl Barth called "the strange world of the Bible." By the same logic we should beware of projecting our modern notions of dialogue on an ancient text. On the other hand, a thousand-year conversation with an eternal God need not result in incoherence. To say, as Norris does, that the unifying core of the canon is theology is correct as far as it goes but is too formalistic. It is the theological truth of the one God preparing for and sending his Son into the world that unifies scripture.

4. *Conversation is oral, not written.* Norris claims that, as a *record* of a conversation, the biblical text is at one remove from the revelatory language-event itself. Because there is a fundamental difference between words and "language" (as in "body-language") or "communication," many simple believers have mistakenly called the Bible "the Word of God." In fact, the Bible as record only stands witness to the fact that communication happened.

I find Norris's distinctions between verbal and symbolic language overdrawn. A literal interpretation that is attuned to matters of genre can detect clues as to how a particular word or phrase is used in context. While the Bible certainly commends the spoken word, preaching itself is seen as expository (Rom. 10:15), and many of the greatest biblical books are explicitly conceived as written works.

Having rejected Norris's particular formulation of scripture as conversation, let me now suggest that my position can accommodate a kind of *lectio divina*, or "sitting under the Word," so long as its truth claims and its salvation-historical thrust are honored. Psalms 1 and 119 provide a biblical image of conversation with scripture, as does Cranmer's scripture collect. In addition, the architecture of George Herbert's poetic work *The Temple* may be a fruitful example from a classical Anglican perspective:

The Temple begins with a long didactic poem called "The Church Porch," which functions much like the Ten Commandments in a catechism class. Only when students have sprinkled themselves with the basic dogmatic and moral precepts of the Bible are they ready to enter into a more creative and fruitful conversation with the loving God of the Bible.

Following "The Church Porch" is a long evangelical poem entitled "The Sacrifice," in which the once-for-all passion of Jesus is narrated with ironic commentary from the Old Testament. The sacrifice of God's Son constantly informs the later poems since, as Herbert confesses, "I have considered it, and find there is no dealing with thy mighty passion."

Finally, the disciple is permitted entry into the mysteries of the church and scripture. The Christian pilgrimage, in Herbert's *Temple*, includes meditation on texts, submission to texts, and transformation of texts in ways that are creative but faithful to the original sense. The final poem, "Love bade me welcome," is a conversation between Christ and the soul, in which the inexpressible gift of his love is offered and accepted. Even here, however, the symposium of believer and divine Lover involves an unequal conversation, which presupposes the sinner's knowledge of moral absolutes and the determinate gospel of the One who bore the blame instead.

Norris's approach to the Bible as conversation is like building the Temple from the top down. Those who seek meaning before truth, symbols before words will, I fear, find themselves in the place of E. M. Forster's elderly pilgrim, Mrs. Moore, as she discovers in India's famed Marabar caves not an echo but an indistinct "boum."

> Suddenly at the edge of her mind, Religion appeared, poor little
> talkative Christianity, and she knew that all its divine words from
> "Let there be light" to "It is finished" only amounted to "boum."
> Then she was terrified over an area larger than usual . . . and
> she realized she didn't want to write to her children, didn't want
> to communicate with anyone, not even with God. She sat
> motionless with horror.

Mrs. Moore may be an apt image of first-world Anglicanism, which has lost confidence in the residual power of the words of scripture to give life and renewal to the soul and to the church.

Review of Ellen Wondra's Paper

I suppose the most obvious point to contest in Ellen Wondra's paper is her rejection of the primacy of scripture: "Liberation theologies do challenge the designation of the Bible as scripture by refusing to uncritically grant the Bible authority." This is what I labeled the "grab-bag" approach: when the Bible affirms the liberationist agenda, it is "authoritative"; but when it contradicts liberation, it becomes part of the oppressive ideology to be overcome. As far as I can see, liberationists place themselves in a privileged position. They do not have to define and defend their assertions about freedom and domination, while those individuals or texts that might critique their assertions come under suspicion of promoting oppression.

One might wonder (and many radical feminists do) if the Bible's bad track record and double messages make it simply too risky to use in promoting human freedom. Wondra argues, however, that scripture does in fact provide a positive set of metaphors that can serve as a two-edged sword, defending against oppressive exegesis *and* irresponsible eisegesis. The key to a liberated use of scripture is "imaginative construal." Imaginative construals work in two ways: first, they provide a metaphorical underpinning for a central reality of Christianity (root metaphor); second, they serve as a check on the credibility of various theological proposals.

Since this idea of imaginative construal is the formal equivalent of what I have called the literal sense of scripture, I would like to see what it looks like exegetically. Unfortunately, Wondra gives no actual examples of imaginative construal in her paper, although her title—"For Freedom Christ Has Set You Free"—is, I suppose, one example (I would call it a proof-text). A literal interpretation of Galatians 5:1 would agree with liberationists that the gospel is the foundation of Christian freedom. According to Paul's gospel, Jesus, by his atoning death, delivers the believer from every earthly power, whether they are the elemental spirits of paganism or the tutor of the Jewish Law (Gal. 4:8-9). The human response of faith includes a willingness to deny oneself, to crucify the flesh with its passions and desires, and to endure this life patiently, awaiting the hope of heavenly glory (Gal. 5:5, 24). While justification is not based on works, the justified life, according to Paul, exhibits a recognizable character, with specific positive and negative content in the works of the flesh and the fruit of the Spirit (Gal. 5:16-24).

My impression is that liberationists would grant that the above exegesis of Galatians is a possible, even historic "reading," but they would maintain that an imaginative construal might go in a very different direction. For instance, the concept of freedom from oppressive principalities might "authorize" a general principle of individual rights, which could then be seen to override the patriarchal specifics of Paul's moral teaching about the works of the flesh.

I encountered just such an imaginative construal at the recent dialogue meeting of representatives of the liberationist *Witness* movement and the evangelicals at my seminary. We concluded our sessions with a Bible study, and our text was Romans 12:1-2: "Present your bodies as a living sacrifice." After a period of silent meditation on the text, one gay member of my group described how his reading of James Nelson's book on "embodiment" had illuminated his understanding of what the text means by "presenting your body" to another person.

A literal reading of the text would take account of the clear emphasis on *self-denial, holiness* as a moral quality with specific content, and *reasonable service* as submission to the divine command. Only by dying to the worldly imitations of fulfillment and trusting the renewing work of Christ's Spirit can one "prove" the good and acceptable and perfect will of God. When I pointed this out, I was told that my interpretation was "dualistic." When I asked whether I was reading Paul correctly, it was granted that Paul too was a dualist. An imaginative construal of Romans 12:1-2, then, could acknowledge the literal sense (Paul's meaning) but "read" the text to a wholly different end.

Am I picking an unfair fight in this example? I don't think so. The liberationist twisting of texts can be found at the highest level of the academy. For instance, I had just finished my commentary on the Book of Esther when I heard at the Society of Biblical Literature a feminist reading by which Queen Vashti was interpreted as a model for emulation because of her assertive refusal to kow-tow to the arbitrary demands of King Ahasuerus. The problem with this reading, from a literal point of view, is that it violates the literary and theological code of the book. Clearly Esther and Mordecai are the heroes of the book and Vashti and Ahasuerus are foils, showing how pagans who do not possess the wisdom that comes from the Law act irrationally and destructively.

Wondra wants scripture to shape the form of theology and to provide limits of what is "seriously imaginable," but she locates the meaning of scripture outside the text itself in an encounter/dialogue between text and reader. The liberated reader brings certain nonnegotiable demands to the table: any textual meaning that "oppresses" is rejected from the start. Only then can the reconstruction of biblical teaching by imaginative construal begin.

How plausible does a reading have to be? I can't imagine, having discarded the possibility of determinate meaning, how one could decide this question except on a utilitarian basis. If it works, that is, if people are "conscientized" by the construal, then it is legitimate. For all the weighty rhetoric, this sounds to me like the function of propaganda. Given the Marxist underpinning of liberation theology, should we be surprised? I do not make this statement as a slur; I assume Ellen Wondra would acknowledge her ideological debts. If classical Christianity and its Bible have been the tool of class oppression (now extended to ethnic, gender, and life-style groups), it must be either repudiated or resymbolized. Imaginative construal, as I see it, is just such a resymbolizing of scripture outside the literal sense of the text.

RICHARD A. NORRIS, JR.: RESPONSE TO OTHER PAPERS

An adequate and useful response to the three other papers presented to the House of Bishops would require more words and more space than either decency or order can allow. In the remarks that follow, therefore, I simply attempt to identify some important questions that after all the discussion seem still to be outstanding. Needless to say, the issues identified arise out of the papers that were presented, and out of their disagreements or differences of emphasis; but what I have to say is not intended to "reply" to anything, but to indicate ways along which the discussion might continue.

The first of these issues is one that was prominent in discussions of the papers both at the House of Bishops and at the subsequent meeting of the Conference of Anglican Theologians; and it turned out to be one on which very little light was shed. I refer, of course, to the question—most prominently raised in Professor Noll's paper—of whether the scriptures are to be "taken" (i.e., read or interpreted) "literally." One reason for the confusion which this question created is of course plain: it is very difficult to *say* what one means by the term "literal." Some progress in understanding might be made, then, simply by trying to elucidate its sense. It is not easy, for example, to define "literal" just as the polar opposite of "figurative," if only because the sorts of speech and writing that people normally take as literal are usually full of metaphor, whether "dead" or living. Perhaps, then, one ought to define the phrase "literal sense" to mean simply "what a sentence says to a skilled speaker of its language"—that is, its "plain sense." But of course there are problems with this definition as well. What a set of English words would have meant to a skilled speaker of Shakespeare's time is not necessarily what the same words would mean to a skilled speaker living in the present; Shakespeare's English has, in effect, to be translated before *we* can understand it well. But the act of translation is an act of interpretation; and this in turn means that the plain sense of a sentence (what it says) is not necessarily its *obvious* sense (what I spontaneously take it to say).

Beyond questions of this sort, though, there lurks a deeper one that has little to do with the question of the "senses" of scripture. Talk of the "literal meaning" of the Bible is, more often than not, an attempt to insist that the scriptures (a) talk about something real (e.g., God, or God's will, or our relation to God), and (b) convey truth about (or: convey the truth of) this reality in *words*. I suspect that most Christians would affirm these propositions; yet at the same time they would understand what they meant by them in different ways. Perhaps it would be useful to explore this issue further, then, not merely or principally in order clarify what might be meant by the phrase "literal meaning," but with view to indicating how it is the case that the Bible *has something to say about God and the human condition* that we do well to attend to.

Less discussion, and perhaps more muttering, were occasioned by introduction of the theme of the "hermeneutic of suspicion" as applied to the Bible. It is perhaps worth noting that, however recent that phrase may be, the sort of practice and attitude it implies are by no means new creations. The Bible has often engendered suspicion in its most faithful exegetes: Philo of Alexandria and Origen, for example, thought the Bible almost blasphemously anthropomorphic in its portrayal of God, and took care to correct it on this score by explaining what it really meant. Liberal interpreters of the nineteenth and twentieth centuries were aghast at the number of miracles reported in the scriptures, and went to some lengths to explain such occurrences in ways that made them comprehensible to "the modern mind." What is more, both of these "hermeneutics" seem largely to have succeeded, in the sense that the scriptures are no longer read or perceived as fundamentally interested in portraying God as an oversized human being or in advertising "violations" of the "laws of nature." It can hardly be a matter for surprise, then, that our age too should find elements in the Bible that evoke suspicion and questions. Furthermore, where it is not so much the Bible as its authorized interpreters that are subjected to systematic suspicion, there is abundant justification for such suspicion to be found in the doctrine of original sin, which can usefully be regarded as the first, and most sweeping, analysis of the source or occasion of distorted communication.

Nevertheless, proposals to adopt a "hermeneutic of suspicion" with regard to the scriptures raise a serious issue. Insofar as they privilege a particular set of beliefs or values (Platonist metaphysics, e.g., or Newtonian mechanics, or feminist social theory), and permit those beliefs or values to sit in judgment on the scriptures, they are bound to evoke a certain suspicion themselves. On the other hand, it is arguable that *no one* approaches the scriptures (or any other literature, for that matter) without tacitly privileging some set of beliefs and values. Is it the case, then, that there is some particular set of beliefs and values that *ought* to be privileged in interpretation of the Bible? And if so, what is it? But then contrariwise, what can one mean by speaking of the "authority" of the scriptures if one has, in effect, decided beforehand what they shall be construed as saying? There is a thicket of problems here that need continued—and open—discussion. For my own part, I suspect that there is a solution to be found in a dialogical understanding of the hermeneutical process; but that suspicion is itself open to question. The fact is, then, that the discussion cannot be left at the point it has now reached in the Episcopal Church. More needs to be said.

CONTRIBUTORS

Frederick Houk Borsch is the Bishop of Los Angeles. Author of over a dozen books, he was formerly dean of the Chapel with rank of Professor in the Department of Religion at Princeton University and Dean and Professor of New Testament at the Church Divinity School of the Pacific.

Linda L. Grenz is the coordinator for Adult Education and Leadership Development for the Episcopal Church. Grenz is the editor of and contributor to *In Dialogue with Scripture: An Episcopal Guide to Studying the Bible*. She received a master's degree in theological studies from Harvard Divinity School (1974) and a master's in divinity from the Episcopal Divinity School (1977) in Cambridge, Massachusetts.

Stephen F. Noll is Academic Dean and Associate Professor of Biblical Studies at Trinity Episcopal School for Ministry. Ordained priest in 1972, he received the Ph.D. from the University of Manchester in 1979. In addition to occasional articles, he is author of *The Intertestamental Period: A Study Guide* (IVP, 1984).

Charles P. Price was educated at the Arnold School, Harvard University, Virginian Theological Seminary, and Union Theological Seminary, New York. He is a Visiting Fellow of Clare Hall, Cambridge University. Price is the author of *Principles of Christain Faith and Practice, Liturgy for Living* (with Louis Weil), *The Gifts of God* (with Eugene Godchius), and *A Matter of Faith*. He served on the Board of Theological Education, on the Standing Liturgical Commission during Prayer Book Revision, on the Committee on Hymn Texts during Hymnal revision, and is currently a member of the Anglican-Roman Catholic consultation and the Board of Examining Chaplains.

Ellen K. Wondra is Assistant Professor of Theological Studies at Colgate-Rochester Divinity School/Bexley Hall/Crozer Theological Seminary in Rochester, New York. She has also written on Christology, on moral authority, and on the theology of inclusive language in the liturgy. She is an adjunct priest at the Church of St. Luke and St. Simon Cyrene in Rochester, and a member of the Anglican-Roman Catholic Consultation in the United States.

J. Robert Wright is the St. Mark's Professor of Ecclesiastical History in the General Theological Seminary, New York City, and a fellow of the Royal Historical Society, London. His most recent books are *On Being A Bishop: Papers from the Moscow Consultation on Episcopacy 1992, Readings for the Daily Office from the Early Church*, and *Prayer Book Spirituality* (all published by the Church Hymnal Corporation, New York City, over the years 1989-93), and *The Anglican Tradition* (with G.R. Evans, S.P.C.K. and Fortress Press, 1991), He has recently served as the President of the North American Academy of Ecumenists.